DATE DUE			

TRAGIC DRAMA AND MODERN SOCIETY

TRAGIC DRAMA AND MODERN SOCIETY

Studies in the Social and Literary
Theory of Drama from 1870 to the Present

John Orr

BARNES & NOBLE BOOKS
TOTOWA, NEW JERSEY

First Published in the U.S.A. 1981 by
BARNES & NOBLE BOOKS
81, Adams Drive, Totowa,
New Jersey, 07512

ISBN 0–389–20226–6

Printed in Hong Kong

For Anne

None of us can help the things life has done to us. They're done before you realise it, and once they're done they make you do other things until at last everything comes between you and what you'd like to be, and you've lost your true self for ever.

EUGENE O'NEILL
Long Day's Journey into Night

Contents

Acknowledgements

I would like to thank the committee of the Una Ellis-Fermor Memorial Research Fund for the award of a grant to assist my research into the Irish theatre at the National Library of Ireland, Dublin.

The author and publishers wish to thank the following who have kindly given permission for the use of copyright material: Associated Book Publishers Ltd (Eyre Methuen Ltd) and Random House Inc., for the extracts from *The Days of the Commune* in *Bertolt Brecht's Collected Plays*, vol. IV, translated by Clive Barker and Arno Reinfrank. Translation © Stefan Brecht 1978. Original work published under the title 'Die Tage Der Commune', © 1955 by Suhrkamp Verlag, Berlin; George Allen & Unwin (Publishers) Ltd, for the extracts from *Plays, Poems and Prose* by J. M. Synge, and *Autumn Fire* by T. C. Murray; John Calder (Publishers) Ltd, with Riverrun Press Inc., for the extract from *The Lulu Plays and other Sex Tragedies* by Frank Wedekind, translated by Stephen Spender; Jonathan Cape Ltd, on behalf of the Executors of the Eugene O'Neill Estate, and Yale University Press, for the extracts from *Long Day's Journey Into Night* by Eugene O'Neill; Jonathan Cape Ltd, on behalf of the Executors of the Eugene O'Neill Estate, and Random House Inc., for the extracts from *The Hairy Ape, Emperor Jones, All God's Chillun Got Wings, The Iceman Cometh* and *Beyond the Horizon* from *The Plays of Eugene O'Neill*; Jonathan Cape Ltd, for the extracts from *The Wesker Trilogy* by Arnold Wesker; Coward, McCann & Geoghegan Inc., for the extract from *The Zoo Story* by Edward Albee; Faber and Faber Ltd, for the extracts from *Look Back in Anger* by John Osborne and *The Party* by Trevor Griffiths; Elaine Greene Ltd, on behalf of Arthur Miller, and Viking Penguin Inc., for the extracts from *Collected Plays*, © 1958 by Arthur Miller; Elaine Greene Ltd, on behalf of Tennessee Williams, and Random House Inc., for the extract from *The Glass Menagerie*; Elaine Greene Ltd, on behalf of Tennessee Williams, and New Directions Publishing Corp., for the extracts from *A Streetcar Named Desire*, © 1947 by Tennessee Williams, *Cat on a Hot Tin Roof* © 1954–1975 by Tennessee Williams, and *Suddenly Last Summer* © 1958 by Tennessee Williams; David Higham Associates

Ltd, on behalf of Michael Meyer, for the translated extracts from Henrik Ibsen's plays *The Wild Duck*, *The Lady from the Sea*, *Rosmersholm*, *Hedda Gabler*, *John Gabriel Borkman*, and for the extracts from Mr Meyer's biography, *Henrik Ibsen: The Top of a Cold Mountain*; Oxford University Press, for the extracts from *The Oxford Chekhov*, translated and edited by Ronald Hingley, vol. 2 (1967) and vol. 3 (1964), and from *The Plays of Georg Büchner* translated by Victor Price (1971); Martin Secker & Warburg Ltd and Harcourt Brace Jovanovich Inc., for the extracts from *The Plebeians Rehearse the Uprising* by Günter Grass, translated by Ralph Manheim; Colin Smythe Ltd, and the Lady Gregory Estate, for the extracts from *Selected Plays* by Lady Gregory; Theatre Arts Books, New York, for the extract from *My Life in Art* by Constantin Stanislavsky, translated by J. J. Robbins, © 1924 and 1952 by Little, Brown and Company; and A. P. Watt Ltd, on behalf of Michael and Anne Yeats, and Macmillan Publishing Co. Inc., for the extracts from books by William Butler Yeats, *Explorations* (© 1962 by Mrs W. B. Yeats), *Essays and Introductions* (© 1961 by Mrs W. B. Yeats), and *Collected Plays* (© 1934, 1952 by Macmillan Publishing Co. Inc.)

Introduction

There are three major events in the history of world drama. These are the emergence of classical tragedy in ancient Greece, the renaissance of the tragic form in sixteenth-century England and seventeenth-century France, and finally the more diffuse tragic drama of modern civilisation, written and performed in the period of industrial capitalism since 1880. The first two forms of tragic writing are universally acknowleged. But until recently, the last has hardly been acknowledged at all. Either modern drama is seen as part of a wider literary transformation of which tragedy is just one of a variety of forms, or else it is dissolved into the individual work of major playwrights and presented as a series of apt comparisons. Since the third major period of drama has just drawn to a close, however, its contours are becoming more apparent and can be judged in historical retrospect. The drama between 1880 and 1966 that we now call modern will in some future epoch no doubt be called by a more generic name. The terms which have been so far suggested, 'bourgeois' or 'naturalist' tragedy, are partial and misleading. The term I wish to use in their place, and shortly to justify, is 'tragedies of social alienation'. The very term suggests that traditional literary modes of interpretation are not sufficient for critical justification, and that presumption is right. Modern tragedy requires both literary and sociological analysis, looking not only at the immediate connections between drama and society but also at the intermediate ones, the connections between drama and social consciousness, and then in turn between varieties of social consciousness and the wider society.

To call drama 'tragic' is to posit the continued existence of a particular mode of writing over a period of two-and-a-half thousand years. It is to suggest both a linear development and a cyclical renaissance. Of course part of the continuity is provided by formal aesthetic rules attributed to Aristotle,[1] which demand a tragic hero with a distinctive weakness causing a reversal of personal fortune, a unity of time, place and action, a tragic climax purging the emotions of the audience, and a realisation by the fallen hero of the true horror of

xi

his fate. At best they have presented a point of departure for the creation of a tragic vision, and in the third period of world-historical tragedy, conformity to these rules is markedly weaker than in previous periods. To circumvent the difficulties of this laxity, the general formula suggested by Raymond Williams seems the most appropriate. The essential tragic experience is that of irreparable human loss.[2] It is a loss felt and performed by actors on a theatrical stage and witnessed in turn by their audience, and usually infused by at least some Aristotelian elements.

The irreparable loss of tragedy is expressed in a variety of climactic events—murder, suicide, madness, disintegration—of either an individual or a group. Death, naturally, is a recurrent feature of tragedy but not a necessary one. It can be enough that the serious wounding of human sensibility cannot be healed. If that loss, and the failure to heal, are conveyed dramatically through the resources of the text and the stage, through the synchronised speech, movement and setting of the dramatic spectacle, then we possess that theatrical totality which is authentically tragic. To speak of this loss purely in itself, however, is not enough. For the loss points primarily to the consequences of the dramatic action, not what generates it in the first place. What does generate it is the predicament of human alienation, of which tragedy is the supreme literary expression. Each of the three major tragic modes contains its own distinctive historical expression of that alienation. The Greek mode is basically divine, the renaissance mode predominantly noble, while the modern mode is fundamentally social. (There is also the less important German middle-class tragedy of Schiller and Lessing providing the historical link between the 'noble' and the 'social' modes, and this we could perhaps call 'virtuous'.) How does social alienation in this context differ from its predecessors? The issues are complex but their understanding is vital, since the mode of alienation provides the necessary context for the dramatic expression of irreparable loss. If this context is not present in the text, the dramatic action portraying loss or suffering is exaggerated and lacks psychological credibility. This results in features which, as often as not, we recognise as melodrama. To understand these modes of alienation and how they work dramatically, some form of historical discursus is required.

Both Greek and Elizabethan tragedy are dramas about past epochs. Because of our closer historical proximity to the Elizabethans, we recognise this more clearly of Marlowe and Shakespeare than we do of Aeschylus and Sophocles. But as Jean Duvignaud has pointed out, the tragic dramatists of the Greek city-states were equally concerned with reconstituting the history of their forefathers as tragic myth.[3] Prometheus and Io, and later Oedipus and Antigone, belong to an antiquity which fifth-century Greeks could recognise as part of a sacrificial struggle for their own collective identity. They are legendary figures. There are two additional similarities with Elizabethan tragedy. Both emerged during a period of imperial expansion which was militarily endangered. The shock of the Persian invasions was as great for the audiences of Aeschyclus as the threat of the Spanish armada was for Elizabethans attending the Globe theatre. In both cases a new empire-building polity was repulsing a threat to its very existence. The shattering historical contradiction was a decisive catalyst to the creation of tragic myth, and produced a second more general point of similarity. Historical tragedy in both periods exhibits a fascination for the past and, at the same time, an affirmation of modernity. The heroic values of the drama are often archaic, but its heroes, in temperament and sensibility, are indisputably contemporary. They belong to an age which had a sense of its own high level of civilised living and its equally ruthless political triumph.

In the second major phase of tragedy, the vantage-point of 'high' civilisation enables the audience to respond to the glory of their country's achievements and the horror of losing it. The tragic doom of legendary heroes provides a salutary point of reference. In Shakespeare the nature of the tragic hero is also of vital importance. The inner dilemmas of personality are juxtaposed with the external obligation to command power over men. The Shakespearean royal persona fuses the nobility of feudal rank with the individualistic sensibility characteristic of Renaissance man in revolt against the traditional social order. Subsequently in the Jacobean tragedy of Webster and Middleton that conflict is lost. The setting of the Italian city-state or Spanish court diminishes the sense of heroic nobility and the drama deals in sensational terms with dissolute sexuality and Machiavellian intrigue. The more direct focus on decadent contemporary obsessions destroys the aura of tragic nobility and replaces it with macabre amoralism. Civilisation is no longer seen at its zenith, but in terms of a disintegration of personality and political morality. The sense of loss, while still explicit, is correspondingly diminished. Racine, writing soon afterwards in the milieu of the French absolutist court, is clearly concerned with a similar kind of disintegration, but by returning to mythology and ancient history recreates the aura of a noble life which the Jacobeans had eroded. The great element of contradiction in Racine's own life, and that of the high social circles within which he moved, was the contrast between the amoral opulence of the Royal court and the severe introversionist morality of Jansenism which he had absorbed during his stay at Port-Royal and which derived its social support from the *Noblesse de Robe*. The trauma of moving from Port-Royal to its cultural antitheses, the theatre and the Court, is expressed in a drama which Lucien Goldmann has termed a 'tragic refusal',[4] where the refusal of the world by the Racinian heroine is linked specifically to the refusal of temptation. The corresponding conflict refracts, at the level of personal passion and its denial, the wider historical conflict between the public patronage of royal absolutism and the private conscience of an emergent bourgeois individualism. While Racine's own conscience was Christian, that of his heroes was pagan.

In the modern period, historical tragedy is still written and is still of vital importance. But it is superseded by the tragic drama of contemporary life, and in turn historical tragedy at its best becomes drama of recent history, a history whose direct influence on the present is readily apparent. Often, as in O'Neill's later works, that historical tragedy is set in an earlier period of the playwright's own life, so that its historicity literally merges into the present. This creates a flow and a unity making the division between historical and contemporary seem artificial and unreal. The concern with recent history is the legacy of the changing social consciousness of the modern age, where the work of Marx and classical sociology has presented us with a new perspective on the transformation of social life and the genesis of those transformations. Men sought out the origins of their present condition in the events of the recent past and the spirit of this enquiry has been absorbed into the drama of the new age where some measure of historical accuracy in dramatic reconstruction replaces the previous traditions of legend and myth. To write directly of contemporary life itself, either in the novel or the play, was also a legacy of a changing consciousness. Novels employing the epic dimensions of narrative form were better equipped for this task than the more concentrated form of the drama, and indeed bequeathed as much to changes in social consciousness as they took from them. The tragic drama of contemporary life postdates the development of tragic realism in the novel, which begins with Stendhal's *Scarlet and Black*, and its scope is limited more by its form. Problems of dramatic form, as we shall see, create difficulties for the development of a tragic political drama, whereas the political novel is one of the basic forms of tragic realism.[5]

Because modern tragedy divides itself between the novel and the play, the third great period of tragic drama does not have the power or intensity of the earlier forms. Taken in conjunction with the novel, however, that artistic parity is restored.

To identify the three modes of tragic alienation is not to construct rigid literary types. Within each mode is contained a struggle of opposites. To see human fate in classical tragedy as wholly governed by divine intervention would be a gross distortion. Within the pantheon of Greek mythology the Gods did have this ultimate power. But in Greek tragedy divine fate is more impersonal. The form of alienation here is close to that deciphered by Feuerbach and Marx in their writings on religion, where Gods are seen as endowed with human qualities alienated from their possessors and objectified as external attributes of superior beings. But this process of alienation only becomes a basis for tragic confrontation when fate is actually defied by the drama's hero. As Nietzsche recognised, the birth of tragedy derived in part from the Dionysian urge of man to create divinity through his own will. The tragic climax of the Greek drama comes when human willing confronts the limits of divine power, and so encounters its doom. But the limit is never recognised until the last moment and the action of the tragic hero becomes, consciously or otherwise, a revolt against divine necessity.

In Renaissance tragedy where the emphasis is transferred from the divine to the human, the internal struggle is, as we have already mentioned, between the resistant individualism of the tragic hero and the privileged position of his royal personage. His consequent fate is, as Duvignaud has noted, atypical.[6] He isolated himself by betraying his privileged role but also by exceeding it. The tragic grandeur of stepping beyond conventions and violating them is not determined by the rank itself but by the individual concern with self. It is a personalised violation. The atypicality here is a form of human alienation, but essentially a distanced one, where the audience witnesses, as in Shakespeare, the growing isolation of the rejected king, beyond the stature of ordinary mortals but no longer commanding authority over them. The theatrical impact of the fate of Lear, Richard II, or Macbeth becomes one of an estranged and doomed grandeur. The nobility, which starts off as an attribute of a fixed rank, becomes through the onset of tragic misfortune the quality of an individual person and is cast free from its social moorings. But precisely by virtue of establishing its individualised quality, it foreshadows its possessor's damnation.

The tragedy of social alienation which begins with Ibsen and ends on a less intense note with Tennessee Williams, Edward Albee and Günther Grass is altogether different from either of the previous two forms. It co-exists with a serious drama which lacks this alienation and expresses instead an ultimate vindication of the social order with which its protagonists are discontented. As often as not, both tragic and serious, or affirmative drama will come from the pen of the same dramatist. For this reason we must look initially not to the playwright but to the text. Often tragedy has appeared in contemporary criticism as an appendage to high moral seriousness in the novel or the play. The crucial generic differences have therefore to be repeatedly stressed, and stressed through examining the precise nature of social alienation in the modern tragedy.

The 'social' component of modern tragedy is no more overriding a feature than the 'divine' or the 'noble' are in its predecessors. The dilemma of the hero is as much psychological as social. John Rosmer or Ella Downey can exert as much fascination for psychoanalysis as Othello or Hamlet. But the context of alienation is indisputably social in a very important sense. The alienation occurs within a family household which is itself socially estranged and internally divided. While the inner conflicts within the household are personal and psychological, the wider terms of reference are social. The household as a collective unit mediates between the individual and the wider society and becomes the filter through which the wider relationship of estrangement operates. There is then, no historical movement from social to personal drama in modern tragedy, as Williams suggests,[7] but rather changes in theme where new forms of social mediation replace older ones as a means of expressing that alienation in theatrical performance.

These changes are in turn related to change in the circumstances of literary genesis. The tragedy of social alienation, as it emerged in Europe, differed sociologically from previous tragedy in one very important aspect. Previous tragedians wrote and lived at the hub of a defined civilisation, its urban centre. The drama of fifth-century Athens, Elizabethan London, and the Paris of the Sun King were all similar by virtue of their centrality. When European tragedy emerges at the end of the nineteenth century, however, it presents us with a new phenomenon of *periphery*. This periphery operates in the life of the writer, the institutional development of the theatres first performing the work, and finally in the themes of the drama itself. The dialectic of centre and periphery, characterised by this centripetal process, is linked to the development of capitalistic industrialisation in the major centres of European power. From 1880 onwards tragic drama originates with Ibsen and Strindberg in Scandinavia, is developed by Chekhov and Gorky in Russia and by Yeats, Synge and O'Casey in Ireland, then latterly by Lorca in southern Spain. The peripheral development presupposes an economic and cultural dependency, (and in the case of Ireland a colonial dependency) making this very rare cultural phenomenon a unique expression of the process of 'uneven development' rarely to be evidenced in any other artistic form. Tragic drama could not have sprung from the major epicentres of European capitalism at this time, nor chosen its tragic protagonists from the urban bourgeoisie of the major nations. For the tragedy of social alienation demanded at inception this geographical transfer to the periphery even if it later came to claim its audience from the civilised and prosperous urban bourgeoisie.

The central theme of the social mode of tragedy is alienation from bourgeois society. But that theme is not static, nor is the alienation a condition of 'being' which remains unchanged throughout the course of the drama. It entails a climactic confrontation between the dramatic personae and the cultural values of the bourgeois social order. We can refer to this climactic outcome as *tragic strife*, but it is important not to confuse it with Georg Lukács' notion of the central collision of the drama reflecting a wider historical struggle of social classes.[8] Tragic strife is not a summarisation of violent struggle although, thematically, elements of that struggle can be present, as in the work of Sean O'Casey. It is the more general dramatic resolution of social alienation, a movement present in the social fabric of the theme and equally in the sequential flow of the action itself. Within this flow the traditional Aristotelian elements are usually incorporated and given social resonance. The reversal of personal fortune becomes a key element in the dynamic process of estrangement, the self-recognition of tragic fate a liberating of social consciousness which comes too late to alter the experience of loss.

The alienation then is structural, but in its literary context differs markedly from the classical formulations of Hegel, Marx and Simmel. It is an estrangement from dominant cultural values rather than the relinquishment of productive powers which Marx saw as the alienated condition of the industrial worker under modern capitalism. But unlike the idealist dimensions of alienation outlined by Simmel, who speaks of an increasing estrangement of the individual from the objective magnitude of cultural products in the modern age, the estrangement is socially located. It occurs within social classes or strata whose material interests diverge from the dominant ruling interests of the society. But the discontent of heroic individuals in such social milieux expresses itself dramatically as alienation from the values of a ruling hegemonic culture, with tragic consequences for the outcome of their own lives.

The connections between the structural and peripheral aspects of tragic alienation change in the course of the modern drama's development. In the movement of tragic drama from the Old World to the New, there is a decisive shift of emphasis towards the proletarian tragedy. This of course had already been established by Büchner, Gorky and O'Casey in Europe. But in the hands of O'Neill and later of Tennessee Williams and Arthur Miller it becomes the dominant feature of American tragedy, whereas in Europe it had been the subordinate one. At the same time American tragedy no longer has the same peripheral relationship to the culture of industrial capitalism as its European counterpart. The switch of emphasis from periphery back to the centre of urban industrial civilisation coincides with the switch of emphasis in the social expression of alienation. But that switch only becomes possible with related changes in dramatic form, changes which undermine the notion of a static and unchanging naturalism as the basic form of the period.

The naturalist techniques which developed during this period revolved around the box stage of the three-walled room. This setting created the illusion of a 'lifelike' representation of domestic environment, but did not in itself constitute a generic 'naturalist' theatre. Rather we must speak of a plurality of naturalist forms used predominantly though not exclusively in the performance of realist drama.[8] Such forms include not only setting but also dialogue and action, and there is no evidence that they have been used together with any real consistency. The early plays of O'Neill, for example, use naturalist dialogue in expressionist settings while the English theatre is notorious for drawing-room drama using limited naturalist scenic design and stylised artificial speech. Most modern drama, even that conventionally labelled 'naturalist', usually makes partial not exclusive use of naturalist forms, and often these are adopted in conjunction with techniques more appropriate to epic or expressionist drama. In modern tragedy the naturalist forms have been predominant but, significantly, in ways which involve either a subtle modification or a subversion of their conventions. In Ibsen especially, who is usually regarded as the naturalist playwright *par excellence*, this is an interior subversion directly connecting the form to the tragic expression.

Such a subversion, then, creates essential changes in the environmental framework of the drama, its dramatic space, which have crucial links with the major theme of alienation. The connection is part of the demarcation between serious and tragic drama, a demarcation often lost by critics in their desire to repudiate a fictitious dogma of 'naturalism' as a genre of synchronised theme and form most suitably adapted, sociologically speaking, to the performance of everyday bourgeois life. It is a critical tendency which posits a doubly false equation – naturalism equals bourgeois drama equals bourgeois life. By illuminating the dramatic space of tragic alienation, this shibboleth can be effectively destroyed. But it must be done in conjunction with a study of the fundamental themes of modern tragedy, most but not all of which have operated within the framework of literary realism. It is naturalism then which refers to form and realism which refers more generally to theme. In the case of the theatre, quite clearly, dramatic realism is going to differ quite considerably from the narrative realism of the novel. The book narrates a fictive world; the stage presents an illusory one. But the common thread of realism in both is what Erich Auerbach has called figural realism.[9] The dramatic persona and the literary character both have a tragic destiny which is socially realised. Far from being a poor relation of the realist novel, realist drama embodies this figural aspect in a different aesthetic form which is itself a unique achievement. In the coming chapters, we have to state precisely what that achievement is.

The internal transformation then of both form and theme are linked in crucial ways. Within this period we have to trace the connections between changes in dramatic space and particular thematic transformations of central importance such as the movement from aristocratic to proletarian modalities of alienation. Equally we have to place these changes in the context of central thematic continuities. One such vital continuity is the inegalitarian status of women in modern society, which works thematically in the plays of Ibsen and O'Neill, Chekhov, O'Casey and Williams, to complement the other modes of estrangement. The absence, outside Germany, of a tragic political drama is more than compensated for here by a tragic tradition creating a new female hero in the context of social alienation. When we move from Ibsen and Chekhov, through Synge and O'Casey, to O'Neill and Williams we can witness the creation of this unheralded tradition, and its relevance to the major thematic changes. In considering first of all one of the most substantial of all modern tragedians, Henrik Ibsen, that relevance becomes immediately apparent.

Part I
The Achievement of Henrik Ibsen

1 Ibsen's Norway

Ibsen's Norway was a predominantly agrarian society, sparsely populated and highly dependent on maritime trade. Insignificant in the arena of European power-politics during the first half of the nineteenth century it had become more progressive and more democratic than most other European countries. But its political situation was extremely paradoxical. In spite of its early democratic achievements, it remained culturally dependent on Denmark long after 1814 when Danish rule officially ceased. In addition it remained politically dependent on its neighbour, Sweden, through enforced union with the Swedish crown. This dual form of dependency coloured its peripheral position within Europe. But the Danish connection also created a division within the country itself. It was divided, linguistically speaking, between a written Danish serving as the official language of church and state, and spoken Norwegian dialects prevalent throughout the countryside. By the middle of the century, this had developed into a cleavage between *riksmal*, an independent reformed version of the official Danish incorporating a substantial Norwegian vocabulary, and the rural *landsmal*, the language of the countryside, giving the Norwegian peasantry a distinct cultural identity which often served as a basis for nationalist aspirations.

Well into the period of rapid industrialisation after 1884, these dual overlapping forms of the relationship between centre and periphery persisted, the one external, the other internal.[1] In the context of protestant Northern Europe, Norway had been a primitive agrarian country, noticeably sluggish in its assimilation of the new material comforts and inventions of an urbanised capitalist civilisation. And while its cities were small and primitive, the internal cleavage between city and countryside was nonetheless strong. This double dialectic, the internal and external, is a crucial key both to the processes by which Ibsen created his realist drama and to the major themes that drama expresses. Cultural isolation sets the parameters for his artistic career; his drama invokes major comparisons of civilisation and wilderness, of a fragile constricted urban existence and the constant proximity of

3

forest, fjord and sea. His drama thus refracts a complex social formation. It cannot credibly be presented as the genesis of the typically bourgeois drama of the last hundred years in Europe. On the contrary, it is a total and uncompromising response to the peripheral nature of the society and the life to which it constantly referred and out of which it was indubitably born. The similarity with Irish drama is immediately apparent. The work of Synge, Yeats and O'Casey contributing in equal if not greater measure to the renaissance of European drama, shared that same context of peripheral dependency. For any social theory of drama the differences between Ireland and Norway are just as important as their similarities. But as far as tragic drama is concerned, their shared predicament is the necessary starting point. And this originates, historically, in the colonial experience.

The Norwegian experience, like the Irish, was one of political subjugation. Yet Norway was never significantly colonised. Thus while economically backward and culturally dependent, it was able to adapt itself politically to the gains of the French Revolution. After the union with Sweden it had adopted one of the most democratic constitutions of its time, modelled on the French constitution of 1791 with an enfranchisement of nearly half the adult population. Moreover it had had virtually no indigenous aristocracy since the Black Death and in 1821 the Norwegian Parliament abolished all orders of nobility. The resulting stable pre-democratic situation, one of representative oligarchy, was flexible enough to adapt to formal liberal-democracy during the period towards the end of the century when the social tensions created by industrialisation were channelled into forms of political discontent. Compared to the Irish uprising of 1916 and its bloody aftermath, the severing of the union with Sweden in 1905, the year before Ibsen's death, was relatively painless.

This position of peripheral dependency and the unique nature of its social and political development were the major dimensions of Norwegian history which we find artistically refracted in Ibsen's work. They form the social conditions for the development of a new prose drama of contemporary life, stretching from *The League of Youth* to *An Enemy of the People* in which naturalist stage conventions are developed in conjunction with the figural realism characteristic of the nineteenth-century novel. More importantly, they constitute the necessary condition for the second major phase in this development—the development of a tragic drama. Ibsen retains the same figural dimensions in the subsequent period from *Ghosts* to *John Gabriel Borkman*. This second and more important phase is often obscured by the reception of Ibsen's work. In Germany and Britain he became popular among intellectuals and middle-class audiences as a serious dramatist of bourgeois life. But the tragic dimension of his drama was diminished by the tendency of his critics and audiences to focus exclusively on the social issues raised by the plays, and to extrapolate these issues from the total dramatic process. In England, this tendency was reinforced by the misleading essay of George Bernard Shaw, *The Quintessence of Ibsenism*. Although Shaw was quick to realise the social challenge Ibsen's work contained, he misrepresented it as a didactic condemnation of all forms of moral and political idealism.[2] Shaw's Ibsen, largely conceived in Shaw's own image, ends up as an apostle of reform and commonsense, a Fabian of the fjords.

This Shavian shibboleth has had a long-standing effect upon critical understanding. It obscured the development of a tragic vision out of the fusion of figural realism and naturalist forms. Amidst all the controversies over modern drama, this development has never been fully recognised or brought to light. Often, realism has been identified with the early 'social' drama as such, and the later tragedies seen as theatrical accounts of a 'personal' or individual fate moving away from realism altogether. It will be argued here, on the contrary, that the tragic and the social are indisputably linked. The tragic vision in Ibsen does not vitiate realism. Rather, it gives a heightened expression to the social and the real. In this view, the most significant 'social' drama is not to be found in *The Pillars of Society*, *A Doll's House*, or *An Enemy of the People*. It is to be found in five 'later' works—*Ghosts* (though written just prior to *An Enemy of the People*), *The Wild Duck*, *Rosmersholm*, *Hedda Gabler* and *John Gabriel Borkman*. The early social dramas are a vital intermediate step in the transition to tragedy but equally stand in their own right. They must be seen as a plateau Ibsen had reached in his attempt to achieve even greater heights of artistic expression. In order to write contemporary tragedy of a higher standard than his earlier poetic and historical tragedies culminating in *Emperor and Galilean*, he had to re-create contemporary heroes in a figural dimension of equivalent stature to Brand and the Emperor Julian. When finally achieved this accomplishment became the major breakthrough into modern dramatic tragedy.

The background to these developments must be sought in Ibsen's personal career and his remarkably insular relationship to European and classical drama. He knew little of the Greeks or the Elizabethans, and took his inspiration from those contemporary developments in the theatre of which he was aware. This placed him at the outset of his career in a web of contradictions whose painful disentanglement was a necessary precondition for artistic development. In Norway, Ibsen came to writing at the time of a great stirring of national consciousness. His first historical dramas, most of them within the genre of Nordic heroism, were a literary expression of this cultural development. At the same time, the genre itself had been developed most successfully in the very country from which many Norwegians wished to culturally emancipate themselves—Denmark. In the first half of the nineteenth century, the Danish Royal Theatre emerged as the focus of Scandinavian theatrical culture. Its dramatic repertoire was particularly enhanced by its productions of the plays of Adam Oehlenschläger who had an immense influence on the early Ibsen. In plays like *Hakon Jarl*, Oehlenschläger provided the inspiration for Ibsen's *Lady Inger of Oestraat* and *The Vikings at Helgeland*. In literary terms, Norway's national awakening was dependent on the very country whose cultural influence its writers and dramatists sought to overthrow. Ironically, it was also through the Danish connection that Ibsen was able to overcome the cultural narrowness of his Norwegian background. A visit to the Royal Theatre in Copenhagen in 1852, his first trip outside Norway, had a profound impact on him. He saw Shakespeare performed for the first time and encountered acting of a standard far superior to that of his native Norway. The Danish theatre had given him what the Norwegian could not—a window onto the drama of the world.

This pattern of experience presents us with a crucial paradox. It meant that in order to become a distinctly Norwegian playwright concerned with contemporary Norway, Ibsen had to abandon the ethnocentric nationalism of many of his contemporaries. The Nordic heroic genre was after all taken from Denmark, from which many of his fellow cultural nationalists wished to rescue their own country. Ibsen escaped this cultural dependency by looking further afield and taking from France and Germany in turn, important dramatic influences which enabled him to make the crucial break with a parochial tradition. The French influence was a necessary evil which Ibsen himself eventually had to overcome. From the work of Eugene Scribe he took the formula of the well-made play with its paraphernalia of tortuous intrigue, overheard conversations, intercepted letters and strained coincidence. It gave him the economy of form necessary for his early social drama, but equally his previous commitment to poetic drama provided a basic resistance against the purely mechanical nature of the Scribean system. The major thematic influences came from German drama. The advanced intellectual development of Germany in the first half of the nineteenth century which, as Marx wryly noted, was in all other respects, backward, became a decisive formative influence.

In the work of Hegel was to be found the major aesthetic doctrine of the age; in the work of Goethe and Schiller, the major tragedy. But it was in more recent developments that Ibsen, with his insular and selective attitude to European culture, found more direct inspiration. He singled out the dramas of Friedrich Hebbel and the dramatic theories of Herman Hettner. Hettner's appraisal of Hebbel's contemporary drama *Maria Magdalene* was particularly significant. This work, basically a play about ordinary village people, raised the possibility in Ibsen's mind of tragic prose drama of everyday life. This had already been accomplished by the unknown German doctor Georg Büchner in his extraordinary drama *Woyzeck*. But Büchner was hardly ever produced in his own century and the available developments of the time in German drama were taken back to Norway where they underwent a remarkable transformation, having been transported, as it were, to the periphery of Europe.

A major contrast between the tragic realism of nineteenth-century drama and that of the nineteenth-century novel immediately presents itself. Tragic realism in the nineteenth-century novel emerged from a previous foundation of serious realist writing and continued to co-exist with it in complex and inter-connected ways. Often, non-realist influences were important. In the case of Emily Brontë, the formative influences upon *Wuthering Heights* of the Gothic genre and the Scottish fiction of Walter Scott and James Hogg were as important as the major tradition of English realism. But the development of the realist novel in England and France paralleled the rise of capitalism and the two revolutions which subsequently transformed it—the political revolution in France and the industrial revolution in England. The genesis and maturation of realism in the novel was at the centre, not the periphery of capitalist development. Seen in this light, the achievement of Ibsen is all the more incredible. It is as if the development of realist drama and the transition from serious to tragic realism is encapsulated within the work of a single person, in cultural isolation from literary tradition and the mainstream of European development. Before Ibsen's death realist drama had already diversified—in Germany, in Ireland and in Russia. But until that time, at the turn of the century, his work stood out as a lone and forbidding achievement.

Once Ibsen had managed to overthrow the Scribean legacy, his tragic drama becomes notable for its transformation of the Aristotelian unities. The compressed form complements the modalities of alienation which are thematically expressed. Expressed sociologically, we can observe an important and dynamic relationship between *tragic sociation* and *tragic space*. To ignore or reduce either of these dimensions, or to overlook their interrelationship is to miss the point of Ibsenist tragedy. The tendency to interpret Ibsen's consistent use of the past as evidence of bourgeois guilt on either his part, that of his heroes, or both author and character, is to miss the point about compression. For although the past is a significant and oppressive fact in Ibsen's work, its re-entry into the contemporaneous situation of the play is a necessary part of a wider process. This process is the dramatic refinement, or purification, by which the single central collision of the play stands out against the background of contemporary everyday life. To this end Ibsen sacrificed the dramatic form, accessible to any audience, of circumstance changing over time and drastically altered the tempo of dramatic action. As a mode of writing this is often over-extended and sometimes results in a stifling lack of theatrical movement. But equally, the inventiveness of dramatic production has not as a rule been equal to the tasks which Ibsen set it. The absence of a Norwegian theatre capable, *ab initio*, of taking up the challenge of its native writer has had wider ramifications for the twentieth-century theatre as a whole.

Before the complex relationship between tragic sociation and tragic space can be fully brought out, we must examine the polarities out of which Ibsen's artistic vision of alienation arises. These are derived from Norway's peripheral position, from the double dialectic already outlined. Three polarities stand out, paganism against Christianity, wilderness against civilisation, the noble against the bourgeois. In his earlier work, Ibsen expressed the conflict of paganism and Christianity romantically and historically. *The Vikings at Helgeland* affirmed the pagan tradition of Scandinavia and the later more ambitious *Emperor and Galilean* continued the assault on Christianity at a sustained philosophical pitch worthy of Nietzsche. But it proved the most unstageable of all his plays. In the realist drama, the polarity is transmuted into a more diffuse kind of tension, the setting up of a pagan 'nature' which ran counter to the Protestant culture of Ibsen's own time. The stifling pietism he had encountered in rural and provincial Norwegian life was a religious expression of growing bourgeois hegemony. In his work it coloured the respectable villainy of provincial figures like Pastor Manders and Doctor Kroll, whose moral hypocrisy was consonant with the conventional bourgeois wisdom of the time. In contrast, his paganism spawned its own dramatic devices, notably the demonic spirit of the trolls and the restless yearning for the sea. Pagan 'nature' is a theatrical aura offering a specific temptation which is significantly unattainable—freedom from the constraints of a bourgeois civilisation. Significantly this kind of tension is very different from the romantic conservatism which had arisen earlier in England and Germany as a response to the twin revolutions, the French and the industrial. There is no rural idyll, no arcadia, no natural organic community being offered. Ibsen's protagonists could only emancipate themselves into a barbaric wilderness.

The link between paganism and wilderness is complemented by a similarly binding relationship between wilderness and nobility. Norway in fact did not have a titled landed nobility. It had effectively been wiped out in Feudal times during the Black Death and the country's later historical tutelage as a Danish colony prevented the formation of an indigenous rural upper class. Ibsen's obsession with nobility as an attribute of life should be seen against the background of its negligible import as a class phenomenon within Norway itself. While a substantial reality underlay the evanescent qualities of the noble in the work of Dostoevsky and Chekhov, Ibsenist nobility is ghostly and incorporeal. His aristocratic heroes such as John Rosmer and Hedda Gabler come from upper-class families but lack what in other societies would pass for an aristocratic pedigree. But in lacking an objective correlative Ibsen places more emphasis on what is dramatically important—the aspiration towards nobility as an attribute of all human life. Here nobility is less a function of material privilege than of superior aspiration within a stifling philistine culture which Ibsen identified with bourgeois domination.

A fourth polarity suggests itself—that of women against marriage. It is, after all, the common thread linking Ibsen's three major heroines, Nora Helmer, Rebecca West and Hedda Gabler. Actually the polarity is narrower and wider than this. Narrower, because often the revolt is against a specific marriage to a specific person without invoking a general principle, but wider because Ibsen inverts the familiar identification of his day with respect to women—the image of the woman as the foundation stone of marriage and family life. Not only did Ibsen subvert the conventional legitimacy of the female role in family life, he produced more positive dimensions of female heroism which were and remain revolutionary from an artistic point of view. They maintain the one sustained link of his tragic drama with the social transformations of the modern age, transformations which in some cases have become actual and in other still remain as potential possibilities for social realisation. This is not to reduce Ibsen to the vapid formula of a 'progressive' or 'committed' dramatist. But taken together with the polarities of alienation stressed above, it effectively demolishes the argument for Ibsen as the prototype of bourgeois drama.

The personal circumstances of Ibsen's career add supplementary weight to the demolition of this myth. Artistically speaking, Ibsen's most productive years were spent in exile. Lasting nearly forty years, from 1864 to 1891, his exile, like that of James Joyce, was self-imposed. But it was also an artistic necessity. The circumstances of Ibsen's life in Norway had made writing finally impossible for him. This was not due to the paucity of theatrical life or his lack of interest in it. Quite the contrary, the number of theatres in Norway at the time was quite high in proportion to the general population and Ibsen became an important theatre director first in Bergen and then in Christiania. Despite these attachments, yet also because of them, Ibsen found that his literary output was grinding to a halt. The puritanism, provincial philistinism and general petty-mindedness of his contemporaries prevented him from accomplishing single-handedly what Yeats was later to accomplish in Ireland. He could not drag the Norwegian theatre out of its torpor and backwardness and at the same time write the plays which would provide it with a new lease of life. In the event he did neither. As an establishment figure in Christiania, he found himself under fire for those very faults he had previously attacked in others as an iconoclastic drama critic. He failed to carry out much-needed administrative reforms, and with inadequate resources at his disposal, he lapsed into producing commercial plays of no value. When he failed to gain a state grant from the Norwegian parliament, he finally ceased writing.[3] By leaving Norway he repudiated a grey future as a barren bureaucratic hack.

The nature and circumstances of his exile are as important as his decision to embark upon it. He went, like Joyce, to Italy. But the transition for him was more immense. The religious, cultural and geographical contrasts were stark. Ibsen found his nourishment in Renaissance art, in the culture which was the seedbed of modern civilisation. Yet his plays of this period are, with only one exception, indisputably Norwegian. The relationship between literary conditions of production and thematic content, between the 'how' and 'what' of drama, were decisively fixed. The period of his transition to prose drama coincided with a longing to return home. But Ibsen, while writing *The Pillars of Society*, rightly resisted it. He wrote most of his major works in either Italy or Germany and returned home only after the completion of *Hedda Gabler* in Munich. In contrast to the domestic cosiness which was adorned the living-rooms of many an Ibsen production, Georg Brandes remarked that Ibsen's own living conditions were truly impersonal, never bearing resemblance to anything which could be called a home. The same homelessness, but within his own country, was to be a personal affliction of Eugene O'Neill. But homeless exile stood Ibsen in good stead. He was to transform not merely Norwegian theatre but the theatre of the world. By staying in Italy he at last put Norway on the map of Europe.

The Beginnings of Tragic Drama

The most distinctive outcome of Ibsen's encounter with German dramatic theory and practice was *Emperor and Galilean*, his long historical tragedy written over a period of nine years in Italy. In it, Ibsen breaks with the Protestant theological obsession which had inspired *Brand* and attempts to vindicate heathenism and apostasy. The Emperor Julian rebels against the growing dominance of Christianity in the Roman Empire and takes drastic and tyrannical methods to roll back the tide of history in a way which anticipates the madness of the later Nietzsche. But the play is immensely long and as a theatrical spectacle almost unstageable. Completed in 1873, it was first staged in 1896 in abridged form. Theatrically, it suffers from its intellectual virtues. Ibsen was the first modern playwright after Büchner to use the theatre as a form for the titanic clash of ideas, and to match it with an extraordinary display of exotic spectacle. The extravagance of Julian's intellectual obsession is outdone only by the extravagance of Ibsen's crowd scenes and his stage directions. Coming from a country where stagecraft and equipment were far behind much of Europe, he produced a play which would have defeated nearly any theatre in Europe because of its vast length and sporadic impracticalities. But the difficulties do not stop there. The central theme shows an imbalance between the abstract and the concrete, between Julian's apostasy and the imperial splendour which surrounds him. The kind of tragic strife that Ibsen envisaged is therefore flawed by this defect. For despite the compelling sense of Julian's emotional involvement with his ideal, intellectual debate slackens the dramatic action and its length dissipates the impact of the tragic denouement.

A further defect of the play lies in the dramatic construction of the hero. Like Brand, Julian is indisputably heroic in terms of the ideal for which he strives. But he is compromised by the tyrannical exercise of political power he uses to attain it. Like Camus' *Caligula*, a ruling position negates heroic potential and loses the sympathy of the audience. In Ibsen's case the sheer tyranny of Julian destroys the cathartic effect of his tragic end, for no pity or sympathy can be offered him. By contrast, modern tragedy begins with the abdication of the tragedy of rank; with the heroic stature of the oppressed, not the oppressor. Through his apostasy Julian joined the ranks of the contemporary intellectual rebels but as pitiless emperor he ramained a tyrant.

Ibsen's first tragic drama of contemporary life, *Ghosts*, can be seen as a movement away from the genre of historical tragedy. At the level of dramatic form, it seeks tragic strife through intensive compression of the plot. Thematically speaking, this development is complemented by a search to express the heroic stature of the oppressed. The heroic figures of the play are its victims—mother and son, Oswald and Mrs Alving. The expansive dramatic form and its Promethean hero are retained only in the affirmative dramas, *The Pillars of Society* and *An Enemy of the People*. This bifurcation is significant. It entailed, temporarily, a partial separation of the heroic and the tragic. In some respects, indeed, *Ghosts* seems closer to classical than to post-Renaissance tragedy. For Ibsen has moved, in the case of Oswald Alving, from the Promethean hero to the heroic victim. A secret modern affliction, congenital syphilis, has been substituted for the vindictive will of the pitiless Gods, synchronising a contemporary content with a classical form. The dramatic development moves the hero, 'worm-eaten from birth', and his audience towards a mutual recognition of his total helplessness, where, at the end, he is reduced to the state of a human vegetable pleading pitifully for the sun. There could be no greater contrast with Brand or Julian, Bernick or Stockmann. The action of the play in that sense seems to move not with Oswald and Mrs Alving, but against them. Victims of bourgeois moral hypocrisy, the aptitude for heroic action is denied them from the very outset.

The main constraint here is the purely physical basis of Oswald's predicament. Though it was realistic, as Auguste Lindberg, the Swedish producer, found to his horror when he visited a Danish hospital for insane syphylitic children, it is an artistic limitation on the tragic vision which Ibsen had created. What he achieved within the framework was remarkable. But congenital disease not merely inflates, in metaphorical terms, the nature of the punishment in relation to the nature of the crime. It reduces Oswald's social circumstance to a purely physical trap. One is reminded of the physical impotence of Jacques in Hemingway's *Fiesta*. In *Ghosts*, the trap is not merely physical but also generational. Despite Oswald's escape into bohemianism, the dependency it sets up is crippling. The hero's final doom is internal to the bourgeois household, within which Oswald, turning insane, remains a prisoner.

One way in which some critics have seen a different tragedy to the purely physical debility of Oswald, is to look at the moral compromise of Mrs Alving and Pastor Mander's hypocritical complicity in her disastrous decision to remain with her husband. But this aspect of the play operates at the level of serious, not tragic drama. The social dilemma is more modest and more narrow, and Mrs Alving has already compromised her heroic stature by accepting the Pastor's advice. The moral hypocrisy of the bourgeoisie is not sufficient to generate by itself a drama of tragic proportion. And the major polarity of the drama, that of nordic Protestantism and French bohemianism presents us with a collision which is merely a clash of attitudes, and not the source of tragic misfortune or reversal. Oswald's dissolute life as a painter is both escape from and revolt against the puritanism of provincial Norwegian life. But since the dramatic irony of the play deems it of secondary importance to the actual congenital source of illness, the revolt is not part of the final reckoning. The circle is finally closed, through heredity alone.

Oswald's *vie bohème* and his disaffection are not sufficient to generate the tragic alienation of the later drama. The play relies on a vision, not of tragic alienation, but of tragic necessity, and that necessity is not, as we have seen, convincingly social. Nor has Ibsen been able to create the tragic space necessary to the modality of alienation. Familial dependency is the all-inclusive metaphor of the one-dimensional stage. Thus, while *Ghosts* has been regarded as the most overtly 'social' of Ibsen's tragedies, it is in fact the opposite. It is the least social. Because it is predetermined, the social action of the protagonists has no decisive impact on its tragic denouement. The play actually works because the recognition of tragic necessity is delayed, and Oswald has refused to accept the truth the doctor has told him. This creates a genuine and remarkable pathos. But only because Oswald is, and will remain the victim of necessity.

In his next tragedy, *The Wild Duck*, the same problem of producing heroes rather than victims, remained. But here, at last, Ibsen was able to create the dimension of tragic alienation that was previously unattainable. By comparison, *Ghosts* represented the crossroads at which modern tragedy stood. It developed a social problematic within the framework of bourgeois life and its tragic strife was genetically pre-ordained. Ibsen had still to create the dramatic space of tragic alienation, establish a two-dimensional frame for dramatic action, and break decisively with the forms of familial and economic dependency characteristic of all the works up to *An Enemy of the People*. A consideration of *The Wild Duck* will show us how that break was made.

2 Wilderness against Civilisation

The heroic victims of *The Wild Duck* are less privileged, more oppressed than Mrs Alving and Oswald in *Ghosts*. But the point at which oppression ends and heroism begins is impossible to detect. Like *Ghosts*, the main dimension of conflict in the play is generational. But not only is it a conflict between generations, it is a conflict within generations. On the one hand there is the conflict between Werle and Gregers, his son, and between Ekdal and his daughter, Hedvig. On the other hand there is the perennial feud between Werle and Ekdal and the tragic confrontation of Gregers and Hedvig. One dimension is superimposed upon the other to make the whole question of victimisation and revolt immeasurably more complex than it was in *Ghosts*. Unlike Ibsen's previous work, this is not a story of one family but of two, and this disrupts the previous pattern of familial integration. There is a separation between family and financial dependency. Ekdal is indebted financially, but not morally, to Werle for the capital to start up his photographer's studio after the humiliation of bankruptcy. Gregers, on the other hand, eschews financial dependence on his father by working in one of the family saw-mills. Yet he is never able to evade completely the consequences of his father's actions. When he leaves his father's employ, it is to live with his father's victims, and deliberately try and undo the wrong his father has committed towards them. Finally, the families are united by Ekdal's marriage to Werle's former servant and mistress, a marriage originally encouraged by the richer man as a further form of his rival's subjugation.

The drama revolves around Gregers' quest to unite his desire for independence with the emancipation of the Ekdal family from his father's clutches. This mutual liberation is not merely materially beneficial to both parties in Gregers' eyes, but also moral proof of an incorruptible courage. The play shows us how, conceived totally in the abstract, his moral crusade comes to grief. Yet this highly abstract and ideal process operates through a concrete material symbol. Gregers' 'claim of the ideal' is obsessively focused on a living being, the wounded pet of a deprived child, on the 'reality' of the wild duck. The play is not, therefore, an exercise in symbolism as some critics have suggested but an exploration of the dialectic interplay of ideal and reality. The wild duck is symbolic of a wider reality. But it is so only by virtue of being a particular kind of bird wounded by the gun of one person and lovingly cherished by another. And here Ibsen introduces in a contemporary realist vein the theme he had represented poetically and historically in *Brand*. That theme is the vast contrast and tension between wilderness and civilisation.

The wounding of the wild duck by Haakon Werle's shotgun points to the ambiguous role of pacification posessed by modern civilisation. The act of pacification is also an act of conquest, the brutal conquest of man over nature. The taking of the winged duck into captivity by the Ekdals is seemingly a more humane version of this same process—of turning the bird into a domestic pet doted on by a child. But this apparent bourgeois domesticity conceals a deeper motive. It is a nostalgic attempt to preserve something of the bird's 'wildness' even in its wounded state. The attachment is not idyllic. It is an attachment to a living being which contains something of a wild and primitive nature. The bird belongs to a natural wilderness which is already being transformed irreversibly by human development. Ibsen brings this out explicitly when Gregers is questioning Ekdal's father about his hunting days in the forest.

Ekdal. . . . How does the forest look up there now? Still good, eh?
Gregers. Not as good as in your day. It's been thinned out a lot.
Ekdal. Thinned out? Chopped down? (*More quietly as though in fear.*) That's dangerous. Bad things'll come of that. The forest'll have its revenge.
Hjalmar (*fills his glass*). Have a little more, father.
Gregers. How can a man like you, a man who loves the open air as you do, bear to live in the middle of a stuffy town, boxed between four walls?
Ekdal. (*gives a short laugh and glances at Hjalmar*). Oh, it's not too bad here. Not bad at all.
Gregers. But what about the cool sweeping breezes, the free life in the forest, and up on the wide open spaces among animals and birds? These things had become a part of you.
Ekdal. (*smiles*). Hjalmar, shall we show it to him?
Hjalmar (*quickly, a little embarrassed*). Oh, no father, no. Not tonight.[1]

Hjalmar's evasiveness and embarrassment are due to the strange attic in which the family keep the wild duck. Their response to the inaccessibility of nature is to capture it under false pretences. The loft is both the 'space' of nature and the means of imprisoning it. In theatrical terms, the loft is an extraordinary device, and quite unique. It is not merely an appendage to Ekdal's studio. It is very much like an appendage to the stage itself. It calls into question those dimensions of bounded space which Ibsen seems to have accepted in most of his work as a necessary feature of the naturalist stage. The stage directions call for it to be 'long and irregularly shaped', 'full of dark nooks and crannies'. It too is a bounded space, a room onstage. But lacking the symmetry and accessibility of Ibsen's typical rooms, it is a jumble lying in shadow. Here, bereft of contact with nature, even with the earth beneath their feet, the Ekdals cultivate their strange captivity of nature. But it is nature as artifice where old Ekdal 'hunts' rabbits and Hedvig lovingly tends to the wounded duck.

In *The Wild Duck*, the loft represents the tragic space lacking in *Ghosts*, the dramatic space of the play's tragic denouement. It is so, however, precisely by being a reflexive illustration of Ibsen's theatrical self-constraint. Since the stage could no more mirror natural wilderness in *Peer Gynt* or *Brand* than it could in *Ghosts*, the loft as a theatrical device illuminates the illusory nature of dramatic space itself. Yet within the context of that illusion, its spatial enclosure presents us with a vivid image of the fragile boundary between nature and civilisation. Wilderness lies beyond the stage but at the same time is incorporated within it. The way in which it becomes crucial to the fate of the two families, the tragic sociation to which it gives rise, has often been overlooked. The wild duck is not important as a symbol in a loft. The loft itself, and the imprisoned animals it contains, are an integral part of the processes of sociation we see on the foreground of the stage. For the hope and joy they inspire in the Ekdal family are living proof to Gregers Werle of the kind of human illusion which he regards as poisonous and wishes to destroy.

Gregers' crusade to transform the life of his father's demoralised victims has been the most controversial issue in the play. The tragic outcome of Gregers' misguided plan has been seen by Shaw as irrefutable evidence of Ibsen's dislike of idealism as such. From this viewpoint, Gregers is a fanatical zealot who, in hoping to save people's lives merely succeeds in destroying them. This is undoubtedly true, and is the key to the play. But the process by which this comes about has been misrepresented. Following Shaw, it has been the custom to attribute to Ibsen a tendentious attack on all idealism as harmful to human life in general. Relling, when he attacks Werle at the end of the play so bitterly, has been seen as the mouthpiece of the author himself: 'Oh, life would be all right if we didn't have to put up with damn creditors who keep pestering us with the demands of their ideals.' But it is much too simplistic to reduce the play to this kind of formula and Shaw unwittingly did much damage in presenting one aspect of the play as its total meaning, and by extension, as the central feature of Ibsen's drama as a whole. The nature of idealism in *The Wild Duck*, as in *Rosmersholm*, is complex and problematical. The conflict is not between idealism and commonsense, but between different forms of idealism and between conflicting views about the material necessities of life.

There is an important duality here. Gregers and his unintended victims each have their ideal view of the world, and at the same time, a view of their own material situation within that world. But in neither case is there a binding unity between the material and the ideal. Not only do these views contradict each other, they are internally contradictory. The picture is one of external conflict and internal division. In his myopic crusade, Gregers preys on the contradictions of the Ekdal family without firstly recognising his own. The desire he expresses to Hedvig of owning a dog which would plunge into the lake and rescue the wounded duck from 'the bottom of the deep' where it has taken refuge, is inherently idealistic. But as an assault on 'the bottom of the deep' which Hedvig so reveres, it is also a crusade *against* an ideal. The full import of this does not become clear however until his long conversation with Hedvig in the third act.

By this time Gregers has come to delve voyeuristically into the secret world of the Ekdals and is particularly fascinated by the half-blind Hedvig, the ungainly but sensitive daughter. He discovers she has no formal schooling but instead nurtures her imagination on old picture books stacked in the loft. As their conversation develops, she tells Gregers the duck is different from other animals in the loft because it is 'a real wild bird' and 'no one knows her':

> Hedvig. No one knows her. And no one knows where she came from.
> Gregers. And she's been down to the bottom of the deep.
> Hedvig (*glances at him quickly and represses a smile*). Why do you say 'the bottom of the deep'?
> Gregers. What should I have said?
> Hedvig. You could have said 'the sea bed', or just 'the bottom of the sea'.

Gregers. Oh, why can't I say 'the bottom of the deep'?

Hedvig. Yes, but it always sounds so odd to me when other people talk about 'the bottom of the deep'.

Gregers. Why? Tell me.

Hedvig. No, I won't. It's silly.

Gregers. Not at all. Tell me now, why did you smile?

Hedvig. It's because I suddenly—without thinking—remembered what's in there. I always think of it all as being 'the bottom of the deep'. But that's just silly.

Gregers. No, you mustn't say that.

Hedvig. Well, it's only a loft.

Gregers (*looks hard at her*). Are you sure?

Hedvig (*astonished*). That it's only a loft?

Gregers. Yes. You are quite certain about that?

(*Hedvig stares at him silently, open-mouthed.*)[2]

Gregers equates the girl's affection for the duck with her interest in old picture books, as an imaginative form of escapism. Her retreat from the public social world is unreal in his eyes, but endowed with a mysterious profundity into which he has been unable to penetrate. The phrase 'the bottom of the deep' signifies for him not only the escape of the duck but that of Hedvig herself. By wanting to rescue Hedvig from it, he wishes to bring her back into the public world, but he can conceive of his mission only in such a way as to actually mystify it.

Thus the loft has a mystical function in his eyes whereas Hedvig, who makes daily use of it, regards it as a real and ordinary place. Gregers, on the other hand, sees in it something much more sinister whose evil force has to be overcome. The play presents us not merely with a moral crusade but with a clash of idealisms in which Gregers blatantly ignores how much the retreat of the Ekdals is due to their past humiliations and reduced material circumstances. He also overlooks the possibility that in trying to rescue Hedvig, like the dog plunging down to drag the duck to the surface, he is complementing his father's original transgression in wounding it—the transgression of civilisation against nature.

His mission to liberate Hjalmar Ekdal is again indicative of his peculiar blindness to human experience. Whimsical and tyrannical by turns, Ekdal is a pathetic defeated figure who wounds his family whenever he feels threatened. Instead of turning Ekdal's hatred towards Haakon Werle, Gregers merely succeeds in turning it inwards onto Hedvig. The idealism then becomes suspect, not based on general principles but highly personalised. He wants to liberate specific individuals and, doing so, succumbs to the temptation of wielding power over them. Hence the warning which Ibsen sounded in his notes for the play: 'Liberation consists in securing for individuals the right to free themselves.' Gregers does not offer a vision of hope. He humiliates Ekdal and Hedvig by increasing their pain. And he unwittingly changes sides in the generational conflict. Wishing to use Ekdal as a weapon against his father, he ends up encouraging his father's victims to victimise his own daughter. In hoping to avenge one form of patriarchal tyranny, he merely encourages another. The irony of this is not lost on the audience either. For during the course of the play Haakon Werle is the one person who does not experience failure or defeat. His son's idealism is never really a threat to him.

Gregers' ideals originate in self-deception and end in catastrophe. But this does not provide proof of the pernicious nature of social ideals. Rather it points to the dangers of their deformation, and ultimately of their betrayal. Gregers' action complements his father's wounding of the wild duck by prompting a psychological parallel—Ekdal's wounding of Hedvig's heart through his rejection of her. Her growing blindness which may be inherited from Werle is significant not only as a physical ailment but also as a metaphor of victimisation. In the following excerpt, she is the main figure of the conversation:

Hjalmar. . . . He [Werle] is going blind.
Gina. Oh, we don't know for sure about that.
Hjalmar. Can we doubt it? At least we ought not to; for there lie justice and retribution. He has blinded many a loyal and trusting friend—
Gregers. I'm afraid he has blinded many.
Hjalmar. And now comes the inexorable, the unfathomable and demands his own eyes.
Gina. Oh, how can you say such a horrible thing? You make me feel quite frightened.
Hjalmar. It is useful to face up to the darker aspects of existence now and then.[3]

At this point Hedvig returns through the front door 'happy and breathless'. The timing of her entrance is exact, a superb piece of dramatic irony. The blinded victim appears before them without any of them recognising it. Shortly, Ekdal and Gregers will conspire in the events leading the distraught girl to take her own life.

The plight of Hedvig is reminiscent of Stevie Verloc in Conrad's *The*

Secret Agent. She is a peripheral casualty of a poisoned idealism. Here, unlike Conrad's novel, she is the sole sacrifice. Werle is not involved, while Gregers and Ekdal can each find excuses for the tragedy of her death. For Hjalmar, she will become in Relling's words 'nothing more than a theme for a recitation' and Gregers can claim that she 'has not died in vain'. The lacerating contempt of Relling at the end of the play, his denunciation of the ideal, is needed to offset their mutual failure to accept responsibility for what has happened. But equally important is old Ekdal's remark that 'the forest has taken its revenge'. Nature, both as innocence and wildness will not be subdued and civilisation has merely won a pyrrhic victory.

Hedvig's fate sets the pattern for Ibsen's subsequent tragic drama—that of suicide. It is suicide as a response to unendurable social circumstance. As a victim Hedvig becomes heroic through the act of taking her own life. The equivocations of Gregers and Ekdal at the end merely enlarge rather than diminish the cathartic effect. The loss is felt to be irreparable. And it is tragic solely through Gregers' intervention. Gregers is a vital link between Oswald Alving and Eilert Loevborg, representing one form of intellectual revolt against bourgeois society. But unlike either of the others, he is the catalyst of tragedy not its victim. His revolt works only in conjunction with what it destroys, namely another form of opposition, mute and residual, which he never comes to understand. And it is the latter which creates the tragic space of the drama, a space which the single dichotomy of intellectual and bourgeois is powerless to accomplish.

The significance of this tragic space is revealed more clearly in a comparison with *The Lady from the Sea*. In his early notes for *The Wild Duck* Ibsen describes Hedvig as 'drawn to the sea'. But this image disappears from the later draughts. Instead it is reserved for the heroine of his next play but one, Ellida Wangel. The mystic attraction to the sea which Ibsen creates here would have been meaningless in *The Wild Duck*. But we need to see precisely why this is so. The wounded duck Hedvig cares for illustrates the tension between nature and civilisation. But the sea, for Ellida Wangel, is the symbol of a mystical freedom, a freedom never really possible for Hedvig Ekdal. Ellida's 'restless yearning for the sea' is an estrangement too, but one without limits. The absence of limits acts as a condition for the possibility of reincorporation since it is bereft of the permanent tension created by a fixed dramatic space. The sea, unbounded and limitless, cannot be reproduced theatrically within the illusion of the stage. As a result the play posits a choice between complete freedom for its heroine and complete dependency on her marriage. When the first is finally rejected, then a return to marriage and re-integration within family life entails an affirmative ending. The yearning for the sea is not only a yearning for the unknown but also a yearning for the unspecified. The nature of her potential rescuer, the American sailor, who is referred to as 'the stranger', is an abstract typification paving the way for the later formulas of Strindbergian and German Expressionism. Thus when her husband successfully persuades Ellida to resist the temptation of 'the stranger' and stay with him, the play ends in bathetic anti-climax. The experience of discontent and yearning is then summarised in a formula which by comparison seems empty and banal:

> Wangel. I feel I begin to understand you, little by little. You think and feel in pictures and visual images. Your restless yearning for the sea—your yearning for this stranger—all that was nothing but an expression of your longing for freedom. Nothing more.[4]

Despite the heroine's yearning for a primitive environment, the ties of the bourgeois family are too strong, and the process of recuperation leads to an affirmative ending devoid of tragedy. But Ellida Wangel was not the only one of Ibsen's heroines, besides Hedvig, to possess this strong tie with a wild untrammelled nature. It is also a feature of Rebecca West in *Rosmersholm*, which provides us with another of the vital links in the development of the tragic drama—the link between nobility and wilderness.

3 The Noble against the Bourgeois/Women against Marriage

Rosmersholm and *Hedda Gabler* are tragedies, and both are connected to earlier non-tragic works. *Hedda Gabler* is a transformation of *A Doll's House*, *Rosmersholm* a tragic reformulation of *An Enemy of the People*. The transformations were not due to conscious dissatisfaction with the earlier work but an artistic blockage in Ibsen's dramatic development. Both the earlier dramas were deemed controversial, not to say scandalous, when they first appeared and they contributed substantially to his popular success. Yet they produced an impasse which could only be overcome by the elevation of his art to the level of the tragic. If we look first at *An Enemy of the People*, we can see a recipe for the stereotyped drama of small-town politics. In order to avoid that temptation Ibsen abandoned political drama altogether in *Rosmersholm*. It is the key to the hiatus between Ibsen's tragedy and the later conventions of the political theatre.

Despite the stature and eloquence of its hero, *An Enemy of the People* remains a 'social problem' drama rather than an authentic piece of political theatre. The provincial setting and Stockmann's role as a conscientious local official considerably narrow its political dimensions. Stockmann's alienation from the political system is not in dispute, but the ensuing strife is very much a conflict *en famille* with Stockmann fiercely opposed to his brother who, as the corrupt mayor of the town, does nothing to ameliorate the pollution of the water supply. Moreover Stockmann himself, through his intense paranoia, reduces every political antagonism to the level of a personal animosity. Only his uncompromising eloquence and his public call for 'a clean sweep' of the political system prevent the conflict from degenerating into small-town bickering. Although Ibsen had found an iconoclastic hero, a contemporary one worthy of Julian Brand, the basis of the play was too narrow upon which to construct a tragic collision between his hero and the society he repudiated. Stockmann endures his increasing estrangement and falls back on the loyal support of his family, cushioned from downfall and ruin. In *Rosmersholm*, the tragic operates at a social level precisely through the shattering of the family household. But where the bourgeois household remains intact, there is no basis for tragic expression despite the political estrangement.

Rosmersholm by contrast is the most enigmatic of Ibsen's plays, perhaps the most enigmatic drama since *Hamlet*. It presents immense difficulties of realisation, and has nothing to rival the sheer theatrical power of Stockmann's public denigration of 'the liberal bloody majority'. Indeed it could easily stand accused of being the most static of all Ibsen's drawing-room dramas, paring to a very minimum the amount of physical movement on stage. Yet there is an underlying movement in the play which has a cumulative strength. Starting from a simple plot the audience is gradually immersed in a situation of increasing complexity where the very process of decoding or decipher-ing the actual meaning of the relationships they witness is constantly undermined by the actual dialogue itself. As a theatrical experience this demands very great discipline on the part of the actors and exceptional concentration on the part of the audience. The play can operate at this level like a psychological detective story and be dismissed for that reason. But it is something more, something which has to be extracted by close interpretation for the tragic denouement to make any kind of sense.

This is the first of Ibsen's contemporary dramas in which the major protagonists are not related by kinship. With the suicide of Beata, Rosmer's wife, the formal dissolution of the family has already taken place. Yet despite this formal release, awareness of the past creates a continuing tension. Beata haunts Rosmer from beyond the grave. The ensuing pain prompts his marriage proposal to Rebecca which is rejected. But there is a more important sense in which family tradition plays a part. Rosmer comes from a respected upper-class family boasting an alternating ancestry of military officers and high clergymen. The setting of the play is the ancestral home and its country estate. Whereas Stockmann came to cultivate an aristocratic contempt of the people, his own life was indisputably bourgeois. The same could never be true of Rosmer, who represents Ibsen's first attempt to introduce the idea of the noble into his contemporary drama.

Significantly, Rosmer was modelled on a Swede, not a Norwegian, the poet Count Carl Snoilsky whom Ibsen had first met in Rome in

1864. With no titled Norwegian nobility to dramatise, Ibsen was forced to use the military and clergy as the background for his own hero. Consequently Rosmer does not possess the heroic dimensions of the hereditary aristocrat. Instead he becomes a much weaker and less compelling figure than Ibsen had originally intended him to be. The ideal which motivates him is for that reason more urgent. Not possessing an inherited title of his own, he nonetheless intends to create one on the basis of the family name. But this ideal of nobility is not a socially exclusive one. Prompted by Rebecca West, it is democratic and universal. It is, as he tells Kroll 'to make all the people in this country noblemen'. In the play, the aura and promise of nobility are more important than actual entitlement, or the material privileges that accrue from it.

Rosmer's 'aristocratic' background is not sufficient in itself to create a sense of alienation from middle-class life. It is reinforced not by his apostasy but by the socially suspect position of Rebecca West as household companion. Rebecca is socially correct and well-educated but of humble origin. Outwardly, her credentials are not in question, but she is emphatically a woman of lesser social status. Moreover she comes from Finnmark, the extreme north of Norway, the periphery of wilderness and myth. The relationship of Rosmer and Rebecca represents a specific conjunction of the wild and the noble. But under the circumstances of their complex relationship, the fusion cannot be sustained. The relationship ends in breakdown and this breakdown is only atoned for by mutual self-destruction, a final and ironic 'marriage' of a couple who find it impossible to marry in life. As the refusal to marry comes from Rebecca alone the play conveys a superimposed opposition. On the one hand we have the failure of a quest to transform bourgeois life and politics through a universal ideal of the noble but embedded within that quest is the female destruction of marriage.

The breakdown of the relationship takes place in the context of external political pressures. Rosmer's failure to justify his apostasy either to the conservative Kroll or the liberal Mortensgaard, renders his proposed political crusade stillborn. This failure to generate practical action in the midst of adversity finally impels Rebecca to lose faith in the man she had once revered. The failure of the relationship cannot be explained solely as a psychological breakdown. It must also be seen in the light of public disapproval both of Rosmer's politics and his ambiguous relationship with Rebecca. The predicament is clear enough. The woman has greater resilience than the man, yet the man has the responsibility to put the plan into action in his own name. Rebecca's own political ambitions can only operate through Rosmer, and his courage is not equal to the task. The die is cast in the very first scene where Rebecca and Mrs Hesketh, the housekeeper, watch Rosmer fail to take the footbridge across the mill-race on his way home, and opt instead for the longer, safer way round. Rebecca, having pledged herself to Rosmer's cause, and thus linked her own fate to his, can only watch helplessly as, despite her promptings, he gradually begins to lose his nerve.

As the action gradually unfolds, it reveals the past decision which Rebecca made in order to prepare Rosmer for his renunciation of religion and his crusade of nobility. Effectively, it is she who has driven Beata to suicide, destroyed Rosmer's marriage and with it the various entanglements of marriage, including the prospect of children, which she regards as debilitating. But it is not a price which Rosmer himself is prepared to pay. His ideal of nobility echoes his idea of their relationship. It is a world of peace and joy. Rebecca believes in the attainment of that ideal through ruthlessness and struggle. When she is preparing to leave him at the end of the third act, the ideal is already in ruins, betrayed by Rosmer's incapacity to accept the harsh means necessary to the realisation of his goal.

The conventional interpretation of the play, and one which was certainly prevalent when it was first produced, saw their relationship as platonic. But there is no concrete evidence to suggest either a platonic or a carnal relationship. Rosmer's denials to Kroll and Mortensgaard about an affair are always evasive and never explicit. Insistence on the purity of their friendship is not incontrovertible proof of the absence of sex. And there is circumstantial evidence, however oblique, which suggests an affair in progress. Rebecca acts the part of a wife or mistress, wearing her dressing gown around the house during the day and calling Rosmer by his Christian name in front of visitors. After their quarrel of the previous night, the following apparently innocuous exchange takes place as Rosmer is on his way out for a morning walk.

> Rosmer. You didn't come up to see me this morning.
> Rebecca. No—I didn't. Not today.
> Rosmer. Aren't you going to from now on?
> Rebecca. Oh, I don't know yet.[1]

To posit a discreet and unassuming affair between them makes more sense of the breakdown of their relationship than to imagine it chaste. Her threat of the previous evening that 'everything has finished' has more resonance and provides the important link between the crusade and personal happiness. It also reveals the extent of Rosmer's anguish. He is not merely hurt because Rebecca has rejected his marriage proposal, but anguished that his present happiness will itself be lost. 'With you', he tells Rebecca, 'I found happiness that was calm and joyful and not merely based on sensuality'. By contrast he recalls Beata's 'uncontrollable sick fits of sensuality', and the 'way she expected me to reciprocate them', feelings expressed when Beata already knew that Rebecca was a dangerous rival trying to take her husband away from her.

In this light, Rebecca's enlighted educational upbringing by Doctor West, with whom she has also very probably had an affair, takes on a rather different hue. She sees her relationship with Rosmer as a determinedly rational emancipation from the purely emotional aspects of sexuality. The emancipation from sexual taboo is ordered and controlled, a matter of personal decision. It does not solve the uncontrollable surge of repressed libidinal energy. Above all, it has no necessity of marriage. Emotional love and legal marriage are the twin opponents of rational emancipation, especially for women. She reacts in horror to Rosmer's marriage proposal, not because it raises the prospect of a physical union, but because it fundamentally violates her rational code. Rosmer has reverted to the very notion of a relationship from which she has so carefully tried to wean him away in the time since Beata's death. But emotionally speaking, it is the only solution he can find to the anguish he feels about Beata's horrible fate. He adopts the bourgeois convention and asks Rebecca to take her place:

> Rosmer. I can't—I will not go through life with a corpse on my back. Help me throw it off, Rebecca. And then let us lay all memories to rest in freedom and joy and love. You shall be my wife—the only wife I ever had.
>
> Rebecca (*controlled*). Don't speak of this again. I shall never be your wife.
>
> Rosmer. What? Never? But—don't you think you could come to love me?
>
> Rebecca (*puts her hands to her ears as though in terror*). Don't talk to me like that, John! Don't say such things!
>
> Rosmer (*grasps her arm*). Yes, yes. It could happen. I can see from your face, you feel it too. Don't you, too. Don't you, Rebecca?

> Rebecca (*again calm and composed*). Listen, now. I tell you—if ever
> you were to speak to me of this again, I shall leave Rosmersholm.[2]

The exchange reveals not only Rosmer's failure to surmount his
guilt and stick to his ideals. It also reveals the failure of Rebecca to
maintain the relationship on the rational self-willed level she had
wished. The earlier exchange between Rosmer and Kroll, where the
pastor mentions Rebecca having in the house books which dealt 'with
the purpose of marriage from the so-called "progressive" viewpoint',
reveal the careful thought and attention which Rebecca had given to
her situation. But in the end, the responses on all sides are emotional.
Beata is driven to madness and suicide. Rosmer, instead of being
emancipated by Rebecca's action, becomes emotionally dependent on
her, slavishly so. And momentarily, when Rosmer mentions marriage,
Rebecca's response is not one of calm repudation but horrified
revulsion. Though Rebecca is rational and controlled, clinical and
manipulative, still she cannot eradicate the life of the emotions or the
forms of personal attachment they generate. Moreover at the beginning of her stay in Rosmersholm, she herself has succumbed to her
emotions, and spent the rest of the time determinedly trying to
overcome their effect.

To start with, she has been seduced by the aura of Rosmersholm.
The ancestral tradition and the noble ideal which Rosmer personified
of her could not be reduced to a rational formula. They had an
emotional attraction which had thoroughly overwhelmed her, despite
the long tutorship of Doctor West. In respose to Rosmer's desperate
accusation that she has merely used him as 'a kind of glove' for her own
purposes, she reveals the 'most important thing of all' about their
relationship, 'the thing that excuses and condemns all the rest'. In one
of the most startling moments in the play, she admits that her rational
freedom has been subverted from the outset:

> Rebecca. I think I could have achieved anything—then. Because I
> feared nothing. I still had a free will. I had no inhibition. I wasn't
> afraid of human relationships. But then it started—this thing that
> broke my will—and frightened me for ever.
> Rosmer. What started? Speak so that I can understand you.
> Rebecca. It came over me—this blind uncontrollable passion—!
> Oh, John—!
> Rosmer. Passion? You—? For what?
> Rebecca. For you.

Rosmer (*tries to spring up*). What!
Rebecca (*restrains him*). Sit still, my dear. There's something else you
have to hear.
Rosmer. Are you trying to say—that you loved me—in that way!
Rebecca. I thought it was love—then. Yes, I thought it was. But
it wasn't. It was what I tell you. A blinding uncontrollable
passion.[3]

The distinction between love and passion is vital. It is the latter
which afflicts Rebecca and whose suppression is the greater loss. The
division is one familiar in the novel of tragic realism, in *Scarlet and
Black*, *The Idiot* and *Anna Karenina*. In modern tragic drama, it is more
rare. And here it comes as a revelation, since we have not been witness
to Rebecca's thoughts. While Rosmer's feelings of love hinder the
development of a free rational relationship, Rebecca's feeling of
passion had initially endangered it with far greater force. Passion is for
Rebecca what his former marriage is for Rosmer—the ghost which
cannot be exorcised. But the elimination of her passion is not merely a
matter of self-control. It occurs all the more easily because the aura of
Rosmer's nobility is itself dispersed by his weakness and failure. Yet the
contradiction between the aura of nobility which instigates the
political goal and the rational quest for emancipation which is part of
the means of attaining that goal remains. Too much attachment to one
diminishes the strength of the other. The passion of Rebecca is doomed
not merely because of her rational approach to life but for reasons
which are more explicitly social.

The political failure in the play is revealing. Rosmer's ideal of
universal nobility is a contradiction in terms. Nobility presupposes
hierachical division and is the cultural product of a society of rank.
When fully democratised, it loses its meaning. The transformation of
passion into permanent love mirrors the dilemma of the transformation of nobility into a universal ideal. In both cases the original and
unique attributes are inevitably lost. Although he does not enter
politics actively, Rosmer discovers soon enough that his idea is doomed
to failure. It has no echo in the political controversies of the day, no
part in the continual dogfight of liberal and conservative typical of
Ibsen's Norway. To either cause Rosmer can give the eminence of his
name but nothing more is demanded of, or wanted from him. When he
tells Kroll of his intention to make a public declaration of his apostasy,
the schoolmaster attacks the conduct of his personal life.
Mortensgaard, the liberal journalist, also finds little of use in such an

apostasy to further his own cause, and as Ulrich Brendel remarks, the future belongs to Mortensgaard, not to Rosmer. It is a future in which there is no possibility for the realisation of Rosmer's dream.

The tragic collision in the play is not of a political nature, for Ibsen's characters usually survive political collision. It is a different kind of collision prompted by Rebecca West. This aspect of the play has always been extremely puzzling. The natural outcome of Rosmer's failure is that Rebecca will leave him. Why then, does she change her mind? In part, it is her recognition that Rosmer's failure is her own failure. It is a failure which finally prompts her, part consciously, part impulsively, to lead them into a surrogate form of defiance which is nonetheless as uncompromising and sacrificial as any act could be. For the audience it comes as a surprise and its dramatic effect is to prompt them to think back over the course of the play, to try and retrace how the ending could possibly have come about. Unlike *A Doll's House*, where the ending creates a similar sense of surprise, Ibsen has not created a discernible pattern of denouement. Indeed, in *A Doll's House* the pattern is clumsy and melodramatic. Here something rather different and more controversial takes place. The explicit truth available during the early part of the play is masked by ambivalence, rationalisation and deceit. It is the contrary movement to conventional denouement where action and confession traditionally reveal or 'clear up' earlier puzzles or mysteries. To present this reversal effectively on stage represents a degree of discipline and ingenuity far beyond most of the theatre companies who would normally present Ibsen in the contemporary theatre.

This latter fact does prompt one major criticism of Ibsen here that the degree of compression in the drama makes it more rewardingly *read* rather than *acted*, and that its virtues are literary rather than dramatic. This kind of assertion is not merely relevant to Ibsen. It must look back to *Hamlet* and forward to Beckett and Pinter. The effort of transcribing a detailed reading of the play onto the stage is immense. Its truth is an intricate mosaic whose shape and nature can never be clearly and unambiguously discerned. The protagonists wilfully pass over important references fleetingly. There is an evasion or withholding of information, a refusal to be specific. That Ibsen created a dramatic language for this conceit, over half a century before the theatre of the absurd, is a remarkable achievement often overlooked. But it also generated internal problems. The uncertainty is not only confined to the audience. It is also part of the anguish of the characters which can no longer be conveyed by the dramatic aside, nor, as in the novel, by the interior monologue.

It is interesting that Freud, who admired the play and was influenced by it, should have overlooked the genuinely Freudian innovation which is presented. For Freud, the important element in the play is Rebecca's past and the ensuing guilt which torments her. By taking Beata's place, she is replicating the earlier Oedipal replacement of her mother in the life of Doctor West, with whom she has an incestuous relationship. But Freud does not give enough credence to the conscious and controlled nature of her decision to leave Rosmer. There are good political reasons why she should do so. It is the sudden change of mind at the end which is unexplained, where she switches in an instant the whole destiny of his life. Ibsen's stated wish that in any production Rebecca should display 'a controlled power, a quiet determination' is very much to the point. Her ability to conceal her feelings and rationalise her actions, as well as her impulsive change of mind, are the result of, and not a deviation from such determination. Rationalisation is not a reflex mechanism of guilt but a considered and complex act of will. Her behaviour in the last act can no more be explained by guilt than Hamlet's actions can be explained by madness. The mysterious woman from the land of the trolls remains the most psychologically complex character that Ibsen ever created.

In the last act, the dramatic interaction hinges on uncertainty. Uncertainty about Rebecca's feelings and motives causes Rosmer an increasing pain he is desperate to relieve. There is a shared, implicit understanding that she can manipulate his emotions and constantly remind him of his dependence upon her. But the power to sow in his mind the seeds of an anguished doubt is even greater:

Rosmer. How do you explain what has happened to you?
Rebecca. It's the Rosmer view of life, —or yours anyway. It has
    infected my will.
Rosmer. Infected—?
Rebecca. And poisoned it. Enslaved it to a law I had not previously
    recognised. You—being with you—has ennobled my soul—
Rosmer. Oh, if only I could believe that!
Rebecca. You can believe it all right. The Rosmer view of life
    ennobles. But—(*Shakes her head.*) but—but—
Rosmer. But—? Well?
Rebecca. But it kills happiness, John.
Rosmer. But how can you say that, Rebecca?
Rebecca. For me, anyway.
Rosmer. Can you be so sure of that? If I were to ask you again now—
    if I were to go down on my knees and beg you—?

Rebecca. Oh, my dearest, please don't speak of that again. It's impossible.[4]

Rosmer cannot believe that he has either ennobled her soul or killed her happiness. On the other hand he lacks the conviction to contradict her. Her calm, assured and damning account reduces him to a state of helpless dependence upon her, yearning for some desperate guarantee of truth he knows he will never be able to attain. Here she defames the ideal of nobility which they had mutually constructed and Rosmer can never be sure whether she expresses a genuine disenchantment or whether she is deliberately killing off the possibility of any further attachment between them. His desperation finally drives him to ask for supreme proof of her 'ennoblement', to sacrifice herself for him. It becomes in his eyes, the last remaining hope for the noble ideal. But even then he draws back from the horror of what he suggests, and it is Rebecca who has to push him forward once more, and for the last time:

Rosmer (*jumps up*). But all this—is madness! Go—or stay. I will believe you—I will take your word for it. This time too.
Rebecca. Words, John! Let's have no more cowardice and running away. How can you take my word for anything after today?
Rosmer. But I don't want to see you defeated, Rebecca.
Rebecca. There will be no defeat.
Rosmer. There will be. You will never have the courage to go Beata's way.
Rebecca. You think not?
Rosmer. Never. You are not like Beata. You don't see life through distorted eyes.
Rebecca. But I see it through Rosmer eyes. The crime that I have committed—demands atonement.
Rosmer (*looks fixedly at her*). Is that what you believe in your heart?
Rebecca. Yes.[5]

The process by which the 'noble' act of self-sacrifice is mutually agreed, is self-defeating. Rosmer will only accept her pledge to act if it has a suitable moral justification. The one she gives him immediately raises the very spectre of evasion and deception from which he has sought deliverance. But he fails to see the contradiction. Her wish to dispense with words in favour of action is undermined by his constant need for verbal justification. The means by which she evades the true expression of her own feelings is, in a very real psychological sense, ignoble. It belies dignity. Once she has decided upon a particular course of action than she is amoral as to the means of attaining it. The ambiguity of her response remains to the end. It is never clear, and cannot be, whether she finally accepts Rosmer's symbolic marriage or whether, in doing so, she is merely luring him to a sacrifice he would otherwise be loathe to make.

The dilemma for Rebecca is very real, and relates to her subordinate sexual status reinforced by her social inferiority. She accepts these constraints in order to gain her ends, and having failed to do so, is left with the tacit recognition of that failure. Yet even her means of atoning for it through self-sacrifice follows the same pattern. She appears to make herself an adjunct to Rosmer's will while at the same time moulding it to her own purposes. The manner of their going retains the pattern of their life. It appears, in view of Rebecca's complicity, as a 'noble' gesture. Yet it is equally the final endeavour of Rebecca to wreak her revenge upon the 'nobleman' who has failed her. The question remains as to whether leaving Rosmer, as Nora leaves Helmer, would not produce the emancipation Rebecca desires, rather than remaining to ruthlessly complete the process of subordinate subversion. But, sociologically, the emancipation from a particular person is not necessarily an emancipation from inequality as a whole. Moreover, Rebecca's attachment to the ideal is absolute. In luring Rosmer into a mutual suicide pact she literally destroys the thing she loves.

Like Hedda Gabler, Rebecca's destructiveness is directed towards something with which she has personally identified but feels has failed her. Yet it is less accessible, less overt. At crucial points the play seems more suitable to television drama than to the stage. For the camera, as a dissecting eye, can reveal the crucial nuance of glance or gesture, make more of the instant hesitation or uncertainty. To project theatrically something of such implosive force remains a challenge which has seldom been answered. One vulgarised version of the play written by Austin Fryers in 1891 had Beata as the main character acting out the role of the 'wronged' wife, thus introducing onto the stage the action which had taken place before the curtain goes up. It was an unthinking answer to the difficulty of compression. But its absurdity illustrates the problem exactly. On the theatrical evidence we have to date, *Rosmersholm* is better read than played. As a prose work, it has an extraordinary poetic density. Despite all the subsequent developments in the theatre, it still gives the impression of throwing into disarray the conventional relationship between dramatic speech and conveyed meaning. The 'mystery' of the play is precisely this breakdown. The 'white horses' of Rosmersholm to which much significance has been attributed, are not in fact meant to convey this mystery at all. Indeed Rebecca West constantly ridicules them. The mystery lies not in symbols but in human thought and feeling which is as masked in Ibsen as the faces of performers in primitive African drama. What culturally disturbs us in our own age is reproduced in dramatic language as a metaphor of performance itself.

Although *Rosmersholm* was not a political drama, its political context cannot be ignored. Before writing the play, Ibsen had made an extraordinary speech on a return visit to Norway, to the Workers Association in Trondheim, his point of arrival. In it he outlined explicitly the basic idea underlying the play yet to be written:

An element of aristocracy must enter our political life, our government, our members of parliament and our press. I am of course not thinking of aristocracy of wealth, of learning, or even of ability or talent. I am thinking of aristocracy of character, of mind, of will. That alone makes us free. And this aristocracy, which I hope may be granted to our people, will come to us from two sources, the only two sections of society which have not yet been corrupted by party pressure. It will come to us from our women and from our working men. The reshaping of social conditions which is now being undertaken in Europe is principally concerned with the future status of the workers and of women.[6]

There are two points to be noted here. *Rosmersholm* had turned out to be the artistic invalidation of Ibsen's belief in a new kind of aristocracy. The play had involuntarily exposed the contradictions of the doctrine, and its tragic vision, its portrayal of tragic alienation, stems very precisely from this process. The second point, which now becomes clear, is the importance of women in Ibsen's drama. Pinning his future political hopes to two main sources, he only succeeded, dramatically speaking, in portraying one of them. No working men ever become major characters in an Ibsen play, even though Rebecca West and John Gabriel Borkman both come from lower-class backgrounds. The shift of emphasis then has to be to women alone, irrespective of class.

The link between women and future social emancipation is therefore vital to his ability to write tragic drama. For unlike Zola, he was incapable of portraying working-class life. The limitation is always there. But it poses greater problems for Ibsen's successors than for Ibsen himself, since his portrayal of the insubordinate social position of women is so central and uncompromising. And it is directly linked to an opposition to the infrastructure of bourgeois social relationships, the family and marriage. For Rebecca West, the opposition is intellectual, for Nora Helmer, it is emotional and for Hedda Gabler it is contemptuous. It links all three women and all three plays. But there remains a very profound difference between the plight of Nora Helmer and that of the other two women, a plight which delineates very clearly the difference between Ibsen's affirmative and tragic drama.

Of the three women, Nora appears to be the only one to emancipate herself. She leaves husband, children and home, and the 'slamming of the door' at the end of the play seems devoid of compromise. By contrast, Rebecca West remains with Rosmer to effect a mutual suicide pact and Hedda Gabler kills herself after she has heard of Eilert Loevborg's ignoble end. It appears then, that Nora's life ends in freedom while theirs end in death and captivity. The crucial differences is that Hedda and Rebecca are playing for much higher stakes. The two men on whom they pin their hopes, Loevborg and Rosmer, are both opposed to the dominant bourgeois values of the day. Nora's dependence on her husband, on the other hand, barely involves any questioning of those values at all. Even at the end, the disaffection remains personal, never really gravitating towards an awareness of the social malaise underlying her domestic predicament. To adopt the terminology of Herbert Marcuse, Nora Helmer remains a one-dimensional woman, while *Rosmersholm* and *Hedda Gabler* are two-dimensional plays.

Rosmersholm and *Hedda Gabler* exemplify rather different forms of opposition to middle-class life. In the former instance the link is between the noble and the peripheral; in the latter between the aristocratic and the bohemian. The links operate thematically through the female hero by demonstrating in each case the social injustice of personal and domestic subordination. But in the Helmer household there is no vital link between Nora and any wider context of opposition. Nora's change of heart at the end involves an indisputable heightening of self-consciousness. But the awareness it brings rests within the limits of social class and cannot transcend them. It is another chapter in the uncomfortable self-enlightenment of the discontented bourgeois which we saw earlier in *The Pillars of Society* and *An Enemy of the People*. But here, in order to produce such an astonishing and unexpected ending, Ibsen forsakes social credibility. There is a confusion of motives which results in a confusion of performance. Here the sound of the slamming door is a superb theatrical illusion. For it helps to conceal the confusion at the climactic moment of the play. Yet when the play is read or seen for a second time, and the outcome known, the incredible thinness of Nora's motivation is readily apparent.

What saves the play at this moment, even on a second or third viewing, is the decisive change in form which Ibsen's writing undergoes. The play is reflexive insofar as the liberation of Nora refracts the liberation of the dramatist himself. In writing of the liberation of his heroine from a bourgeois household, Ibsen simultaneously liberates himself from the well-made play. Until the middle of the final act, the writing is riddled with the familiar contrivances of the *pièce bien faite*. There is a whole series of unlikely coincidences and the familiar gratuitous fluctuations of economic fortune. Ibsen's personae perform, for the most part, like lifeless puppets. Ibsen identifies with Nora in wishing to escape from the banal meaningless charade of a certain kind of domestic theatre in which he feels himself trapped. When Nora wants to abandon Helmer, Ibsen wants to abandon him too. In his impatience to be rid of the Scribean legacy, he overlooks credible grounds for his heroine's departure, and the question, totally unanswered, as to what her subsequent life could possibly be. Moreover, the resolve to leave is compromised by her final suggestion to Helmer that 'the greatest miracle of all' would be 'that our life together could be a real marriage'. As the hope still lingers, there can be no real transformation of sensibility.

By contrast, Hedda Gabler has shunned the accepted sensibility while resigning herself to the imprisonment which accompanies it. This is not merely the result, however, of a perceptive and sensitive nature, but also of class upbringing. The critical spirit and the disaffection arise from the sense of social distance which Ibsen explicitly outlines in the stage directions concerning Hedda's appearance: 'Distinguished, aristocratic face and figure. Her complexion is pale and opalescent. Her eyes are steel-grey with an expression of cold, calm serenity.' The aura of a higher social rank is immediately fixed. So is her predicament. Yet the precise nature of her 'aristocratic' background should not be overlooked. She is undoubtedly upper class, the daughter of a famous general, but not from a titled family and not from the landed nobility. The specific social peculiarity of the Norway of her time is the springboard for tragic creation. It would have been impossible to create her tragic counterpart in the England, France or Germany of the same period. Norway, with its urban upper class and predominantly rural population presented a contrary picture to those European countries where the landed aristocracy continued to thrive in a society based on industrial capitalism. Nor is her bourgeois husband a personal threat to the wealth or power of the aristocracy. Far from it, he is an academic hack, and one of the few really comic creations in Ibsen's work.

The Tesman household has its own contradiction. Their house is a distinguished town residence, belonging formerly to an eminent politician, and bought by Tesman at great expense to accommodate Hedda's superior social standing and superior tastes. Yet it becomes stultifying for Hedda because it is the place of marriage and the place of captivity. Intended as an acknowledgement of Hedda's sensibility it becomes an oppressive prison. Yet within it, she retains an inner freedom and a cultivated sense of distance from which the dramatic space of tragic alienation springs. The achievement here is to make Hedda fearful of acting with resolution, yet at the same time, the prime mover of destiny in the action. Moreover her contradictory nature is never reduced to a domestic neurosis. The dramatic emphasis is exactly the opposite. She *ennobles* that neurosis. It is a sustained act of flamboyance on her part, a striking and deliberate contrast to Strindberg's *Miss Julie*. The social superiority of Strindberg's heroine is an artefact. In showing her degrading seduction by a household servant, Strindberg undermines her position as mistress of the house without questioning the authority of its owner, her absent husband. The neurosis here is in the writing itself. Strindberg was unable to separate the personal defects of his heroine from a general misogynist obsession. Ibsen, by contrast, portrays the neurosis of his heroine in a plausible social context where it co-exists with the very positive qualities of composure and perceptiveness. Through this figural co-existence, Hedda proceeds to break down the sympathy of the audience as soon as she engages it, creating an alienation-effect which forces the audience to think very closely about the contradictory impulses in her personality.

Her coldness is not, then, reducible to an overriding sexual frigidity. It is a combination of aloofness and neurotic recoil from the traumatic sexual experience of her marriage; and it is an outcome of her previous failure, with Eilert Loevborg, of passionate involvement. The constant pressure of Judge Brack is based on a recognition of Hedda's potential hedonism, and on the knowledge that she had married Tesman because, as she puts it, 'I'd danced myself tired'. By hinting at an affair, he suggests a conventionalised hedonistic alternative to passion, but only succeeds in making Hedda recoil even further. This is not to say that Hedda cannot be wilful when she wants. She is knowing about flirtation and herself can create a sexual *frisson* through her coquetry. The dangerous firing of the pistol in the direction of Judge Brack as he enters cryptically by the back garden is the case in point. But his consequent probing of her domestic discontent brings him no closer to his adulterous goal. Even as Hedda confesses, the personal distance is maintained and the enigma of her unease remains:

> Hedda. People who are only interested in one thing don't make the most amusing company. Not for long, anyway.
> Brack. Not even when they happen to be the person one loves?
> Hedda. Oh, don't use that sickly stupid word.
> Brack (*starts*). But, Mrs Hedda—!
> Hedda (*half laughing, half annoyed*). You just try it, Judge. Listening to the history of civilisation morning, noon and—
> Brack (*corrects her*). Every minute of one's life.
> Hedda. All right. Oh, and those domestic industries of Brabant in the Middle Ages! That really is beyond the limit.
> Brack (*looks at her searchingly*). But, tell me—if you feel like this way on earth did you—? Hm—
> Hedda. Why on earth did I marry George Tesman?
> Brack. If you like to put it that way.
> Hedda. Do you think it so very strange?
> Brack. Yes—and no, Mrs Hedda.
> Hedda. I'd danced myself tired, Judge. I felt my time was up— (*gives a slight shudder*). No, I mustn't say that. Or even think it.
> Brack. You've no rational cause to think it.
> Hedda. Oh, cause cause—(*looks searchingly at him*).[7]

Two things become clear from the exchange. In remarking rather ambiguously that 'people who are only interested in one thing don't make the most amusing company', Hedda is indirectly rejecting the very overtures that Brack is starting to make to her. Secondly, her reference to 'love' as that 'stupid sickly word' is the most decisive judgment in the whole play. It does not merely refer to marriage but to the wider question of passionate involvement, which she had failed to establish with Loevborg prior to marriage. Her repudiation of passion places her close to Rebecca West. But whereas Rebecca had overcome her passion for Rosmer through rational means, Hedda's response to her failure is rather different. She sublimates that passion, and it re-emerges not as the rational wilfulness characteristic of Rebecca, but as a combination of neurosis and idealism within an aristocratic sensibility. The romanticised world of 'love' either in marriage or adultery is alien to her. 'The triangle is completed', Brack remarks on hearing her husband return. 'And the train goes on', she replies acerbically. There is here a passive resignation to the inevitability of married life prompted by the fact that she is, in her own words, a 'dreadful coward'. But there also develops involuntary and tragic resistance to it. While she can never be as ruthlessly rational and consistent as Rebecca, the fusion of neurosis and idealism in her personality leads her to invite danger and to tempt fate to the point where she can no longer control it. The main figural characteristic is not the titillation of her idle imagination, which Ibsen had suggested in his preliminary notes for the play operate through the manipulation of Loevborg. It is the intrigue which quickly gets out of control and operates as an external fate before which Hedda becomes powerless. This is the dramatic key to the reversal of fortune, that of Loevborg as well as her own, and to the self-recognition at the end of a truly tragic predicament.

Like Rebecca West, her social position is constricted by the limitations of her sexual role and by her desire to channel her ambitions within the framework of that limitation. Hence she actually achieves as a result of her intrigue with Loevborg the very goal she thought impossible—'having the power to shape a man's destiny'. In both Hedda and Rebecca one finds contrasting aspects of a complex dialectic between the social position of the woman and the figural qualities of the man she seeks to control. Rosmer is Rebecca's social superior whereas Loevborg is Hedda's social subordinate. Yet ironically Loevborg proves to be a more worthy and more 'noble' cause than the weak apostate Rosmer who has the aura of nobility attached to his family name. The differing figural stature of the man in each case is of immense dramatic importance. The success of *Hedda Gabler* as a performed work lies partly in the genuinely heroic characteristics of Loevborg, a heroism Rosmer never possesses until the final decision to commit mutual suicide. In the later play there is, by contrast, a superimposed tragic fate as first Loevborg and then Hedda separately meet their death. The sharing of tragic fate in *Rosmersholm* is intricate but theatrically too dense for really effective performance. In *Hedda Gabler* that tragedy works because tragic fate is separated socially as well as dramatically. The tragic space is created out of the circumstance where the modalities of alienation, the aristocratic and the bohemian, periodically intersect, where they are never entirely separate, but never entirely conjoined.

The dramatic movement from tragic alienation to tragic strife then works within the space of this spasmodic sociation, where the destinies of the two heroic figures are finally and indissolubly linked. It is this sociation, rather than the individual qualities of the dissolute writer or the domesticated aristocratic lady, which provides the basis for the tragic experience. It lies ultimately in how Hedda responds to Loevborg's work. It is the work of someone who is both a dissolute bohemian and an intellectual genius. His book has to be seen as a triumph, a masterpiece of its kind. Not only does it provide a contrast to Tesman's dry pedantic 'domestic industries of Brabant'. It has a boldness and totality untypical of academic life in general. Hedda recognises the Faustian quest for mastery, dealing not only with 'the forces that will shape our civilisation' but also 'the direction in which that civilisation may develop'. Yet the personal price he has paid for this achievement is severe self-constraint. Ibsen contrasts the position of Hedda with that of Thea Elvsted very ironically in this respect. While Hedda fears adultery, Thea has the courage to leave her husband and devote herself to Loevborg. But by doing so, she has domesticated and reformed him, depriving him of those Dionysian qualities which Hedda had encouraged. Hedda's scheme to remove him from the sphere of Mrs Elvsted's influence is a deliberate attempt to prevent the kind of compromise with bourgeois life of which she herself stands indicted.

Her attitude here is much more than one of jealous revenge. At the same time it does not exclude such a base motive. Ibsen constructs his heroine in such a way that the profoundly ideal ambitions she possesses coincide with and complement the more ignoble aspects of her character. Rather than provoking a crisis of conscience, as occurs in the reformist social drama, they fuse perfectly in Hedda's response to Loevborg's manuscript once it has fallen into her hands. As she holds the misplaced manuscript in her hands, the metaphor of creation is never far from her mind. She links the creative work with childbirth, and for that reason destroys it. The imagined metaphor is not merely one of giving birth, but giving birth under conditions of imprisonment. As she cries ecstatically 'I'm burning your child, Thea!' and starts to throw the pages in the stove, she identifies the manuscript with the domestic trap set for Loevborg by Thea Elvsted. The act of burning the book is malevolent, but perversely idealistic too. The intuition behind it goes beyond the analogy with childbirth in her own imagination. It shows a profounder desire to destroy *the least compromised of all written things*. The emphasis here is on 'compromised'. However iconclastic, however subversive, however profound, for her Loevborg's work is compromised by the abandonment of the Dionysian image and domestication by a 'poor little fool', a married *bourgeoise*. The aristocratic spirit in Hedda cannot tolerate Loevborg's dilemma, the dilemma of all talented bohemians in a capitalistic culture. She cannot endure the fact that he must sacrifice his Dionysian qualities for the advancement of his intellectual ambitions. Her imperious manner demands both simultaneously, and avenges itself upon the impossibility of obtaining them.

The dramatic flow of the play incorporates Hedda's failure to push Loevborg forward towards a 'noble' Dionysian destiny. Her tragic recognition of that failure comes from the gradual realisation that the only destiny he can assume is one socially appropriate to his dissolute life. He is incapable in that life of sustaining the idealised image she has of 'a crown of vine leaves in his hair'. The recognition is a staged one. After Loevborg's arrest in a brothel she dispenses with the Dionysian image, but retains the hope of a 'noble' suicide. But when he dies of gunshot wounds, shot in the groin in the very same brothel by his own revolver, the nobility has evaporated. The pure and noble gesture of a bullet through the head to which Hedda had coaxed him, has been replaced by 'a mean and ludicrous occurrence'. The tragic experience is retained but its social meaning is transformed since it is no longer in Hedda's control. Because, socially speaking, she cannot accept the tragic horror of Loevborg's death, the way is then clear for the tragic climax of her own suicide. The social recognition of a 'noble' suicide would have saved her from a similar fate. But since that recognition must be withheld, there is little or nothing to stop her. With Brack still clamouring for a *menage à trois* and the prospect of marriage to Tesman stretching on indefinitely, the consequence is clear. 'Not free', she cries. 'Still not free.' It is she, the aristocratic daughter of a famous general, who uses her father's pistol to shoot herself through the head. In so doing, she executes the noble fate which is socially appropriate to her but not to the debauched genius whose death preceded her own.

The final catalyst comes not from Judge Brack's veiled threat of blackmail, though that of course heightens her sense of desperation. It comes from the attempt of Tesman and Mrs Elvsted to reclaim Loevborg's work for posterity. In trying to reconstruct the book she has burnt from the author's remaining notes, they suggest the possibility of a further and more lasting dilution of Loevborg's talent again beyond her control. Even death, however ignoble, has been no protection against *embourgeoisement*. There is then the final recognition that all the horrifying destruction has been in vain, all noble gestures empty, all

suffering worthless, with the same aimless, boring and oppressed life
still to be lived.

Unlike Ibsen's other tragedies, *Hedda Gabler* conforms thematically but *not* spatially to the dialectic of centre and periphery. The
setting is an urban residence, probably in Christiania itself, the house
of a former cabinet minister bought by Tesman at a price he could not
afford to satisfy his new bride. There are no dramatic metaphors of
periphery available, and instead the emphasis is on coterminous
action. But Hedda and Loevborg, the two tragic figures, are each
designated a different dramatic space. Once she makes her entrance in
the first act, Hedda rarely leaves the stage. The whole episode of
Loevborg's downfall, however, occurs *in absentia*. This duality, within
the dramatic form, complements the duality of the tragic alienation
about which we have already spoken. Loevborg's forays offstage, away
from the upper-class residence, constitute a specific descent. They are
sexual and social encounters with the vulgar and dissolute, which
Hedda personally disdains but recognises as part of the integral
personality of her protegé. A similar aristocratic conceit can be found
in Yeats's cycle of poems *The Three Bushes*. It is the anti-sensuous
rejection of, but dependence on, a vulgar material world. The contrast
between Hedda's fate as a presented one, and Loevborg's as an
absented one, highlights the thematic paradox of the play. It portrays
the upper-class woman as captive to bourgeois domesticity and male
ambition, but conceals the less privileged world which triggers off the
downfall of its heroine. The Unities to which Ibsen again scrupulously
adhered, triggered off in this instance a rather unique polarity.

When he moves back once more to the male hero, all the polarities of
which we have spoken, wilderness and civilisation, noble and
bourgeois, women and marriage are transformed and transcended.
But this proved to be possible in one play alone, the penultimate work
of his career and as it turned out, one of the most popular, *John Gabriel
Borkman*.

4 The Synthesis: John Gabriel Borkman

In the early realist drama, Ibsen had twice sought to create a contemporary hero with the status and grandeur of *Brand* but within a thoroughly naturalistic setting. Bernick and Stockmann are Brand's successors, the ambitious bourgeois of contemporary Norway, one a ruthless magnate, the other a heroic reformer embroiled in the great social issues of the time. But by comparison with Brand, their stature is markedly diminished. For a start, their world is too provincial. The majestic grandeur with which Brand roves the vast expanses of his native land is replaced by stifling and claustrophobic provincial life beset by petty social obligations. It is an arena in which they can dominate but also a stranglehold from which they cannot, as epic heroes, truly break free. Of the two, it is Stockmann who takes the more radical course—the calculated break with the local community. Bernick in *The Pillars of Society* poses a slightly different problem. How valid is it artistically to construct a portrait of 'the heroic capitalist'? Despite his moral faults, yet also because of them, Bernick is intended to be just such a hero. Yet the end product is artistically compromised. While celebrating Bernick's ruthless triumph, his hero's success is coloured by such hypocrisy and deceit that Ibsen cannot fully condone him. The result is a theatrical compromise. Bernick, despite his faults, is allowed to succeed. But he is not allowed the public adulation of the people. Instead he confesses his failings publicly and promises to reform himself. The ending is hollow and unconvincing and the drama's probing into the hypocrisy of bourgeois morals cannot compensate for its dramatic failure. Bernick lacks heroism but equally Ibsen stops short of transforming him into the villain the logic of his ruthless materialism suggests. The dilemma has been a general one for modern literature. If the moral defects of the practising capitalist are uncovered, it suggests he can only attain heroic stature as a diluted villain.

Ibsen's turn to tragic drama had meant a shift away from the focal points of political and economic life, a move away from centre to periphery in which the expression of tragic alienation became possible. The last realist work, *John Gabriel Borkman*, reinstates the centrality of capital. But it still retains the tragic vision which Ibsen had sought and found on the periphery. The mature Ibsen, nearing the end of his life, is at last able to draw his heroic capitalist to a point of tragic strife. The complex reasons for this need to be enumerated. In the first place Borkman is portrayed as a capitalist in old age and financial ruin. His marriage has been destroyed, his son has rejected him and yet he still entertains the thought of making a triumphant financial comeback on the threshold of death. He is the Lear of the modern stage, stripped of his crown and his kingdom. But it is the nature of the kingdom which is so vitally different, and which is the key to the tragic vision of the play.

Borkman's lost kingdom has no royal title attached to it. Moreover it has never become a substantial reality in his life. It has remained an unrealised dream, becoming more remote as Borkman's financial failures leave his life in ruin. By virtue of being a social fiction, however, the vision of the kingdom becomes a theatrical fact. The whole play is woven around it. It is the material symbol of the failure he has never accepted, the mythical domain he is doomed never to possess. This is the key to the tragic estrangement, the sense of what might have been but is no longer possible. Such an estrangement does not relate directly to personal success. It goes beyond that, to the potential goodness which Borkman surmises could have come from his triumph, not for himself or his family but for humanity in general. The operation of capital remains the central reality of the play, but this double distancing from it, the looking back to the past and to a wider vision of humanity, transform Borkman into a tragic figure. For many, Ibsen has set a precedent for bourgeois drama as a whole, the creation of a capitalist magnate with a genuinely tragic fate. But in the history of modern drama, Borkman is an exceptional, not to say unparalleled, creation. He spawned no genuine successors.

The way in which Ibsen sabotages familial dependency in the play is also strikingly unique. Borkman and his wife inhabit different floors of the same house, totally devoid of contact with one another. This agreement to lead separate lives gives them a kind of freedom from each other, but only the freedom to live in separate prisons. Though they can escape from each other, they cannot escape from the past. The spectre of Borkman's ruin continues to haunt them. Their link with the future, through their son Erhart, is also cut. The younger man has no intention of atoning for the crimes of the previous generation. He completes the dissolution of the family by going off against their wishes with an older married woman. The break is not only with the Borkman household but with its all-pervasive joylessness. For Erhart there is no turning back.

If Borkman had been totally rejected on all sides, there would be no basis for tragedy. But Gunhild, his wife, and Ella Rentheim, her twin sister and Borkman's former mistress, retain some hope in him. Both wait for 'the sick wolf' pacing the floor above to return. Gunhild's price of forgiveness is actually slight. She sees her own ruin in terms of the public scandal and Borkman's secrecy. She is affronted not by the crime, but by Borkman deceiving her about his financial deception. Ella Rentheim, on the other hand, is more directly the victim of Borkman's actions. Marital deception is not a sufficient basis for tragedy so it is the double deception of wife and mistress, simultaneous violation of married love and passion which personalises the nature of the crime. Its reverberations are much wider than the petty hypocrisy of Nora Helmer's cover-up for her husband. Ibsen makes clear the very profound relationship between personal and financial failure. Borkman's betrayal of Ella Rentheim is the key link with the failure to attain 'the power and the kingdom and the glory'.

For this reason, the play is not a purely social drama, a conscious attempt to portray the contradictions of finance-capital. Ibsen's haunting fear of bankruptcy, dating from the financial ruin of his father in 1835 when he was a seven-year-old child, was no doubt a significant biographical feature in the writing. Yet Ibsen is less concerned to show the mechanisms of faulty investment than he is to show their consequences. The main tension in the play is between Borkman's limitless ambition and the dictates of economic necessity. It is a necessity which Borkman does not, and cannot, recognise if he wishes to aspire to his 'kingdom'. This lack of recognition, this deliberate turning away, means that he ascribes his failure to the personal treachery of other people. But the terms in which he does so reveal his enslavement to the risk-taking process which has already destroyed him. Here he is with Foldal, the clerk, awaiting the impossible recall to former glory.

> Borkman. I was so close to my goal. I needed only eight days to consolidate my position. Every deposit would have been redeemed. All the money I used so boldly would have been back in its place. All the stupendous enterprises I had planned were within a hair's breadth of being realised. No one would have lost a penny.
> Foldal. My word, yes, how you nearly succeeded.

Borkman. And then in those crucial days I was betrayed. (*Looks at Foldal.*) Do you know what I hold to be the ultimate treachery a man can commit?

Foldal. No, tell me.

Borkman. Not murder. Not robbery or perjury. Those are crimes one commits against people one hates or is indifferent to.

Foldal. What is it then, John Gabriel?

Borkman. The ultimate crime is to abuse the trust of a friend.[1]

Borkman fails to see the connection between the crimes he dismisses and the crime he calls 'the ultimate treachery'. The abuse of trust is not merely an injury inflicted on him: he has previously inflicted it on others. It is part of the robbery and perjury he has already committed. At one level, he has abused the trust of Ella Rentheim by giving her to a rival as the price of his financial ambition. 'You bartered me!' she accuses him. 'Traded your love to another man! Sold my love for the chairmanship of a bank!' The crime of which he claims to be the victim is the one of which he is the perpetrator. It is not merely a result of personal failing, but derives from the necessity of the economic system to which he has sold himself as a slave. He accepts its evil consequences by relinquishing control over the events he has instigated. The contradiction is fundamental. Borkman has limitless courage and free will, an unshakeable belief in his power to shape the destiny of the world. But the means to which he must of necessity resort undermine him in his hour of triumph. He becomes their helpless victim, condoning to the end of the methods which have destroyed him.

The tragic circumstance of Borkman's plight actually arises through lack of self-recognition. He is unable to realise his failure is absolute and continues to hope for a redeeming success. Discussing with Foldal the success of the cabinet minister who betrayed him, Borkman makes it clear that he sees his own downfall as nothing more than a grimly comic farce:

Foldal. But he climbed.

Borkman. And I sank.

Foldal. Yes, what a tragedy—

Borkman. Yes. Yes, when I think about it, it seems almost as tragic as your play.

Foldal (*innocently*). Quite as tragic.

Borkman (*laughs quietly*). But if you look at it another way, it really is a kind of comedy.[2]

This limited recognition is linked to his myopic attitude to the women who have stood by him. Ella and Gunhild are seen as the fatal hindrance to his ambition and the Strindbergian echoes are intentional. 'Women!' he proclaims to Foldal. 'They corrupt and pervert our lives. They deflect us from our destinies, rob us of our triumphs.' But unlike Strindberg, Ibsen does not let his hero have the final word. Nor does he allow him to become the vehicle of mysogynist fantasy. Ella's unexpected visit undermines his delusion and restores the tragic dimension to his life.

Like Borkman, Ella is unable to perceive the true link between the public and private aspects of Borkman's former life. But at a personal level, she spells out the nature of Borkman's crime against her. His delusion of female treachery is dramatically dispelled:

> Ella (*moving closer to him*). You are a murderer! You have committed the mortal sin!
> Borkman (*retreats towards the piano*). You are raving, Ella.
> Ella. You have killed love in me! (*Goes towards him.*) Do you understand what that means? The bible speaks of a mysterious sin for which there is no forgiveness. I've never understood what that meant before. Now I understand. The sin for which there is no forgiveness is to murder love in a human being.
> Borkman. And—*that* you say I have done.
> Ella. You have . . . You are guilty of double murder. The murder of your own soul and mine.[3]

Despite this, their respective obsessions with the past diverge and cannot be reconciled. Ella can think only of personal betrayal and Borkman of public aggrandisement. And Ella, like Borkman, deludes herself as to the future. Incurably ill, she wishes Borkman's son to bear her own name as a lifeline to the future. But like Gunhild, she too is the victim of Erhart's determination to free himself absolutely from the Borkman household. His elopement signifies the death of the already divided family. The break with the past, with bourgeois morality, but also with the unrelenting austerity of Ibsen's own stage, is complete.

The full significance of the break is revealed in the final act when Borkman leaves the prison of his upstairs room never to return. The leaving is part of the delusion. He goes to assume control of his visionary 'kingdom'. The ambition and the ruin of that vision belong to finance-capital. But the vision itself transcends the means which destroy it. Borkman was a miner's son. His origins lie outside the trap of the corrupt world within which he has operated and they sustain the vision beyond the feeling of 'a life wasted'. Early in his life he had discovered a poetry and an inspiration in man's relationship with nature, and this is what he wishes to preserve. After her recital of the *danse macabre* he tells Frida Foldal:

> Borkman. Sometimes my father took me with him into the mines. Down there, the iron ore sings.
> Frida. It sings?
> Borkman (*nods*). When it is broken loose. The hammer blows that loosen it are the midnight bell that sets it free. And then in its own way, the ore sings—for joy.
> Frida. Why does it do that, Mr Borkman?
> Borkman. It wants to be taken up into the daylight, and serve humanity.[4]

What flaws the ideal of serving humanity is the sense of ownership, of possession. It remains 'my' kingdom. The new kind of relationship he envisages between man and nature is embryonically a socialist one. But it is flawed by his monomania, the exaggerated sense of his indispensability to the process as a whole. As a heroic capitalist who has become a heroic failure, he is still unable to distinguish finally between the task of serving humanity and the duty of serving his investors. The lack of insight is crucial to his plight. For without realising it, Borkman has given himself as a burnt offering to the very process he imagined would redeem him and make him great in the eyes of the world.

The leaving of the upstairs room to claim his kingdom is then a movement towards a goal as well as a movement away from voluntary imprisonment. The upstairs room symbolises the conventional three-walled room of the naturalist stage within which Ibsen had so scrupulously observed the Unities. Though he had located a tragic space beyond it, he now makes the metaphor of the prison explicit and frees his hero altogether. Faced with the prospect of being locked out of the house by the maid if he does not return, Borkman immediately makes his new allegiance clear: 'I shall never go under a roof again. Out here in the night air, it's good! If I were to go up to that room now, the walls and ceiling would shrink and crush me, crush me like a fly—'.[5] True, in previous plays, *The Lady from the Sea* and *Little Eyolf*, the dramaturgical emancipation had already taken place. But it had only done so because at crucial points Ibsen abandoned his figural framework. Here the emancipation occurs within the frame. The final act of the play is the culmination of his tragic writing. The change within the last act, from the open courtyard to the rugged mountainous landscape, is as momentous as the previous emancipation from the upstairs room. And the stage direction, as Borkman walks away from Ella, is one of the most significant in the whole of his work: 'They enter the trees on the left, and gradually disappear from sight. The house and the courtyard fade away, and the landscape, rugged and mountainous, slowly changes, becoming wilder and wilder.'[6] The break is both Borkman's: 'Nearly three years before the trial; five in the cell; eight upstairs; sixteen years in prison', and also that of Ibsen himself. His movement is at one with that of his hero. There can be no going back.

Borkman and Ella reach a small clearing high in the forest from which they can see the vast landscape beneath them and the mountain peaks beyond. It reaches back to the world of Brand. But Borkman is an old man. The effort of conquest is beyond him and the effort of climbing has taken the last ounce of strength from his body. Yet before he dies, the vivid images of memory come to assume their own dominion. It is wrong to see them as mystical symbols. Their terms of reference are the real productive relationships of man and nature and what these could possibly become. It is in these terms that we must grasp the meaning of Borkman's kingdom:

Listen. Down there by the river the factories hum. *My* factories. Listen how they hum. The night shifts are working. They work both day and night. Listen, listen! The wheels whir and the pistons thud, round and round, in and out. Can't you hear them, Ella?

and moments later:

I feel them, those buried millions, I see those veins of iron ore. Stretching their twisting branching enticing arms towards me. I've seen you all before like shadows brought to life—that night when I stood in the vaults of the bank with the lantern in my hand. You wanted to be freed. And I tried to free you. But I failed. Your treasure sank back into the darkness. (*Stretching out his hands.*) But let me whisper this to you now in the stillness of the night. I love you where you lie like the dead, deep down in the dark. I love you treasures that crave for life, with your bright retinue of power and glory. I love you, love you, love you.[7]

This marks the end of Ibsen's long isolation as a writer from the primary productive forces of human existence. Equally it marks the artistic transcendence of the polarities of the earlier work, of city and country, wilderness and civilisation, noble and bourgeois, women and marriage. The treasures of Borkman's kingdom underlie all of them. As Borkman walks high into the mountain clearing, the tragic space of the earlier works dissolves before a new freedom. As the vision of the kingdom is finally enunciated, tragic alienation ceases. In its place is emancipation and unity. But the price of overcoming alienation is Borkman's death.

The vision of the kingdom also incorporates the new Norway which has come about towards the end of Ibsen's life—the beginning of rapid industrialisation, the exploitation of the rich sources of raw materials. Such factors were also to change the nature of Norway's peripheral dependence and to pave the way for its economic and cultural integration into Europe as an independent nation. In these circumstances there was no literary successor to Ibsen. Between 1885 and 1914, there ensued a sustained attempt to do justice to Ibsen's genius in the Scandinavian theatre. William Bloch in Denmark, Gunnar Heiberg and Bjorn Bjornson in Norway all contributed memorable productions of his realist drama.[8] But the problem of literary creation remained. Ibsen had no successors in Norway, and in Sweden the later expressionism of Strindberg paved the way for the influence of non-naturalist techniques, notably those of Max Reinhardt and Gordon Craig. By the time of the First World War, in fact, Scandinavian theatre looked directly to theatrical influences from other parts of Europe, most notably Germany. Of the Scandinavian countries, Norway had once more become the least thriving and the least active. Apart from Ibsen, realism was practically dead as a dramatic form.

It is customary to attribute the movement away from Ibsen in the European theatre to Strindberg and the transformation which took place within his drama. But of more significance was the institutional predicament of Ibsen. He had written in exile and the Norwegian theatre built itself into a modern theatre by the *post hoc* performance of his work. There were few institutional links fruitful to the development of his work. On achieving fame, he kept his artistic distance from the directors who produced his work. Significantly, the best contemporary productions were of the earlier non-tragic drama, in particular *An Enemy of the People*. Bloch's production at the Danish Royal Theatre in 1883 and Stanislavsky's production at the Moscow Arts Theatre were both memorable events and landmarks in the development of the naturalist stage.[9] But the tragic drama took longer to gain due recognition and realism was already being challenged in both theory and practice by other forms of theatre. The kind of revolution which Ibsen had produced in drama was inevitably continued elsewhere and Ibsen's true artistic successors were, without exception, playwrights of other nations.

The closest writer to Ibsen, culturally and geographically, was Strindberg. But Strindberg's career cannot be taken as evidence of a transcendence of Ibsenist drama any more than, from the opposite viewpoint, the two writers are twin exemplars of Scandinavian realism. The connection with Strindberg is more complex. In the first place Ibsen had responded to Strindberg's early realism and himself superseded it in *Hedda Gabler* and *John Gabriel Borkman*. The proximity of Ibsen, as well as the trauma of his own marriage, must have influenced Strindberg's move away from naturalist conventions. Comparatively speaking, however, there are profound thematic differences within the realist drama of the two writers. These can be related, though indirectly, to the different histories of Norway and Sweden. Unlike Norway, Sweden had been an absolutist state for more than two centuries and, under Gustavus Adolphus, one of the most powerful in Europe. For Strindberg the idea of nobility had a different resonance than if did for Ibsen. It was more militaristic and authoritarian, an echo of a more distant past which had never been part of the Norwegian experience. This meant that Strindberg's themes contradicted his use of progressive forms. The facile identification of Strindberg's bold experimentalism with Sweden's subsequent development into the most advanced social democracy in Europe has obscured the reactionary aspects of his work. As far as aristocracy goes, the emphasis of fixed rank displaces the Ibsenist striving for the universally noble, and its main effect, dramatically speaking, is upon the portrayal of women. Despite all the contemporary agitation for female emancipation, Strindberg thought he had discovered a deeper truth in his theatrical images of modern women as 'naturally' subordinate and incapable of attaining genuine freedom or equal status with men.

From this standpoint Strindberg tries to subordinate social to sexual hierarchy. *Miss Julie* is the prime example. Through her demeaning seduction by a servant the aristocratic heroine is 'exposed' as naturally inferior, and Strindberg considered that by introducing a lower-class hero, he had followed the French naturalists in casting off the shackles of middle-class drama. But the play is not about a class war or even a personalised representation of it. It is about a sex war in which the explicit presence of the boots of the absent Count onstage during the whole of the play expresses an allegiance to both sexual and social hierarchy. By attacking the position of an emancipated aristocratic lady, Strindberg had attempted to strike a blow against those undermining the principle of aristocracy in its full male authoritarian and traditional sense.

Strindberg's switch to Expressionism aided his particular talents and obscured his greatest weaknesses. In all his plays the subjective vision of the male hero is always the most compelling, despite the gross distortion of the social fabric often needed to achieve it. The pattern is set out in *The Father*. The very personal vision of life is compelling but at the same time utterly disturbed, set as it is on the borderline between neurosis and art. In later German Expressionism and perhaps even in the *Damascus* trilogy, the vision actually displaces the character at the centre of the play. The latter is delegated to a secondary and abstract role and the audience is invited to share in the compelling but unreal logic of the dream. To see this as the genuine breakthrough into the modern theatre is misleading. Its main development was into the more abstract and more objective forms of German expressionism, which in turn reached a theatrical impasse and provoked, in counter-response, the epic theatre of Piscator and Brecht. The limitation of Strindberg is seen more easily by comparison with the painting of Munch or Kokoshka. Here the expressionist method was used to enlarge the figurative dimensions of art and represented a step forward in the history of painting. But theatre invariably imposes a distance between the spectator and the hero which has to be overcome both technically and thematically by the actor's performance. It has no equivalent of the novelist's 'point of view' which can lead us, through indirect speech, into the mind and sensibility of the character. Strindberg's attempt at such direct exposure through dramatic speech can be compelling and equally disturbing, but the sense of distance is always there. The attachment of an expressionist method to the exploration of the human unconscious ultimately led him to a pathological vision of the world.

This pathology leaves a question mark hanging over the advance represented by Strindberg's new techniques. In the dramatic portrayal of women and its relationship to issues of social injustice, Ibsen by comparison appears to offer great promise of a new relationship between drama and society. But he inspired no coherent movement as such to counter the Expressionist movement deriving from his Swedish antagonist. The development was more dispersed and tangential. While there was an obvious recognition of Ibsen's work, subsequent tragic drama often involved a conscious attempt to cast aside the fetters judged to be a part of the Norwegian's theatrical forms. The theatre in Russia, Ireland, Germany and the United States has its own history, its own social relevance and institutional relationships. The kinds of tension generated by the historical development of these countries were more than equal to the creative tension which the legacy of Ibsen produced and what resulted was an elective affinity between literary influences and the contemporary conditions of social life.

In subsequent theatrical history there was an institutional feature significantly lacking in Ibsen's own case—a close organic relationship between the new playwright and a new theatre. Unlike Chekhov or Gorky, Ibsen had no Moscow Arts Theatre, unlike Synge and O'Casey no Abbey, and unlike O'Neill no Provincetown Players. Even when he returned from exile, his reputation assured, he was still a remote figure and did not co-operate in the production of his plays. His earlier experience of the Norwegian theatre was perhaps still too close. For there he had tried unsuccessfully to be an artistic monolith, incorporating into his own person the diverse roles of critic, administrator, producer and writer. Although he was eventually received with enthusiasm in Norway, he was best understood and performed outside it. His most satisfactory interpretors were Bloch, Duke Georg von Saxe-Meinungen, Stanislavksy and Aurelién Lugné-Poe. None of them were Norwegian. In the British Isles where his work, after immediate vilification, became the most popular serious drama in performance, his most perceptive critics were Shaw, William Archer, Edward Martyn and James Joyce. None of them were English. And no one, critic or producer, could really grasp the totality of his work. The nearest to do so was the young James Joyce, and he was a novelist. Of the producers Bloch and Meinungen preferred the early realist work, Lugné-Poe gravitated towards a symbolist approach and Stanislavksy confessed his bafflement at the later tragedies. The drama was subject, inevitably, to a process of fragmentation, where producers and audiences in different countries admired different things. His overall acceptance in Europe was reflected in the first six months of 1891, when there were twenty-one major productions of his work, a fact casting doubt on Henry James' misleading reference to his 'lonely provincialism'. Isolated he may have been, but in spite of this the tag of provincialism rings as hollow as ever, a poor substitute for the generic attribute of tragic alienation.

Ibsen's contribution to modern tragic drama was to apply the Unities to the context of contemporary everyday life. But in doing so, he also undermined the domestic tragedy of the middle class typical of the German theatre before him. His tragic drama attacks and dissolves the centrality of the family household and of domestic values. German domestic tragedy from Lessing to Hebbel had asserted artistically the middle-class revolt against aristocratic domination already expressed in the philosophy of the Enlightenment. The villainous aristocratic seducer of the virtuous bourgeois woman was a recurrent German theme. In *Hedda Gabler* Ibsen reversed the sensibility pertaining to the attributes of the two antagonistic classes. But he did so in a situation where middle-class values had already replaced aristocratic values in the life of Western Europe. His tragic drama is not therefore about the affirmation of middle-class values but of resistance to them. It represents an expression of alienation from middle-class life and a heightening of resistance towards it. But unlike German drama, this takes place at the periphery of Europe where the social distancing is greater and the cultural isolation is crucial. By that very token however, the artistic continuity of Ibsenist drama is rendered inoperative. The increasing economic and cultural incorporation of Norway into Europe blocks a later repetition of the same artistic process. Elsewhere the development of tragic drama entails the same radical break with the past, but one in which Ibsen is both part of the impetus towards the break and a part of the tradition with which the break is made.

Part II

Directions from Ibsen:
Russia and Germany

5 The Everyday and the Transient in Chekhov's Tragedy

Modern Russian drama, from the time of Ostrovsky, has been invariably overshadowed by Russian poetry and the Russian novel. Anton Chekhov, the greatest Russian dramatist of the period, does not possess the same literary stature as Tolstoy or Dostoevsky and no later Russian playwright can compare with Mandelstam, Akhmatova, Tsvetayeva or Pasternak. Russian drama, as a phenomenon of cultural periphery, never spearheaded the process of artistic achievement as drama had done in Norway, Sweden and Ireland. The Russian transformation of European literature had already taken place when Chekhov turned to writing for the stage, and though Chekhov as a dramatist broke quite radically with traditional Russian theatre, the themes of his drama are more directly linked to the legacy of the novel than to a previous body of dramatic work. The clearest dramatic link is with Ibsen but even this undoubted influence is secondary to Chekhov's place as a writer within Russian literature and Russian society. While Chekhov's work and his relationship to the Moscow Arts theatre is as important to modern drama as any of the other major national developments of the period, it differs by operating partially in the shadow of the greatest peak of literary achievement reached in the novel form.

At the time Chekhov wrote, Russia was still an absolutist state governed by an autocrat on behalf of a landed ruling class. Yet it was also a country where the peasantry had been recently emancipated from serfdom to form a class grouping whose political loyalty could no longer be taken for granted, and where industrial investment was promoted and encouraged by the state in the interests of Russian modernisation. Turgenev, Tolstoy and Dostoevsky had written their major work during a period when the social and economic power of the landed ruling class seemed relatively stable. But in the period between

1890 and 1905 when the first Russian Revolution occurred, it had become clear that this class was entering a period of irreversible decline which made its political power more tenuous than over. Tolstoy and Dostoevsky both prophetically sensed the ultimate collapse of the Russian aristocracy, and their tragic vision had stemmed from their feeling, that, nonetheless, nobility was, either actually or potentially, an unrivalled source of human goodness and honour. This 'aura' of nobility, which take radically divergent forms in Tolstoy and Dostoevsky, is bluntly rejected in Chekhov, who sees in the life of the landed gentry and the provincial intelligentsia a growing malaise of boredom and social superfluity. The gentry live without purpose, the intelligentsia without a cause. The structure of feeling central to Tolstoy's and Dostoevsky's concern with the noble, that of passion, is dissolved by Chekhov in the very process of writing. His personae are generally incapable of passion. Their usual fate is a mutual boredom in which the links between passion, nobility and human destiny are all torn apart.

This new thematic development in Russian literature simultaneously necessitated a new theatre capable of producing a drama which contained new forms to accommodate its central themes. Chekhov's work found its match in the Moscow Arts Theatre of Stanislavsky and Nemirovitch-Dantchenko, founded in 1902 after a famous marathon discussion between the two men lasting eighteen hours. The theatre was as important in encouraging and performing Chekhov's work as the Abbey Theatre in Ireland was, at approximately the same time, in promoting the controversial drama of John Millington Synge. Both theatres in their own way had an important relationship through the drama they performed to coming transformations of their respective societies—Ireland with its national rebellion and war of independence, Russia with its class revolution, the first phase of which occurred soon after Chekhov's death, in 1905. In Ireland, the relationship was direct and continuous; in Russia it was more oblique. After Chekhov's death there was a vacuum in contemporary writing which lesser writers like Gorky and Andreyev could not replace. The period between 1905 and 1917 is one in which Stanislavsky's theatre extended its repertoire and theatrical prowess, but could not find a dramatist of vital contemporary importance to replace Chekhov. Thus paradoxically, Chekhov was closer to the pulse of revolutionary transformation than lesser dramatists who, unlike him, went on to live through the experience of it.

The formation of the Moscow Arts was instrumental in rescuing

Chekhov from a growing despair which he had felt until that point about his new career as a dramatist. 'Never will I write these plays', he asserted in a letter to Nemirovitch-Dantchenko, 'or try to produce them, not if I live to be 700 years old'. The premature confession of failure prompted the sympathetic director to seriously consider the new kinds of theatrical discipline which Chekhov's earlier drama demanded. In subsequent discussions with Stanislavsky one dominant theme emerged—the emphasis on collectivity. This was an emphasis necessary not only, as we shall see, in actual performance but also in rehearsal and in the general organisation of the company itself. Chekhov's emphasis in the plays on the theatrical ensemble as a collectivity is mirrored in the attempt of the Moscow Arts, like the Dublin Abbey in its first years, to consider itself a collectivity of theatrical workers. The rejection of the star system and dilletantism of the traditional Russian theatre with its predilection for the well-made play was correspondingly inevitable.

In the relationship between Chekhov and the Moscow Arts, there were then strong organic connections between theme, form and theatrical institution. To start with, Chekhov clearly wanted his theatre to be a theatre of everyday life. Influenced by the manifesto of the French critic and playwright, Maurice Maeterlinck, *Le Quotidien Tragique*, he moved away from the theatre of the grand gesture and the momentous event to present life 'as it is' on stage. This was not drama as a mirror of everyday life, but drama as performance in which a new theatricality of everyday life was to be created. Chekhov's drama portrayed a mundanity theatre had previously ignored, and this revelation was equal in stature to the dramatic portrayal of lower-class life in Hauptmann's *The Weavers*, Tolstoy's *The Power of Darkness*, and Gorky's *The Lower Depths*. Chekhov, however, did not deal with lower-class life and confined his themes broadly speaking to social milieux with which he was personally familiar. Thus the radical breakthrough in theme and form is circumscribed by conventions of class and culture. It is precisely within these conventions that Chekhovian *ennui* thrives and generates a universal appeal which goes beyond them. The achievement is all the more remarkable when we realise that such conventions were shortly to disappear from the face of Russian life.

The usual stage setting for Chekhov's work is the country estate. In *Three Sisters*, which is the exception to the rule, the Prozorov's house is in an isolated county town, hundreds of miles from Moscow, and very probably in the Urals on the edge of European Russia. The dramatic confrontation between intellect and landed interest is geographically isolated, even more than in Turgenev or Tolstoy. But despite the continuity with these latter two writers, there is an important use of dramatic form which suggests, by contrast, the work of Dostoevsky. Chekhovian drama is a convocation in which all the dramatic personae participate. By and large, the stage is collective and the characteristic emphasis of Ibsen, the sustained single focus of two people speaking to one another, is often relinquished in favour of a more complex confrontation. There is constant interruption, continual movement of people back and forth from the wings to the stage, the rapid shifting of focus onstage from one conversation to another, and generally the effect of a theatrical kaleidoscope of interaction. Chekhov effectively dramatised one of the main features of Dostoevsky's narrative form—the simultaneity of events. It is in this context that we find the two central features of Chekhov's style which separate him from Ibsen—the generality of mood and the use of the dramatic convocation. The diffuse quality of *ennui* pervading Chekhov's plays illustrates both usages very clearly. Boredom is expressed not merely by the hero or heroine, but by anyone who happens to be onstage. It is part of the collective ambience. Moreover, the dramatic convocation, in a typically Russian manner, breaks down the barriers of privacy and spatial deference more typical of middle-class society in Western Europe. Out of a different social space is created a new kind of dramatic space. There is little deference, hesitation or walling-off of social encounters. Instead there is a fluid intermingling and extreme informality of manners which makes Ibsen seem at times stiff and untheatrical by comparison. For this reason, there is never any sense of intrusion or invasion of privacy. The inhabitants of Chekhov's country-house have a resigned openness to social encounter.

The clearest example of this can be seen in the third act of *Three Sisters*. Set in the bedroom shared by Olga and Irena, it shows a variety of people moving in and out at will. Although the movement here is specifically related to the progressive resignation of the sisters in the context of the play, it also illustrates the wider point about their disinclination to punish any kind of social intrusion. Moreover Chekhov was clearly not attempting to shock his audience by such devices but to show them as natural conventions of everyday life. There is here a complete erosion of the conventions of attentiveness present in Ibsen's work. In the plays of the Norwegian writer both the audience and the non-speaking actors on stage are listeners, hearing not only the spoken word, but often searching out the truth behind the speech itself. By contrast, Chekhov's onstage listener often does not listen at all, even when being directly addressed. The garrulous confessional idiom of his drama is the antithesis of *Rosmersholm*, where the speech is totally elliptical. The Chekhovian persona openly confesses inmost feelings, which then become public property but a public property treated with indifference and neglect rather than hatred or sympathy. Thus the confessional idiom, while entailing some democratisation of the stage, also dissipates the central focus of Ibsenist drama—the dramatic dyad of speaker and listener. And this leads in extreme cases to a dispersal of dramatic tension, diffused throughout the collective household, and seldom concentrated, fatefully, upon specific encounters. Stanislavsky, who identified both the strength and weakness of this dramatic form, systematically set out in his production of Chekhov's work to explore its theatrical possibilities.

The Russian director's concern with what he termed 'the intuition of feeling' stemmed directly from the contrast between Ibsen and Chekhov. 'Chekhov's characters cannot be shown', he claimed, 'they can only be *lived*'.[1] The intuition of feeling entails the lived sympathy of the actor for his persona, a total immersion of self in his stage identity. With Ibsen's work the process is more difficult precisely because so much is withheld and ambiguous. For this reason, Stanislavsky mistakenly regarded Ibsen as a symbolist writer and only had real theatrical success in his production of *An Enemy of the People*. The success of the play was due in part to the ease with which the grim implacable Stockman struck an immediate chord in the hearts of many revolutionary Russians who saw it. But that success was also made possible by the total accessibility of the hero, whom Stanislavsky played so effectively. From this point of view, it was the most Chekhovian part that Ibsen ever wrote, and did not present the same difficulties of dramatic compression as the later work, difficulties which the bemused Stanislavsky found insuperable.

It would be true to say that generally the Stanislavskian emphasis on the intuition of feeling and the self-immersion of the actor in his role derived largely from the lack of attentiveness implicit in Chekhov's dramatic form. The open expression of feeling, regardless of circumstances, lent itself precisely to this highly individualised mode of acting. At its worst, it degenerates into self-indulgence. Stanislavsky, however, did manage to forge out of it a radically new theatricality. It then becomes clear how Chekhov's drama provided the context for Stanislavsky's insistence that his actors turn their backs on the audience as if they did not exist and how he was able to give them the following advice: 'You must not live on the stage for the purpose of entertaining the spectators, you must live for yourself.'[2] The new theatricality had to combine a social and a spiritual reality, in which constant movement and social encounter were the context for the sustained expression of personal sensibility.

The importance of such a style cannot be divorced from social and historical considerations. Stanislavsky's success was specifically appropriate in the first instance to the Russia of his own time. The success with Chekhov is thrown even more into relief by his failures with Ibsen and Shakespeare. In retrospect we can see Chekhov's most creative period of writing as being the start of an age of transition. The everyday life he sought to capture was the everyday life of a transitional age with its concealed transience. Universal in its theatrical appeal, it was trapped, thematically speaking, in space and time. Chekhov's everydayness is the twilight of the Russian gentry. Boredom is then a personal and psychological indication of its declining social influence and relevance, and the drama shows a transformation from the superfluous man to the superfluous class. One of its strengths is Chekhov's ability to demonstrate this superfluity as a growing process, a malaise which develops over time. He thus dispensed with the unity of time so vital to Ibsen but concentrated even more upon the unity of place. Indeed the unity of place is cemented by a strongly focused *identity* of place, in which the change that occurs happens not only to Chekhov's personae but to the setting they inhabit, the landmarks of their existence, the dramatic space they occupy. The social change which lies at the foundation of the drama is captured most explicitly in the dissolving aura of the country estate.

The question of tragedy in Chekhov's work is more complex than the general question of realism. Chekhov never called any of his plays tragedies. *Ivanov* and *Three Sisters* were designated 'dramas', *The Seagull* and *The Cherry Orchard* 'comedies', while *Uncle Vanya* was called 'Scenes from Country Life'. It was Stanislavsky who regarded the 'comedies' as genuine tragedies, an inversion which Chekhov could never accept. Most critics and producers have taken Chekhov at his word and followed his nomenclature. Others have suggested a compromise formula such as 'tragi-comic' or 'comic tragedy' to emphasise the interweaving of comic and tragic elements and the breakdown of traditional forms. But the paradox was, as Stanislavsky realised, that Chekhov had written tragedies and called them comedies while the works he considered to be more serious dramas did not possess the same tragic dimensions. While comedy is evident in all his work, on two occasions, *The Seagull* and *The Cherry Orchard*, Chekhov became, to use the title of one of his lesser known stories, 'a tragedian in spite of himself'.

In both these plays, Chekhov intensified the break made by Ibsen with previous tragic forms. The major innovation was the organic link between tragedy and everyday life. This possibility had been suggested to Chekhov by Maeterlinck's *Le Quotidien tragique*, but Maeterlinck's ideas were incoherent and presented no explicit formula. In a negative sense, however, they reinforced the development which had taken place in Chekhov's earliest dramatic writing. Maeterlinck had rejected the grandeur of classical tragedy suggesting that its modern counterpart could be created out of modern everyday life. It was Chekhov alone who achieved this in any substantial way. But he did so at a price. His tragic vision was at times hindered by the conscious and wilful devaluation of grandeur. This was not only a matter of theme but also of form. When declarations of passion are ignored and rejected, quarrels and conflicts treated as being of no importance, what occurs is the artistic rejection of a previous theatrical convention. The ubiquitous desire to repudiate form in this way often flaws the dramatic development. It works detrimentally, though at different levels, in *Ivanov* and *Three Sisters* where drama of everyday life does not significantly develop into tragedy.

It seems highly likely that Chekhov's method of wilful devaluation did create a tension in his dramatic writing and this in turn led ultimately to tragic expression. In this sense *Ivanov* and *The Wood-Demon* are the precursors of *The Seagull*, just as subsequently *Uncle Vanya* and *Three Sisters* prepare the way for *The Cherry Orchard*. Of the later work, *Three Sisters* stands out in its own right and raises the most difficult questions about the dividing line between the serious and the tragic. But the cumulative artistic tension prior to *The Seagull* has much clearer contours. It derived, for a start, from the lack of public success, particularly of *The Wood Demon*. But it was augmented by Chekhov's own feeling that *Ivanov* had not been properly performed and, given the state of the Russian theatre, was unlikely ever to be so. There were then, the biographical intimations of artistic failure, of standing on the verge of a new kind of theatre with a new dramatic form, yet being denied. In *The Seagull* the artistic self-doubt was used reflexively as a central theme of the play. Yet it could not have been sustained dramatically without another kind of transformation, and this raises the whole question of turning 'everyday life' into a theatrical experience.

Ivanov represented an attempt to overhaul one of the major themes of the nineteenth-century Russian novel—that of the 'superfluous man'. Chekhov diagnosed the malaise of his hero in a letter to Alexei Suvorin:

> Ivanov is a nobleman who has been to university and is in no way remarkable. He is easily excitable, hot-headed, strongly inclined to be carried away, honest and straightforward—like most educated noblemen . . . His past, like that of most Russian intellectuals, is wonderful . . . The present is always worse than the past. Why? Because Russian excitability has one specific quality: it quickly turns to weariness . . .
> Disappointment, apathy, frayed nerves and weariness are the inevitable consequences of excessive excitability and this excessive excitability is to a great degree characteristic of our young people.[3]

Yet Chekhov proceeds to vulgarise the theme which had been presented with such accomplishment by Turgenev. To begin with, the intellectual context is lacking. There is no discussion of ideas, no concern with politics, and consequently, no model of experience in relation to which Ivanov can justifiably feel superfluous. The conflict in Turgenev between life and ideal, however slight it was at times, is replaced here by a general mood of petulant resignation. Not only does the lack of idealism make Ivanov an anti-hero; it contributes to a dramatic looseness in the play itself, a felt absence of tension only sporadically broken by Ivanov's inarticulate rage. The anger occasionally vanquishes the boredom and disgust of the daily round, but it has no language, no voice. Its eloquence is negative, its predicament unchanging.

The effect on the style is to create a figural stasis beneath a ritual homage to dramative development. The hero's disgust is incapable of change and his life is a constant refusal of involvement. Linked to this refusal are all the devices by which Chekhov cruelly deflated the conventional melodrama of the forbidden love affair. But as a repudiation of false dramatic convention for portraying passion, they themselves have a purely negative function and in turn become easily recognised and stereotyped. Here is the scene where Sasha, his mistress, comes back to him, knowing of his wife's fatal illness:

Sasha. Is it your fault that you fell out of love with your wife? Perhaps, but one can't help one's feelings, and you didn't want your feelings to change. Is it your fault she saw me telling you I loved you? No, you didn't want her to.

Ivanov (*interrupting*). And so on and so forth. In love, out of love, can't help one's feelings—that talks's so cheap and vulgar, it's no help.[4]

The emotions of discontent that 'talk' is unable to convey, cannot themselves be expressed any better by the hero. There is no dramatic speech to supplant that which Chekhov has rejected. The rejection of romantic sentimentality is rightfully there, but the resulting disaffection is nihilistic. Ivanov's verbosity stems ironically from trying and failing to say that which in his own terms, can never be said.

Confronted with this void of nihilism, Chekhov then falls back on the one ideal he could never reject—the ideal of art. *The Seagull* is the outcome of a conscious nihilistic despair in conflict with the impetus towards a major artistic breakthrough in the history of drama. Chekhov's art in desperation discovers a hidden treasure in danger of being buried forever, the ideal of artistic creation. This meant a decisive break with the idea, and possibility, of the tragic daily round. *The Seagull* embodies a continuous tension between life and art which can never be resolved. Artistic striving cannot be reduced to the one-dimensional monotony of the provincial daily round. Even as failure it constitutes 'fate'. Chekhov was thus pulled back towards a traditional Aristotelianism. *The Seagull* exhibits peripeteia, recognition and catharsis in a work its author called a comedy. What is so remarkable about the work is not the presence of comedy but the transformation from one dramatic form to its opposite in the same work. The failure of Treplev's play is initially the subject of mirth but eventually the object of tragedy. The change moreover is not occasioned by extraneous circumstances. It is entirely organic.

From the beginning it becomes clear that the dominant sensibility of the previous drama is to be relegated here to second place. In a small sub-plot, we encounter the figure of Savorin who, like Ivanov, feels his life to be hopeless and wasted. More realistically, however, he is an older man and of minor importance. In a similar way, Medvedenko the schoolteacher and Masha the estate manager's daughter, echo the failed relationship of Sasha and Ivanov. But they are there merely to set the scene for a very different kind of relationship, a difference foreshadowed by this encounter at the beginning of the play:

Masha (*looking back at the stage*). The play will be soon.
Medvedenko. Yes. Nina Zarechny will act in it and Constantine

Treplev wrote it. They're in love and this evening they'll be
spiritually united in their effort to present a unified work of art.
But you and I aren't soul-mates at all. I love you. I'm too
wretched to stay at home and I walk over here every day, four
miles each way, and it just doesn't mean a thing to you. And that's
understandable. I've no money, there are a lot of us at home, and
anyway why marry a man who doesn't get enough to eat?
Masha. What rubbish. (*Takes snuff.*) Your loving me is all very
touching but I can't love you back and that's that.[5]

The performance of the play then takes place. It destroys at one
blow the supposed spiritual unity to which Medvedenko had referred.
Treplev's failure is Chekhov's gain. The play is a comic *tour de force*. But
its dramatic function is rather different from 'The Slaying of Gonzago'
in *Hamlet*. In Shakespeare's tragedy, the King and Queen recognise
the true meaning of the play with a genuine horror. But Treplev's play
has no recognisable meaning for his audience at all. It has an intended
impact, certainly, which his audience can decode as an attack on
existing theatrical conventions, but beyond that it can present them
with nothing they can recognise. For critics to see the play within the
play as an exercise in decadent symbolism is therefore to miss the point.
It has two contrary impulses, the portentous symbolism of Nina's
famous speech and the total naturalism of the stage itself which, as
Treplev puts it is, 'just a curtain with the two wings and an empty space
beyond. No scenery. There's an open view of the lake and the
horizon.'[6] Theme and form diverge grotesquely. Both are rejections of
the traditional theatre but remain incompatible since they represent
the opposite extremes of realism and symbolism, and reflect a wider
hiatus within Russian literature itself. The artistic dilemma is genuine,
but Treplev's immature attempt to resolve it merely appears to his
audience as unintentionally comic and ludicrous.

The failure of his relationship with Nina stems directly from the
artistic debacle. Nina is not interested in the pain of creation but in the
mystique of success. Several days later, Treplev still feeling humiliated,
comes to realise this and jealously contrasts his own uncertain status
with that of Trigorin, a writer of established reputation. Their
competition for Nina throws into relief their respective strengths and
weaknesses as artists. Treplev possesses inspiration without craftsmanship and Trigorin craftsmanship without inspiration. But the contrast
goes deeper. The play enacts the consequence of that contrast in terms
of their respective lives, and reveals the damage done by the artistic

deficiency in each case. The weakness of Treplev's work haunts his life and makes him the tragic victim of his own failure. Trigorin's deficiency leaves his success intact, but makes victims of his admirers. Nina is the direct victim of his tendency to use people in order to compensate for lack of genuine inspiration.

The contrast between the two writers works dramatically through the fate of Nina who is as vital a link between them as Hedwig is to Gregers and Ekdal in *The Wild Duck*. The crucial turning-point in the play, the beginning of Nina's misfortune, comes with her disenchantment with Treplev and her growing attraction to Trigorin. Midway through the second act, Trigorin enters making notes for his next story and immediately deposes Treplev in her affections. While Treplev confesses his total failure to Nina, Trigorin is jotting down professional observations from a previous encounter with Masha:

> Treplev. It all started that evening when my play was such a stupid flop. Women can't forgive failure. I've burnt the thing, every scrap of it. If only you knew how wretched I am. Your coldness terrifies me, I can't believe it, it's as if I'd woken up and found this lake had suddenly dried up or soaked into the ground. You say you're too simple to understand me, but what is there to understand? My play failed and you despise my inspiration and think me a dreary nonentity like so many others. (*Stamping.*) All this is only too clear. It's as if someone had banged a nail into my brain, damn it—and damn the selfishness which seems to suck my blood like a vampire. (*Spotting Trigorin, who walks in reading a book.*) There's genius for you. Struts about like Hamlet. Carries a book too. (*Sarcastically.*) 'Words, words, words'. The great luminary hasn't come near you yet, but you're smiling already, your whole expression has melted in his rays. I won't stand in your way. (*Goes out qiuckly.*)
> Trigorin (*making a note in his book*). Takes snuff. Drinks vodka. Always wears black. Loved by schoolmaster.[7]

When Trigorin takes over the conversation he confesses his utilitarian approach to art with the cynicism of a Russian Maupassant. Nina fails to see his limitations and feels a privileged witness of the mystique of artistic success. Treplev can have no mystique for her as he has had no success, but with Trigorin, there is the voyeuristic fascination with the way in which he exploits his everyday life for the 'higher' purpose of art. The technique he expounds is an essential part of the craft of fiction, but he elevates it onto a pedestal and makes it into something totally self-conscious and contrived. What for most writers is intuitive, what makes each of them 'a snapper-up of unconsidered trifles' is distorted by Trigorin into a habitual exploitative act. 'I try to catch every sentence', he tells her, 'every word you and I say and quickly lock all these sentences and words away in my literary storehouse because they might come in handy. Then when I finish work, I rush off to the theatre or go fishing.'

The contrast and division between the two writers is a struggle for art itself. The seagull Treplev shoots is not therefore a symbol of Nina's fate, nor a clumsy imitation of Ibsen's 'wild duck'. The ontological status of the bird is never finally decided. Instead it is the focus of the unresolved artistic struggle between the two men. In the first instance Treplev claims to have killed it because its fate will soon be his own. But Nina, on seeing the bird laid preposterously at her feet, rejects the meaning he assigns to it. 'You're touchy lately', she tells him, 'and you always talk so mysteriously in symbols or something. This seagull's a symbol too, I suppose, but it makes no sense to me, sorry.' The rejection is at two levels. Not only does she reject the nature of the connection, but also the crudity of the symbol. Later, however, Trigorin, on seeing the symbol, offers a more artistically polished version of the seagull's symbolism. But he relates its fate to Nina, not Treplev:

Nina. What are you writing?
Trigorin. Nothing, just a note. An idea for a plot. (*Putting his book away.*) A plot for a short story. A young girl like you has lived all her life by the lake. Like a seagull, she loves the lake, and she's happy and free like a seagull. But the man happens to come along and wrecks her life for want of anything better to do. As happened to this seagull.[8]

Its significance only becomes clear at the end of the play. As Nina tells Treplev of the failure of her career as an actress and of her affair with Trigorin, she constantly repeats, as if in delirium, 'I'm a seagull. No, that's wrong.' And later Trigorin, who thought up the story of the seagull, can no longer remember the incident at all. When Shamrayev produces the stuffed bird out of the cupboard, the writer's mind remains blank. On this occasion he had not after all transformed life into art. The story he envisaged had taken place in his own life. Having ruined Nina, the symbolic referent of that act becomes superfluous and unrecognised by the artist. But the haunting image lingers on in the minds of the victims. It is their intertwined fate which has translated Trigorin's artistic symbol back into life as a nightmarish reality. While Trigorin is oblivious to any meaning the bird may have had, Nina has to resist the horrible temptation to view it as the symbol of her failed life. The life of the symbol has passed out of the writer's imagination into his victim's experience. In the beginning, art has imitated life, but thereafter life has to resist the temptation to imitate art.

The specific tragic unity from which Chekhov necessarily departs is that of time between the acts. Nina has to live out her romantic infatuation with Trigorin in a real world, bearing his child, being deserted by him, and failing in the acting career upon which she had gambled so much. And when Treplev sees her again in the final act he has to respond to this experience. The response is not merely that of a jealous rival, recognising Trigorin's treacherous nature. It is the tragic recognition that nothing can be done to heal the wound of time. For her, Treplev's play, once a fiasco, is now a happy memory in the light of what has subsequently happened: 'When you see Trigorin', she tells Konstantin, 'don't say anything to him. I love him—love him even more than before. A plot for a short story. I love him, love him passionately, desperately. Wasn't it nice in the old days, Constantine? Do you remember? What a life it was—so serene and warm, so happy and innocent. What emotions we felt—like exquisite delicate blossoms.'[9] The reminiscence refers the spectator to what has already taken place on stage, and the sense of tragic experience it evokes, comes from that change over time.

Linked to this abandonment of the unity of time, is a significant change in the expression of tragic alienation. Whereas Ibsen built up, through dramatic compression, from a identifiable alienated predicament to a denouement of tragic strife, the climax of *The Seagull* involves the recognition of alienation itself. The transformation from the comic to the tragic mood as a change in form encapsulates a simultaneous change from social integration to social estrangement. To begin with, Nina and Treplev are socially integrated, and Chekhov's setting of the landed estate, his thematic embrace of privilege, deny the initial estrangement which is ceded in Ibsen precisely through compression. The estrangement in Chekhov therefore arises out of the unexpected transformation of social circumstance, essentially out of what happens between the acts away from the protected environment of the country estate. Within that environment the sense of pain and humiliation becomes a source of rich comedy, as in the scene where Treplev's mother changes the bandage on her son's self-inflicted head wound, only for them to end up trading insults over their respective contributions to the theatre. Laughter ensues because of that protectiveness and because there has not yet been change in fortune through change over time. Once that occurs and the passage from innocence to experience is irreversible, the estrangement is tragic. Treplev's suicide is the realisation that everything has failed and that nothing can be redeemed.

The tragic alienation we find in *The Seagull* differs too from that in Ibsen for important sociological reasons. Not only does it have an indirect bearing on European society in the widest sense, it also has a direct bearing on Russia, which differs more significantly from industrial Europe than Norway. While Ibsen's Norway was a largely agrarian bourgeois society, Chekhov's Russia was still in a process of transition to agrarian and industrial capitalism. The landed gentry and notables in his work have direct links with the political power of the absolutist state, and are not therefore typically bourgeois, either in the entrepreneurial or the professional sense. This makes the aristocratic alienation of *Rosmersholm* and *Hedda Gabler* something which in the Russian context would have been a contradiction in terms. The landed aristocracy had direct access to the levers of political power to protect their wealth and privilege. The artistic alienation in *The Seagull* is an estrangement from the culture of the landed ruling class rather than from the substratum of bourgeois philistinism which, in Western Europe, would have condemned Treplev's dramatic efforts with even greater vehemence. Therefore the experienced alienation, though embryonically anti-bourgeois, takes place in a rather more select and privileged social context. Only in *Three Sisters* and *The Cherry Orchard* does the development of bourgeois life become manifest, and possess dramatic centrality. We might then expect both these plays to conform to a more typical sociological pattern of tragic drama. We find, however, that while one conveys a tragic experience, the other ultimately does not. By looking at this more closely, we can discover one further factor differentiating the two dramas. *The Cherry Orchard* is the quintessential drama of the country estate, *Three Sisters* the sole work of Chekhov's to dispense with that favoured setting. By examining the difference more closely, it is possible to see how important the setting of the country estate is to the tragic space of Chekhov's drama, and how, once he leaves it, Chekhovian tragedy is no longer possible.

Three Sisters was probably written soon after the completion of *Uncle*

Vanya, and is a substantial improvement upon it. The latter, a revised version of *The Wood Demon*, still possesses in abundance the major weaknesses in Chekhov's writing. There is a privileged collectivity in which individual differences are blurred. There is a shared generality of mood in which speeches are often interchangeable, and there is the futility of the daily round where resignation and the loathing of life reign supreme. The deflationary technique, the 'anti-theatricality' is negative, and when high seriousness intervenes, as in Astrov's ecological concerns, the effect is verbose and tendentious. One only has to compare Astrov's pontifications about the destruction of nature with the organic metaphor of wilderness in *The Wild Duck*. By changing to a bourgeois family household in a provincial town, Chekhov seems in *Three Sisters* to have created a much more fecund dramatic space to replace a setting which *Uncle Vanya* seemed to have finally exhausted. There is a return to the precedent set in *The Seagull* where the reversal of fortune is seen through change over time, and where the resulting fate of the three sisters can be seen as the outcome of their resistance to the middle-class family household. The theme takes us closer to Ibsen, and the context seems once more to be alienation from bourgeois society.

The theme is simple enough. The sister-in-law of the three women connives to remove them from the family household and to leave it free for her husband, her children and herself. The husband is too weak and too resigned to prevent her, and the sisters themselves are stoical about their fate, rather than resistant to it. In the use of a town house, and particularly the bedroom setting for the third act, Chekhov is able to convey an increasing sense of claustrophobia and the stifling atmosphere of provincial imprisonment. At the same time, it becomes clear as the play develops that the constituent elements of tragedy are not present. There is a dramatic movement towards the collective displacement of the sisters, but this is not equivalent to the alienation of Nina and Treplev. For the fate of dispossession works towards the very goal the sisters themselves desire, the longing for Moscow expressed by Olga and Irena at the beginning of the play:

> Irena. To go to Moscow, to sell the house, have done with everything here and go to Moscow.
> Olga. Yes, to Moscow! As soon as we can.[10]

The displacement moves them in the same direction as the utopian longing. Their desire to escape to Moscow is undercut by attachment to home and stoic compromise with provincial life. The utopia is reduced to an undifferentiated desire for freedom from the quotidien, a utopia which, once achieved, brings no more happiness than the predicament in which it originated. Vershenin tells the two sisters the story of an imprisoned French minister:

> Vershenin. The other day I was reading the diary of a French minister written in prison—he'd been sentenced over the Panama swindle. He gets quite carried away with enthusiasm writing about the birds he sees from his cell window, the birds he's never even noticed when he was a minister. Now he's let out and of course he takes no more notice of birds than he did before. Just as you won't notice Moscow when you live there. We have no happiness. There's no such thing. It's only something we long for.[11]

From then on, the theme is not resistance but endurance, a melancholy endurance in which the sense of fate is extremely stoic. In their rootedness within an oppressive environment the sisters resemble Brecht's Mother Courage and to a lesser extent the Jewish families of Clifford Odets and Arnold Wesker. But they do not have the strength to endure, or the developed strategies for survival. When Olga hears the fire engine rushing to the fire at the beginning of the third act, she comments, 'How horrible. And how thoroughly tiresome too.' She cannot relate the danger of fire to her own fate, or allow the emotion it evokes to displace the suffocating *ennui* of the daily round. In truth, she cannot really respond at all.

While the sisters, like Ibsen's later heroines, reject the conventional bourgeois pattern of marriage and family life, they cannot endow their choice with any degree of fatefulness. Chekhov, moreover, devotes himself in the last act to a conscious theatrical deflation of destiny. The attack is again against a previous dramatic form, deliberately playing down the importance of the duel between Tusenbach and Salony. Thus the fateful 'nobility' which the duel would suggest in conventional melodrama, is reduced here to the 'muffled sound of a distant shot' offstage. But in relegating the death of Irina's betrothed to a secondary role within the drama, Chekhov also destroys the sensibility of loss. Before the duel, Irina admits she does not love her fiance, who in turn is unable to tell her of his intentions. 'I'll be back in a minute, my dear', he says feebly. The deliberate bathos entails a numbing of response, and all that is left is the sadness of resignation. This in Chekhov's theatre remains a powerful *gestus*, but is bereft of tragedy. Sociologically, there is a contradiction too in the military setting. While wishing to divest his stage of the elements of nobility and destiny, Chekhov equally wishes to portray the military officer stratum of the garrison town with a dignity appropriate to their social status. Thus the social and theatrical aspects of the drama are mutually incompatible. While the institutional attachment to the power of the landed aristocracy is there, the aura of nobility is absent—a reversal of *Rosmersholm*. The personal attachments of the sisters to the military operate dramatically as a mode of social incorporation within the ruling order, however indirect, and thus pre-empt the possibility of their displacement occupying a dramatic space identifiable as tragic. By taking everydayness to the limits of felt suffering, Chekhov unintentionally explodes the contradiction of the tragic daily round. And of all modern playwrights, he conveyed in this particular work the most intense theatrical expression of a human loss which is not ultimately tragic in terms of its own form.

Yet, this was not the basis of a new form, either in his own work, or in that of his successors. *Three Sisters* remains unique while his last drama, *The Cherry Orchard*, is a return to tragic drama as strikingly original in its own way as *The Seagull*. The theme of dispossession is similar to that of *Three Sisters*. But the dispossession is not an internal conflict of the household. It is collective and total, involving a whole way of life. Instead of melancholy stoicism, there is a different sensibility—the feeling of an end of an era, of an age coming momentously to its close. The play was the most prophetic of all Chekhov's work, an artistic signalling of the coming Russian Revolutions. In *Three Sisters*, there are also prophetic elements, notably the vision of society based on productive labour and uttered mainly by those whose lives were unproductively wasted. But in *The Cherry Orchard*, the prescience is more organic. The lament for a dying world comes from the lips of those who have everything to lose and the visions of a new age from the lips of those who have everything to gain.

The humour of the play, Gaev with his billiard shots, Trofimov with his galoshes, must be thought of as a comic moment set against historical necessity. The cherry orchard is doomed to destruction. But the gradual eclipse of a whole way of life does not lead to the two-dimensional tragic space of alienation and strife characteristic of Ibsen, of *The Seagull*, and later of O'Neill and Williams. The movement is coherent and unified, sustained consistently by the note of tragic *lament,* a modality which we also find in Synge's contemporaneous work *Riders to the Sea.* It is not the individual persona but the collectivity and their environment which is doomed, and the loss is shared harmoniously in a remarkable dramatic statement of human solidarity. Reflexively, the theme loops back onto the new dramatic form Chekhov had created and Stanislavsky put into effect—the collectivity of the ensemble rooted to a fixed dramatic space. With the loss of that environment, the collective identity disintegrates. Yet significantly, because that environment is directly rooted in a particular social class and a particular way of life, the solidarity can, for the duration of the play, cut across class dimensions. As we shall see, that solidarity and its transience finds brilliant dramatic expression.

The Cherry Orchard produces a major change in emotional response. The response is no longer to boredom and the daily round but to the factual, and matter-of-factual, process of dissolution. It is in the integration of subjective feeling and objective process that Chekhov proves so masterly. This is achieved by simple dramatic juxtaposition. When the family arrives back at the estate from Paris, Anya's joy is anxious and overwhelming:

> Anya (*fondly, looking through the door into her room*). My own room, my own windows, just as if I'd never been away. I'm home again! I'll get up tomorrow and run straight out into the orchard. Oh, if I could only go to sleep. I didn't sleep at all on the way, I was so worried.[12]

But when she meets Varya, she hears the truth bluntly:

> Anya. Well, how is everything? Have you paid the interest?
> Varya. What a hope.
> Anya. My god, how dreadful.
> Varya. This estate is up for sale in August.
> Anya. Oh, my God.[13]

The juxtaposition is not merely left there. It is progressively deepened as the play continues, but the sequence is reversed. Next we get Lopakhin's sober assessment of the orchard's financial value followed by Mrs Ranevsky's childhood memory of the nursery in which she used to sleep, then the vision of her mother walking through the orchard in white. Lopakhin meanwhile explains his scheme for dividing the orchard into building plots and leasing them out for summer cottages:

Lopakhin. You'll get at least ten roubles an acre from your tenants every year. And if you advertise right away I bet you anything you won't have a scrap of land left by autumn, it'll all be snapped up. In fact I congratulate you. You're saved. The situation's magnificent and there's a good depth of river. But of course you'll have to do a spot of tidying and clearing up. For instance, you'll have to pull down all the old buildings, let's say, and this house— it's no more use anyway is it?—and cut down the old cherry orchard—

Mrs Ranevsky. Cut it down? My dear man, forgive me, you don't know what you're talking about. If there's one interesting, in fact quite remarkable thing in the whole county it's our cherry orchard.

Lopakhin. The only remarkable thing about that orchard is its size. It only gives a crop every other year and then no one knows what to do with the cherries. Nobody wants to buy them.

Geyev. This orchard was even mentioned in the Encyclopaedia.

Lopakhin (*with a glance at his watch*). If we don't make a plan and get something decided, that orchard—and the whole estate with it— is going to be auctioned on the twenty-second of August, you can make up your minds to that.[14]

Lopakhin, like a true businessman, is blunt and practical. Considerations of a past life cut no ice in financial transactions. The gesture of looking at his watch is much to the point. Time is passing, a constant echo and re-echo through the whole play, and cannot be put back. But the ruthlessness of social transformation, which Lopakhin represents factually and rationally up to a point, must also have its personal repercussions. Once the fate of the orchard is more or less sealed, then the nostalgia for it becomes more poignant and compelling.

In this respect, Mrs Ranevsky's response is unique in tragic drama. She tries to drown necessity in innocence and laughter.

Gayev (*opening another window*). The orchard is white all over. Lyuba, you haven't forgotten that long avenue, have you. It runs on and on, straight as an arrow. And it gleams on moonlit nights, remember? You can't have forgotten?

Mrs Ranevsky (*looking through the window at the orchard*). Oh, my childhood, my innocent childhood! This is the nursery where I slept and I used to look out at the orchard from here. When I woke up every morning happiness awoke with me, and the orchard was just the same in those days. Nothing's changed.

(*Laughs happily.*) White! All white! Oh, my orchard! After the damp dismal autumn and the cold winter here you are, young again and full of happiness. The angels in heaven have not forsaken you. If I could only shake off the heavy burden that weighs me down, if only I could forget my past.

Gayev. Yes, and now the orchard's to be sold to pay our debts, unlikely as it may sound.

Mrs Ranevsky. Look! Mother's walking in the orchard. In a white dress. (*Laughs happily.*) It's mother.[15]

The apparition, reminiscent in colour and function of the white horses of *Rosmersholm*, turns out to be a small white tree leaning to the side, with the shape of a woman. The response of Mrs Ranevsky operates at two levels. She responds to harsh financial reality by expressing personal loss and recaptures the past at the moment when all discussion is of the future. She expresses resistance to change through recollected happiness of childhood, and by doing so, juxtaposes innocence and experience. The balance here is crucial. In the context of the play as a whole, it possesses a classical harmony representing the summit of Chekhov's dramatic achievement.

The dramatic balance mirrors the profound social contrasts which give the play its historical importance. It is maintained with the introduction of Trofimov, the student radical, who (according to political predilection) is played either as a revolutionary prophet or a ridiculous student. He is both. He constantly fails to find his galoshes *and* gives the magnificent speech proclaiming that 'All Russia is our orchard'. The balance is not merely maintained within the characterisation. It also works between the characters themselves. The social contrast is multi-dimensional. Trofimov and Lopakhin represent alternative futures for Russia, and alternative successors to the aristocratic world of the Ranevsky's. The balance has to be found both in their relationship to each other and their separate attachments to the Ranevsky family. The rivalry between the *arriviste* bourgeois and the revolutionary student is dramatically comic, but despite their personal idiosyncrasies, their convictions are absolute. Personal failings humanise them. That is to say, they place them in the context of human fallibility. But it does not undermine their social importance. Both have an organic relationship to the social world which the Ranevsky family by contrast has lost through its growing superfluousness.

In the last act, as the work on the demolition of the orchard commences, the alternatives they represent are brought more clearly into focus:

> Lopakhin. I put nearly three thousand acres down to poppy in the spring and made a clear forty thousand roubles. And when my poppies were in flower, that was a sight to see. What I'm trying to say is, I've made forty thousand and I'd like to lend it to you because I can afford to. So why turn it down? I'm a peasant, I put it to you straight.
>
> Trofimov. Your father was a peasant and mine worked in a chemist's shop, all of which proves precisely nothing. (*Lopakhin takes out his wallet.*) Oh, put it away, for heaven's sake. If you offered me two hundred thousand I still wouldn't take it. I'm a free man. And all the things that mean such a lot to you all, whether you're rich or poor—why, they have no more power over me than a bit of thistledown floating on the breeze. I can get on without you. I can pass you by. I'm strong and proud. Mankind is marching towards a higher truth, towards the greatest possible happiness on earth, and I'm the vanguard.
>
> Lopakhin. Will you get there?
>
> Trofimov. I shall. (*Pause.*) I'll either get there or show others the way.
>
> (*There is a sound of an axe striking a tree in the distance.*)
>
> Lopakhin. Well, good-bye, my dear fellow. It's time to go. You and I look down our noses at each other, but life goes on without bothering about us.[16]

Despite their comic idiosyncrasies, Lopakhin and Trofimov both represent social forces which are wider than themselves, and their personal unimportance cannot obviate this objective attachment. Instead of producing the tragic collision of conflicting social classes, concentrated in the personae of epic protagonists, as Lukács might have wished, Chekhov subsumes them within the dramatic ensemble. The contrasts are clearly expressed but the mood of social harmony predominates. It predominates as a tragic lament for the loss of the house and the orchard and even Lopakhin and Trofimov, who objectively undermine the way of life which the Ranevskys dearly cling to, themselves become part of the fabric of lament.

'Without the cherry orchard life has no meaning for me', Mrs Ranevsky tells Trofimov. 'As you know,' he replies, 'I feel for you with all my heart.' The mood is not one of resignation or futility like the previous two plays, but of a transient solidarity lasting only as long as the process of loss is collectively endured. In the third act, the evening of the ball builds up to its climax when Lopakhin comes back to announce that he himself intervened at the auction to buy up the orchard. Yet the dancing which precedes this is much more than festive interlude. It actually expresses the felt solidarity of the ensemble. The partners are not romantically paired, and Mrs Ranevsky dancing with Tromifov suggests the total matching of social opposites. The sustained image of elegant movement, of the intertwining of social and musical harmony, is a prelude to Lopakhin's disastrous news with which the ballroom suddenly empties. Mrs Ranevsky is left there alone with him, weeping. The effect of joy turning to sadness is to sustain the note of lament, which is not an explicit choric statement but a mood enduring and growing in spite of the comic interludes and the joyousness of the dance.

The short-lived harmony of Chekhov's characters is a function, not so much of life itself but of the stage on which he has placed them. His creation of the ensemble derives from his use of dramatic space. But only in this work does it find its objective social correlative. The common experience is one of historical transformation. In performance it cuts across class divisions for the brief duration of its communal life. But at the end it still leaves those divisions intact. This evocation of the passing of a way of life would have been impossible within the conventions of Ibsenism. True, Ibsen hints at it and obliquely directs our attention to it. But Chekhov displays it in front of our very eyes. The spatial metaphors of the play also differ significantly from Ibsen. In *John Gabriel Borkman* Ibsen consciously broke his naturalist confinement by sending Borkman out into his 'kingdom'. But here, though Chekhov as in his other plays uses an exterior setting for one act, the exterior is not in the orchard itself. It is in the open steppe from which the orchard can be seen in the distance, just as in the first act it can be seen from the nursery of the house. The orchard is a form of cultivated nature which in the Russian context mediates between wilderness and civilisation. The scenes on the open steppe and in the nursery symbolise the two polarities, opposing perspectives from which the cherry orchard is viewed as a nearby image of the world which will be lost.

By constantly evoking the image of imminent loss and the collective estrangement it entails, the link with tragic alienation is maintained, in a muted form perhaps, but still tangible as a felt predicament. In the familiar pattern of *embourgeoisement* of Chekhov common to much of the

English theatre, *The Cherry Orchard* has been reduced to a period drawing-room comedy in which the sustained note of lament and the feeling of loss have been removed. Historically, Chekhov has usually been performed as a Russian variant of the 'high society' English play which came to monopolise the commercial English stage from late Victorian times. But the inherent universal appeal of this particular play actually overcomes accepted conventions of class and class imagery. At no time did this become more apparent than during the Russian Revolution itself. With its prophetic insight and its dramatic sense of social transformation, it could be seen as relevant not only to revolution but to the dialectical tension which ensued between that process and art itself. Stanislavsky, in his memoirs, recalls a production of the play on the eve of the October Revolution, no doubt exaggerating and romanticising its impact, but still drawing attention to the vital connections an audience can make for itself between the theatrical performance and the life outside it to which it must necessarily refer:

> On that night the soldiery was gathering around the Kremlin, mysterious preparations were being made, grey-clad mobs were walking somewhere, some of the streets were completely empty, the lanterns were out, the police patrols removed, and in the Solodovnikovsky Theatre there gathered a thousand-headed crowd of common people to see Chekhov's 'Cherry Orchard', in which the life of that class against whom the common people were preparing for final revolt was painted in deep and sympathetic tones.
>
> The auditorium, filled almost exclusively with common people, buzzed with excitement. The mood on both sides of the footlights was one of worry. We actors, in our make-up waiting for the performance to begin, stood near the curtain and listened to the buzzing of the audience in the thickened atmosphere of the auditorium.
>
> 'We won't be able to finish the performance', we said to each other. 'There will be a scandal. Either they will drive us from the stage or they will attack us.'
>
> When the curtains parted, our hearts beat in the expectation of a possible excess. But—the lyricism of Chekhov, the eternal beauty of Russian poetry, the life-mood of country gentility in Old Russia, caused a reaction even among the existing conditions. It was one of our most successful performances from the viewpoint of the attention of the spectators. It seemed to us that all of them wanted to

wrap themselves in the atmosphere of poetry and to rest there and bid peaceful farewell forever to the old and beautiful life which now demanded its purifying sacrifices. The performance was ended by a tremendous ovation, and the spectators left the theatre in silence, and who knows—perhaps many of them went straight to the barricades. Soon shooting began in the city.[17]

From 1905 to 1917, the production of dramas of Russian contemporary life declined from its high pinnacle of the previous six years. There were new productions of Ibsen and Hauptmann from abroad, Alexei Tolstoy's historical tragedy *Tsar Fyodor*, and successful stage adaptations from the novels of Dostoevsky. But there was no organic link between the development of the new Russian theatre and the Russian revolutions of 1917 during this period. Gorky, sometimes seen as the key figure here, has had his historical position distorted by his re-emergence as a political and intellectual celebrity in the Soviet Union. His best work *The Lower Depths* was produced before the 1905 revolution when he was working in close conjunction with the Moscow Arts Theatre. This play belongs apart from his subsequent work, and has its rightful place in both proletarian and tragic drama. Thematically it was a continuation of Hauptmann's *The Weavers* and the Goncourts' *Germinie Lacerteux*, an attempt to bring the lower classes onto the bourgeois stage as a collective hero, using distinctively naturalistic techniques. Stanislavsky's assiduous forays into the Moscow underworld, similar to Zola's first-hand visits to the mines of north-east France in preparing *Germinal*, provided the necessary background to the famous Moscow Arts production. But though the work gave Gorky the label of a proletarian dramatist, this was the only play of his for which such a label can be justified. Prior to it, he had written *A Respectable Family*, a Chekhovian version of petit-bourgeois family conflict, and after it the central personae of his dramatic work were usually members of the intelligentsia or the mercantile bourgeoisie.

The latter, especially, remained the central reference group for his dramatic work from *Vassa Zheleznove* and *The Zykovs* to his most famous drama of the Soviet period *Igor Bulichev*. It also characterises what is often considered his most revolutionary political play, *Enemies*. In all these works there is explicit conflict between provincial intellectuals and the cruder, more ruthless self-made men whose prototype Gorky had known in his own life. The predominant viewpoint is that of the latter group from whom Gorky usually drew his heroic prototypes.

The political irony of this is very obvious. Gorky was involuntarily favouring an emergent social grouping whose dominance within his drama is in distinct contradiction to his political views demanding their abolition. This incongruity in his work lasted right into the Soviet period. But as Bulichev's timely death from natural causes in 1917 makes clear, it was possible to portray them heroically as long as they remained historical figures of the pre-revolutionary period. This provides the key to the absence of tragedy in Gorky's work after *The Lower Depths*. There is no social basis for the necessary estrangement of tragic alienation. His prototypical hero is too closely allied to the emergent mode of capitalist production. And in Gorky's portrait of this fraction of the bourgeoisie there is a clear ambivalence. He wanted to expose its repressive brutality but still showed a perverse admiration for its stubbornness and ruthless dynamism. There is then a compromised sense of loss which in the later work becomes nostalgia, and the didactic formula for creating heroes is often to surround them with specimens of their own class. This becomes at best a negative yardstick of authenticity. It means that Gorky could never create a Russian equivalent of John Gabriel Borkman or his 'kingdom' since the heroism he portrays necessarily lacks Ibsen's vision of a wider redemptive power for all humanity. His scrupulous adherence to the familial household as collectivity, shorn of the Chekhovian aura of the country estate, makes him essentially a bourgeois dramatist despite his revolutionary connections and his decisive role in founding the doctrine of socialist realism.

Enemies (1904) is actually no exception to this rule, and for that reason cannot be regarded as a successful politicisation of the apolitical themes of *The Lower Depths*. Though the plot concerns a violent workers' strike the action is still seen through the eyes of the bourgeoisie. The workers remain peripheral and mysterious while Gorky concerns himself by and large with the internal crises of conscience within the bourgeois household between those with a social conscience demanding a greater understanding of the workers' situation and the outright reactionaries demanding immediate reprisals after the death of Mikhail Skrobotov. It would be untrue to say that by making the workers a shadowy force, Gorky explicitly hoped to avoid the heavy hand of Tsarist censorship, since he never expected the play to be performed in Russia anyway. But there does appear to be an unnecessary degree of evasion, almost as if the dramatist had unwittingly internalised the prescriptions of the political censorship to which he was so bitterly opposed. As far as his outstanding achievement is concerned we are thrown back on the beginning of his dramatic career, to the writing of *The Lower Depths*.

Thematically, *The Lower Depths* presents a social life about which Chekhov could never have written. But this hiatus should not obscure the figural continuity between this text and the work of Ibsen and Chekhov. It recalls to mind both *The Wild Duck* and *The Seagull* since it charts the contradictions of life and ideal and represents Gorky's own reaction against what, in his mind, were the over-idealised portraits of the Russian lower classes in Tolstoy and Dostoevsky. Through the figure of Luka, Gorky attempts to deny the redemptive power of a rootless social idealism and to reveal instead its capacity for causing suffering and destruction among the dregs of humanity. But the figural commitment does not have the same depth or complexity as *The Seagull* or *The Wild Duck*. The result is an aborted tragedy where Gorky creates the dramatic space necessary for tragic climax but then removes the central persona from the stage in the last and crucial act.

The difference between Luka and Trigorin or Gregers Werle becomes readily apparent. There is no organic attachment between Luka's own life and the process of destruction he instigates. Though Trigorin and Werle can necessarily distance themselves from the consequences of their action, there is never a complete break and they are still there to witness without recognition the suicides for which they are partly responsible. Luka's disappearance from Gorky's play after the end of the third act is, by contrast, arbitrary. We see his idealism creating bitter mutual distrust within the lodging house, a distrust fomented very credibly under conditions of extreme human degradation. But because Luka is not there to witness it and to refuse it recognition as tragedy (as Gregers does with Hedvig's death) the dramatic action lacks a true conclusion. The role of Satin is vital here. His tendentious moralising fills in the space vacated by tragic climax, a didactic substitute for the desertion by the dramatist of his own play. The figural problems here combine with the problems of dramatic form. Satin's famous speech about the nature of Man is really epilogue, not denouement, an extrinsic moral judgment on the dramatic action crudely incorporated into the play itself. Stanislavsky pointed out the problems by comparing it with Ibsen's *The Enemy of the People*. Recalling his respective roles as Stockmann and Satin for the MAXT productions in the following way, he wrote,

In Stockmann I did not think of politics and tendency and they created themselves. In Satin I thought only of the social and political importance of the play and that did not pass over the footlights . . . there took place a movement towards my habitual theatricality, and I began to play not the role but its result, the tendency, the idea, the gospel of Gorky.[18]

Although *The Lower Depths* was claimed retrospectively as a classic of Russian realism within the Soviet Union, it never became the model for a proletarian drama of Soviet theatre because no such drama ever emerged. Moreover the Moscow Arts, which has had such a global impact on twentieth-century theatre, became something of a fossilised institution in the new Russia, still highly influential and still successfully adapting classics of European fiction for stage performance, but no longer an innovative theatre with innovative dramatists. The talent was still there among actors and producers, but the theatre itself, as Bulgakov has amusingly revealed in his novel *Black Snow*, was one of the most privileged artistic institutions in the new state, displaying a political and aesthetic caution which made it highly conservative. The external problem of state patronage was complemented by the more intrinsic problem of the theatre's response to the vast transformations of revolution and civil war. Clearly the epic dimensions of the realist novel were more suited to the literary portrait of such events in their totality. The forms of compression present in the naturalist techniques of the realist theatre were a decisive limitation, especially on those figural dimensions relating the social to the political levels of experience. The theatre then became a vehicle for the adaptation of novels to the stage, but produced no new major writers who were dramatists in their own right. Other theatres, such as those of Meyerhold and Vakhtangov sprang up to enlarge the dimensions of theatrical experimentation but these represented an alternative aesthetic direction for which eventually they were forced to suffer the political consequences. That the Moscow Arts did remain intact to maintain continuity with an earlier tradition meant that it performed a vital aesthetic role during the period of artistic persecution from 1928 onwards. But its power to survive, as opposed to all those artists and groups who perished, testified equally to its lack of vitality and to the lack of any significant power of artistic renewal. Theatre had become one of the less dangerous literary forms of the Stalinist era, and for that reason, one of the less important.

6 Germany's Political Theatre: The Rise and Fall of Historical Tragedy

From 1880 onwards there developed in the German theatre two alternative routes to modern tragedy. One was through Hebbel and Ibsen, the other through Georg Büchner. The playwright in whom both routes converged was Gerhart Hauptmann, who has been generally recognised as the leading naturalist writer in the German theatre between 1875 and 1900. Initially influenced by Ibsen, Hauptmann's famous political drama *The Weavers* (1885) shows an unmistakable turn in the direction of Büchner, whom Hauptmann had read but never seen performed. Indeed, although Büchner preceded Ibsen historically speaking, his literary impact postdates him. Büchner's two major works, *Danton's Death* and *Woyzeck*, both written in the 1830s, were not produced for the stage until the turn of the century some seventy years later. By that time Ibsen had already made a tremendous impact on German drama and Hauptmann's reputation as Germany's leading dramatist had already been established. Yet the posthumous emergence of Büchner drastically altered the course of German drama. The initial development of the so-called 'Naturalist' school of drama, both as a source of plays and as a critical movement, waned after 1900 as Strindberg's work made its mark and as the plays of Frank Wedekind hastened the transition to Expressionism. While Büchner was clearly influential in the development of Expressionism, he was also instrumental in the development of the new political theatre of Piscator and Brecht which superseded it. Indeed his seminal influence on the development of modern drama has been as great, in its own way, as that of Ibsen.

Why was it that Ibsen's impact in Germany was intense but short-lived, while Büchner's has gradually gained strength right up to the present day? Part of the answer lies in the literary response to Ibsen's work. This was immediate and spontaneous. Contemporaneous with the success of Ibsen on the German stage from the first production of *The Pillars of Society* in 1878 to the staging of *Hedda Gabler* in 1891, Hauptmann produced a series of contemporary dramas about German provincial life, which have often been referred to as domestic tragedies.[1] Among the most outstanding of these were *Before Dawn*, *Michael Kramer*, *Lonely Lives* and *Rosa Berndl*. In their format and choice of theme they copied Ibsen's early realism fairly closely. But they suffer from a rather stuffy provincialism (much of Hauptmann's drama of this period was based upon incidents from his life in Breslau) and they lack historical dimension. The domestic tragedy effectively broke with the tradition of historical tragedy of Goethe and Schiller but the loss of the historical consciousness proved to be a stumbling block in the German context which it had not been in either the Scandinavian or the Russian context. That loss does much in fact to explain why the German variant of Naturalism was so short-lived.

Before considering modern historical tragedy and its use of political themes, it is important to see for what reason domestic tragedy in Hauptmann's case, and sexual tragedy in Wedekind's case, failed to achieve the intensity and scope of Ibsen's artistic vision. In Hauptmann's case the dramatic space of tragic alienation is clearly missing from the early plays. The closer the thematic links with Ibsen, the greater the failure usually was. In terms of the wider dimension of European drama and European society, what could be witnessed here was a movement back from periphery to centre, a greater dependency of Hauptmann's heroes upon an expanding capitalist society. The dependency is a deceptive one. Paradoxically, Hauptmann's male heroes are more detached from the material process of social development than Ibsen's. At the same time they are less alienated, and consequently less tragic. The Ibsenist polarities, derived from contemporary Norway, of wilderness against civilisation, the noble against the bourgeois, and women against marriage, are never reproduced in the work of the German playwright. Instead civilisation, marriage and bourgeois life are the dominant modalities. Of course they are problematic and at times intolerable. But generally the external space of tragic alienation is replaced by the inner space of the troubled conscience in the male hero.

This modification should be seen in the context of Germany's economic and political development. In the period of the Second Reich when Germany became an expansionist nation and a major industrial capitalist state, the industrial bourgeoisie still lacked any significant share in political power. The evanescent aristocratic spirit which haunted Ibsen was an oppressive political reality in Germany where the reactionary Junkers were the major bastion of Imperial power, and provided the cream of the country's military élite. In the authoritarian middle-class household the subjugation of women was as great as anywhere in Western Europe, and in Hauptmann's work itself intimations of the wilderness of Western Norway are replaced by the stuffy provincialism of Breslau and small-town Silesia. The troubled conscience, unreconciled with the external realities of German life is driven inward towards subjective despair, a despair lacking in objective correlative. It is fitting that Hauptmann's prototypical hero should be the academic intellectual. Uncompromised by material success he can, like Johannes Vockherat in *Lonely Lives*, retreat to a private protected world lamenting his predicament but unable to alter it. The inner space of the introverted hero is then closed off from external expression since it is never properly translated into dramatic performance. For want of adequate means of expression, the domestic tragedies tend to languish in their own *Weltschmerz*.

Lonely Lives reproduces the theme of *Rosmersholm*, but places it in the context of the extended bourgeois household where Vockherat has instigated a relationship with the Rebecca West figure of Anna Mahr, but must simultaneously face his parents who accuse him of atheism and his wife who accuses him of neglect. By trying to make explicit the variety of nuance and ambiguity in Ibsen's play, Hauptmann empties the theme of all dramatic resonance. In place of the haunted and aristocratic country house is the respectable urban family residence riddled with domestic squabbling. The inner space Hauptmann hoped to create for his hero is doomed from the outset. But that failure is indicative of a more general contradiction. Hauptmann was hailed as a naturalist but his selection of social themes took him back to the sanctity of a German idealism uncompromised by the commercial or material interests of a mundane world. His is the realist drama of power-protected inwardness, the fairly unique privilege afforded to prestigious German intellectuals up until the outbreak of the First World War. Paradoxically, this privileged idealism of Hauptmann's heroes leads not to romanticism but to a very positivistic outlook on modern life. Vockhert and Alfred Loth, the 'socialist' investigator of *Before Dawn*, are both proponents of a ruthless social darwinism, and committed disciples of Ernst Haeckel. The cult of inwardness allows them to propagate doctrines of the survival of the fittest for a public world to which they do not themselves belong. Here Hauptmann faithfully portrayed an intellectual tendency of his age. Yet dramatically speaking, his veracity is counter-productive, for it destroys his attempt to create a genuinely contemporary tragic hero.

The same problem had previously affected German historical tragedy. Schiller had remarked of the Orestes created by Goethe in *Iphigenie* that 'his condition becomes an overly long and unrelieved torment without an object'. The recurrence of this idealist dilemma in a naturalist form was new in German tragedy. It was so pressing, in fact, that Lukács, writing in 1909, took it to be symptomatic of bourgeois drama as a whole. In retrospect, however, we can see it as specific to Germany where eighteenth-century tragedy had been more advanced than in any other European country. The cultural achievement of this, and the greatness of German philosophy, in a country materially less advanced than England or France, has often been noted. This disparity between cultural and material development, which Marx commented on at length in his early writings, is modified but not eliminated by Germany's rapid industrialisation during the Second Reich. The cultural problematic which Lukács discusses analytically and Hauptmann portrays artistically, comes from that complex of factors which according to Helmuth Plessner made Germany a 'retarded nation'.[2] The conservative intelligentsia supported the ruling alliance of reactionary landed and military interests during a period when economic power had passed into the hands of the industrial bourgeoisie. In return the state protected academic privileges and scholarship, and also art itself where it was not directly subversive. This unspoken concordat was rationalised by the academic mandarins of the time as a necessary defence of a superior German culture against the base influences of Anglo-Saxon commercialism.

In this context, the Expressionist movement which succeeded Naturalism after 1900, was more overtly oppositional in its stance towards the ruling order. It also tried to find a radically new artistic solution to the problem of German inwardness. In painting, the work of Edvard Munch and Oscar Kokoschka projected inner feeling and emotion onto external objects. The language, themes and stage sets of Expressionist drama attempted to do the same. Unfortunately many of the dramatists, including Toller and Barlach, were concerned to create average social types rather than individual personae, destroying the figural elements so vital to the success of expressionist painting. One dramatist who stands uneasily between Ibsen and Hauptmann on the one hand, and the Expressionists on the other, is Frank Wedekind. Wedekind's work highlights the problem of the transition. In the Lulu plays, *The Earth Spirit* and *Pandora's Box*, he tried to produce a drama of sexual tragedy in opposition to the domestic tragedies of Hauptmann. While there were substantial links with Ibsen and the early Strindberg, Wedekind had already begun the process of figural decomposition which was characteristic of Expressionism.

Like Ibsen and Hauptmann, his work was immediately controversial. Moreover Wedekind had deliberately set out to shock his middle-class audiences. He justified sexual tragedy by claiming that it was a means of exposing the hypocrisy of bourgeois morality, and by making a plea for a higher human morality based on the recognition of sexual need. He also wanted to portray the way in which the ruling classes used sexuality as a means of personal domination over others. What Wedekind actually wrote, however, was less a tragedy of sex and more a drama of sexual exploitation. In his work, people are portrayed as usable objects, whose common characteristic is to manipulate or be manipulated. His famous heroine Lulu, the prostitute, is known as a *femme fatale* but as Wedekind admitted, was almost completely passive and exploited just as much as she exploits. The geometry of sexual exploitation tends to reduce Wedekind's personae to ciphers. The opulent social ambience, rendered as grotesque, makes it impossible to sympathise with the sexual predicament of any of the protagonists. The one exception is the lesbian Countess Geschwitz whose unrequited love for Lulu almost acquires a sense of noble desperation in the last scene of *Pandora's Box* as she dies protecting her friend from a homicidal client. Unlike his critics, and the German judges who banned the play, Wedekind saw Geschwitz as the tragic heroine of the piece. But the finished text actually undermines his vision. In trying to portray the sexually tragic nature of 'the curse of abnormality', he thought it necessary 'to personify in the most telling possible form the vulgar mockery and shrill derision which is the uneducated man's reaction to this tragedy'.[3] In the play, many of the other characters consequently ridicule the sexual desires of the Countess, particularly the brutal acrobat, Rodolfo. Unfortunately that tone of ridicule dominates the play, and the writing lacks any felt understanding of her sexual desires to counter it. Not until Tennessee Williams created Blanche Dubois in *A Streetcar Named Desire*, did tragic drama based on the explicit sexuality of the female hero finally arrive on the modern stage. There it contained specific forms of class and cultural confrontation basically lacking in Wedekind's portrayal of the upper middle classes and their parasitical acolytes. By contrast, as the work of Heinrich Mann and Carl Sternheim testifies, the comic portrayal of that same stratum of German society at the time, worked very effectively indeed.

The failure of the two variants of tragedy, that of Hauptmann and that of Wedekind, had a specific social context. The inwardness of high German culture never provided the basis for a genuine social estrangement. In the fiction of the period, it often produced the passive problematic hero who occupied the attention of the young Lukács. But as Lukács realised, the inward and inactive nature of this fictional hero fell short of tragedy. The dramatist's dilemma was to revitalise the tragic vision in an age of growing social consciousness where religion and myth were no longer credible supports, and where at the same time, the themes of everyday bourgeois drama seemed too trivial to sustain the grandeur of classical drama. Lukács's solution was once again history:

> History is meant as a substitute for mythology, creating artificial distances, producing monumentality, clearing away trivia and injecting a new pathos. However the distance to be gained by projecting back into history is more conscious than formerly, and it is for this reason less spirited and forced to appeal more to the facts, forced because more timid, to cling more strongly to empirical data. The essence of historical distancing is that it substitutes what happened long ago for what happens today. But always one event takes the place of another; never does a symbol replace reality.[4]

The renaissance of the historical drama under changed terms of reference was the German response to the incompatibility of the tragic vision and contemporary bourgeois life. It attempted to forge a dramatic space compatible with the procedures of 'historical distancing' and superior to the conceit of inwardness which as often as not, had ended in sentimental pathos. It was also the occasion for a politically conscious drama unrivalled in the history of the modern theatre. The first great historical and political tragedy of the modern age was Büchner's *Danton's Death*, written some thirty years before *Emperor and Galilean*. Its novelty lay in its focus on *recent* history, a focus to be repeated in *The Weavers*, *The Days of the Commune* and *The Plebeians Rehearse the Uprising*.

These four plays, stretching over a period of a hundred and thirty years, are the pinnacle of achievement in the political theatre, linked closely to each other over that long period by a common dramatic tradition. How is it possible to conceive of them as 'political' theatre? Essentially they are plays about political revolt which portray direct, often violent opposition to established authority. As dramas of recent history, the events portrayed are a simultaneous comment on past and present, and on the connections between the two. They differ from previous historical drama by making the fabric of political revolt recognisably social in origin, not just an instance of conspiracy or intrigue. This is an achievement which is for the most part lacking in *An Enemy of the People*. Social discontent is made politically meaningful in the most general sense, as a central challenge to the legitimacy of the authority it opposes. There is, however, a crucial difference here between the plays of Büchner and Grass and those of Hauptmann and Brecht. The former are quintessentially tragic while the latter adopt, in contrasting ways, dramatic alternatives to a tragic denouement. The difference is a crucial one. All modern historical drama in Germany is influenced to some extent by Büchner, yet none of the later dramatists are legitimate successors to the Büchnerian tradition. For Büchner was above all a tragedian whose work was much closer to the Aristotelian tradition than his successors and yet fits neither into the conventional categories of epic or realist theatre. In the modern context, his work is unique, and despite his immense influence, he stands alone.

Placing Büchner historically is a difficult task. His work, written between 1835 and 1837, stands outside the modern period but was only given its first performance at the turn of the century. The first production of *Danton's Death* was in Berlin in 1902, well after the successful productions in Germany of Ibsen's major work. Yet as written texts, his two tragedies had strongly influenced Hauptmann and Wedekind before they were ever put onto the stage. The time-span of his work is thus unique and remarkable, only finding its true place in the German theatre with the famous productions by Max Reinhardt of *Danton's Death* in 1916 and *Woyzeck* in 1921, but acting as a major influence on the departure from Ibsenist realism well before that time. There are elements in Büchner's work which can be used to justify the turn to expressionism *and* the subsequent reaction against expressionism to be found in the epic theatre of Piscator and Brecht. But this movement and counter-movement, while furthering the use of dramatic forms which Büchner had seminally developed, also ignored major aspects of his artistic legacy. His main achievement had been to create an intense sympathy for his lower-class or revolutionary hero while creating a new dramatic form. The treatment of Woyzeck or Danton is the antithesis of the alienation-effect by which Brecht later attempted to distance his audience from his main personae. The audience are meant to sympathise with the plight of the doomed hero but on the basis of the social and political understanding with which the play presents them, rather than by pure sentiment.

The Expressionist and the Brechtian theatre were to take contrary strands of this formula for their own use. The expressionists tried to retain the audience identification with expressed emotions but forfeited the social understanding. Brecht developed dramatic techniques for enhancing that understanding but forfeited the engagement of sympathy. While Büchner was a catalyst to major innovation, his own kind of theatre did not develop in any significant way. The reason for this cannot be reduced purely to the question of literary influence. The development of German society from the turn of the century to the rise of fascism is equally pertinent. During that period Germany was transformed into a society of mature industrial capitalism and beset by political conflicts of an intensity far greater than during Büchner's own life or the second half of the nineteenth century. It could no longer be seen as a society peripheral to the major economic and political developments of the age, as it was temporarily during the brief span of Büchner's lifetime. As political theatre, Büchner's influence was transformed into different forms of drama such as those of Toller and Kaiser which stressed the centrality of the industrial and technological age, and the theatre of Piscator and Brecht which stressed the centrality of class struggle within capitalism. In the flourishing German theatre of the post-war period, the figural aspects of sympathy became submerged either by the exaggerated theatricality of external oppression or replaced by an aesthetic of distanced judgment. The fact remains that as a tragic dramatist, Büchner produced sympathetic heroic figures in Danton and Woyzeck never to be repeated with the use of epic forms.

Büchner provided then an alternative to two very different kinds of drama. The first which preceded his was the Idealist refinement of Shakespearean tragedy, specifically the work of Goethe and Schiller, which transformed Elizabethan tragedy into a pure nobility of speech and character. The second, which came fifty years later, was the realist drama of Ibsen and Chekhov with its commitment to naturalist forms. Büchner revived the vulgar, the demotic and the sensual which his German predecessors had ignored and retained the open, episodic structure of the Shakespearean theatre. The lower-class persona became a serious dramatic figure unconstrained by the dramatic space of the three-walled room. The episodic structure enabled Büchner to present a variety of successive scenes in the city, seemingly fragmented at first, but revealing cumulatively the constituents of a total vision. The tempo, in both *Danton's Death* and *Woyzeck* captures the varying rhythms of urban life. These forms were later developed by Brecht into more complex and enduring techniques. But Büchner had presented the basis for a figural not a gestural theatre and in that, the difference was irreconcilable.

In his political writings, Büchner's concern with the poor revolves around the deprived peasantry of his native Hesse and his political activities were largely directed towards this rural environment.[5] But his plays, especially *Danton's Death*, written under threat of prosecution for his radical activities, are closer to the urban environment. While it can be said, therefore, that as a critic of society, Karl Marx was more prescient writing a decade later about the emerging industrial proletariat, it could nevertheless be said that in his drama, Büchner had already embodied this shift of focus which was unconsciously at odds with his political commentary. Certainly *Danton's Death*, as a political drama, is on a par with the writings of the early Marx on the French Revolution. Whereas Marx saw it as a bourgeois revolution consummating the separation of state and civil society, Büchner's play presents the consequences of this in human terms. The revolutionary leaders are unable to control their lower-class following because of the immense social hiatus between the two classes. For Büchner that failure, presented in the conflict between Danton and Robespierre, was the basis of tragic destiny. This was not an attempt to replace history by fate, but a recognition that henceforth tragic fate was inescapably the consequence of human history.

There is a danger here that his revolutionary protagonists, as leaders of a middle-class revolution, should be stranded between the social and noble modes of tragedy. But the essence of Danton's tragedy is that he can assume the mantle of nobility for that brief historical moment before death by guillotine finally sweeps him away. The more he distances himself from the turbulent processes of revolution, the more he comes to possess a doomed nobility. Robespierre, on the other hand, the founder of a Republic of more Virtue, becomes villainous precisely through his grim revolutionary righteousness. But this embellishment of the traditional division between hero and villain cannot be contained by a drama which resorts purely to political intrigue. The volatility of the *sans-culottes*, the urban mass, is decisive. The appeal to the masses, and the attempt to manipulate them is not only the new key to political success, it is also the key to political survival. In the political unravelling of the play, the noble and social modes are linked. Danton assumes a tragic nobility by recognising the material and sensuous nature of a world in which as an individual he is helpless, and which has no metaphysical or teleological meaning. He is the victim of a triangular conflict between individual freewill, social necessity and cosmic anomie.

On the surface Büchner appears to reduce the conflict between the two rivals to stereotypes of sexual decadence and relentless puritanism. But the choice is not ultimately between Epicurean pleasure and incorruptibility. It is between the limits which Danton imposes on his own sensuous being and the idealism of Robespierre which has already been corrupted by power. For Danton the latter is a fraud:

> Robespierre, you are infuriatingly righteous. I would be ashamed to wander between heaven and earth for thirty years with such a priggish face, for the miserable pleasure of finding others less virtuous than myself. Is there no small secret voice in you whispering just occasionally: 'You are a fraud'?[6]

Danton's own flaw, by contrast, is to constrain the nature of his material being, substituting sensuality for sensuousness in the much wider sense. As the price of sexual pleasure he has abdicated his concern with wider human issues, leaving the way open for the dictatorial designs of Robespierre, even though he senses these cannot ultimately succeed. For him his rival's failure is a material one, in which the guillotine becomes a substitute for the satisfaction of the needs of the masses. 'You want bread and they throw you heads!' Danton shouts in his defence before the revolutionary jury. 'You thirst and they make you lap the blood from the steps of the guillotine!'

Danton's retreat into sensual pleasure has been seen as fatalistic and therefore lacking in heroic proportion. But this initial alienation from the revolutionary process is later transformed into tragic strife when he recaptures his revolutionary eloquence and denounces the current leaders at his trial. The process of imprisonment and trial actually advances his recognition of the higher meaning, and meaninglessness, of revolution. Büchner's materialism is not an optimistic vision of human capability. The recognition of the materiality of the world, especially in a revolutionary situation, is a felt experience of anguish and uncertainty. There is no external adjudicator, no metaphysical plan, and no life after death. In contrast to Robespierre's view of himself as a redemptive Messiah, Danton's atheism is a cosmic anguish in which he can trace no historical pattern of redemption.

It is before his trial, in prison with other revolutionaries, that he reaches the full agony of this insight. Not only human life but the cosmos itself in chaos, and life just a transient moment of that chaos:

> That damned argument: something cannot become nothing, there's the misery. Creation has become so broad, there's no emptiness.

Everything is packed and swarming. The void has destroyed itself: creation is its wound. We its drops of blood and the world the grave in which it rots.[7]

Danton's anguish here is closer to the atomic age than to the Enlightenment or the age of progress. It possesses a tragic horror in which the revolution seems to mirror the formlessness of the void out of which all creation comes. Yet despite this horror, Danton revitalises his hopes and defends the achievements of his own life. His own tragedy lies not in that horror but in the fact that he can rebound from its nadir only when it is too late. His resurgent optimism already accepts the inevitability of his own death:

Danton. . . . Let the flood of revolution cast up our bodies where it chooses. Our fossilised bones will serve to crack the skulls of kings.
Herault. Yes, so long as there's a Samson to swing our jawbones.

and again:

Danton. When history comes to open its graves, despotism may choke on the smell of its corpses.
Herault. We stank enough when we were alive. You're making phrases for posterity, Danton. They're no concern of ours.[8]

The balance between optimism and despair is, as Herault's retort shows, a very fine one. Danton and his supporters cannot know at that moment what posterity will think of them or what legacy, if any, they have bequeathed to future life on earth.

The uncertainty, rather than leading to fatalism, prompts Danton to make one last effort at his trial to condemn the leaders of the revolution and exonerate his own role in its making. The passage of recognition then transforms his posture from one of scepticism to defiance. His first major insight into Robespierre is accompanied by a desire for escape:

Robespierre is the dogma of the revolution; you can't put a pencil through him. It wouldn't work. We didn't make the revolution. The revolution made us. And even if it did work, I'd sooner lose my head than cut off other people's. I've had enough of it. Why should we human beings fight one another?[9]

Later at his trial a more considered realisation of Robespierre's rule leads him to defiance, because he can now see it as a hideous injustice which has to be fought:

One day the truth will be acknowledged. I see a great misfortune overwhelming France. It is dictatorship. It has torn off its disguise, it carries its head high, it strides over our dead bodies. (*Pointing to Amar and Vouland.*) These are the cowardly assassins, these are the ravens of the Committee of Public Safety! I accuse Robespierre, Saint-Just and their hangmen of high treason![10]

The realisation comes too late. The revolution devours its own, and in doing so, eventually destroys itself. Danton's end is noble because it shows his defiance in spite of his aristocratic aspirations to a private decadence. The tragedy lies in the internal conflict between the vice and the virtue, the former alienating him from the fight and the latter subsequently returning him to it.

The theatricality of rival eloquence, his own on the one hand, that of Robespierre and Saint Just on the other, is significant here. The protagonists have to sway not only the revolutionary tribunal, but also the masses for whom Danton now has nothing but contempt. To them, whose function is like that of unruly spectators occasionally invading the political stage, Danton has to be the more suspect because of his conspicuous opulence; an accusation which could never be made of Robespierre. The latter wins because the masses hate the luxury of wealth and sensual pleasure more than the corruption of power. If we see the play as being at an intermediate stage between noble and social tragedy with its Shakespearean imagery on the one hand and its modern political themes on the other, it clearly veers in the direction of the social when its total impact is considered. Danton's aristocratic inclinations are a material choice, not a matter of natural rank, and are judged by the masses on a material basis. They have no legitimate basis in an age proclaiming the virtues of equality and fraternity. Danton's exclusive materialism is based upon a more universal one which in turn condemns it. Yet it includes that recognition of material human want which Robespierre's distorted idealism wilfully obscures. Danton is thus more archaic and more relevant than the man of virtue whose zealous attitudes, once moderated, became the basis for the cultural values of middle-class society.

Woyzeck, the first working-class tragedy ever written, poses much greater problems about the relationship between a realist theme and epic forms. It is shorter and more fragmented, the dialogue terse and sparse, and appears on first sight to lack overall coherence. Since the final version was never truly completed before Büchner's death, there seems to be an analogy here with Michaelangelo's unfinished figures struggling to force themselves out of semi-sculpted stone. There *is* coherence in the play but it is neither rounded nor explicit, and the dramatic problem here is one which cannot be explained away by Büchner's untimely death. It was inherent in the kind of tragic drama that Büchner was trying to write. It was a play about contemporary life, based upon a murder committed by a real Woyzeck in Leipzig some fifteen years earlier. Despite the short-term difference, there is no attempt at historical distance or retrospective writing. The drama appears to be in the present, to be contemporaneous with the writing of it. It therefore lacks the clarity of perspective in *Danton's Death*, which focuses on a major historical process. But the short, rapidly changing scenes, the terse colloquial dialogue, the use of the fairground and of the popular songs suggest a culture within which Woyzeck's voice cannot have the articulate eloquence of his social superiors. The lower-class culture has a poetry on the periphery of discursive speech. Within this there is a pain at finding an expression for feeling, a pain most deeply felt within Woyzeck himself whose feelings of rejection, jealousy and rage are the most painful of all. The compression gives the tension to his compulsion to kill which cannot find verbal outlet. Like the early proletarian heroes of Eugene O'Neill, Woyzeck in searching for his destiny is also searching for his voice. Nothing could be further from the measured eloquence of Danton or St Just.

The difficulty of the drama is in maintaining a dialectic between fragment and totality, and at the same time identifying with the affliction of the hero within the framework of oppressed social circumstance. Brecht's response, as we shall see, was to develop the former by using forms incompatible with the exercise of sympathy. And the gestural techniques he developed also involved an historical or geographical displacement of theme which meant that he never confronted the contemporary reality of his own society in the way that Büchner had done. A rather different response can be found in Hauptmann's work *The Weavers*. While he never developed Büchner's epic forms as Brecht did, he made a significant advance on Büchner in using a collective rather than an individual hero. The replacement of an isolated individual on the verge of madness with an occupational group on the verge of destitution is a significant advance. Yet the drama is historical, and though influenced by the contemporary conditions of Silesian weavers which Hauptmann had witnessed at first hand, it relies for its thematic credibility on a specific kind of conflict which took place forty years earlier during a less advanced period of economic production. Although Hauptmann was writing in the 1890s the weaver's revolt in his play is closer to the violent protests of the English Luddites earlier in the century than it is to the struggle of the industrial working class organised under the auspices of German Social Democracy. It takes place at the birth of industrial capitalism not during the later period of rapid ascendancy, and the difference is crucial.

As a concerted form of political action, the uprising had no immediate historical precedent in Germany, especially since it occurred several years before the 1848 revolution. The source of the agitation, handweavers whose wages were depressed by the introduction of new machinery, was part of a process of rapid displacement of workers which, as Marx noted, increased rapidly with capitalist development. Hauptmann's weavers, whose culture Hauptmann captured in his intensive use of regional dialect and custom, operated within a predominantly rural environment contrasting both with the epic, urban rhythms of Büchner and the machine-age theatricality of Expressionists Ernst Toller and Georg Kaiser. Although Hauptmann's drama is collectivistic, it does not enter the world of the factory or the modern machine and adheres on the whole to conventional naturalist forms used in the earlier domestic tragedies. In this pre-industrial world, what we see are not machine wreckers like the Luddities of Ernst Toller's later historical work, but destroyers of the domestic world of the employers. The key scene here is in the fourth act when the weavers invade the drawing room of their employer Dreissiger who is the major manufacturer of fustian in the district. The target is the owner, not the machine.

The invasion develops out of a confrontation in the previous act. In the local inn, the younger weavers dispute with their more cautious elders over the best means to pursue their grievances. The cry of revolt wins out and the invasion of Dreissiger's house is the result. The fusion of theme and form here is doubly significant. Not only is it an open portrayal of class struggle on the bourgeois stage, but also a symbolic transformation of the conditions under which that stage had previously operated. The weavers' invasion destroys the privacy and the security of the middle-class drawing room. For the weavers it is a new world. Girls try out the sofas, whole groups admire themselves in ornate mirrors, then study the portrait paintings and stand on the chairs. Soon they begin to smash the objects in their possession and the scene ends with the imminent destruction of the living room by the mob. The expropriation is symbolic in theatrical terms; yet in thematic terms, it is real. Hauptmann had clearly not relinquished all naturalist forms, since his authentic use of Silesian dialect is crucial to the depiction of class struggle. But he had symbolically annihilated the stage conventions of the domestic tragedy which characterised his previous work. The play presents a kind of opening both into new themes of lower-class life and new forms, both expressionist and epic, which were seen to follow.

In breaking so decisively with the domestic tragedy, however, Hauptmann also compromises the tragic form itself. In his previous drama it would be true to say that, by and large, he diluted it beyond theatrical credibility. Here, the ending of the play is ambiguous, emphasising the strangely compromised stoicism of the old weaver Hilse, who is accidently shot at the window of his work room, looking out at the conflict between the weavers and the soldiers. Old Hilse is intended to symbolise a kind of ancient wisdom, counselling an acceptance of the misery of the human condition. His sudden death is given the auspices of tragedy, but he himself has no heroic qualities. Hauptmann tries to suggest through his unexpected death the violation of a natural religious order of things, in which Hilse is the sacrificial victim and the weavers the reckless culprits. But this strange quietistic message, preceded by Hilse's claim that the fate of mankind is alone decided on Judgment Day, not only disrupts the dramatic rhythm of the play, it effectively destroys its meaning. It is almost as if Hauptmann, in exorcising the idealistic inwardness of his domestic tragedies by political realism, is forced to retreat even further inward to discover a mystic quietism inaccessible to the forces of revolt. *The Weavers* already contains elements of the sensibility which drove Hauptmann away from realism into historical verse tragedy, and even later, politically, into Nazism.

The Weavers is, strictly speaking, neither tragic nor didactic drama. The ending is too compromised to be the former and too ambiguous to be the latter. Didactic theatre in fact developed out of a departure from traditional naturalist forms, and while it certainly left its mark in the Expressionist theatre, it was not until the work of Piscator and Brecht in the twenties that it led to a distinctly new kind of political theatre. This theatre had its foundations in the political triumph of Soviet communism and the development of the German Communist

Party attached to the Third International. The early work of Soviet experimentalists in 'agit-prop' drama sparked off the development of a political theatre designed to influence political opinions and to enhance the communist cause. In the work of Erwin Piscator, this became predominantly a form of documentary theatre which relied heavily on specific historical events. Bertolt Brecht went beyond this, however, by developing a political drama which did not base itself on actual historical incident but invented its own history for doctrinal purposes, concerning itself less with historical verisimilitude than with theatrical effect. Brecht's *Lehrstücke*, although didactic, were nearer to fable than to documentary and presented the audience not with a packaged political formula but with the obligation to make a political judgment on the drama they had witnessed.

Political theatre, however, was one aspect among many of Brecht's vast body of work, and at times, the least successful. Though never a Party member, Brecht's drama was heavily coloured by the ideological practices of the communists during a period when they claimed sole and exclusive representation of the working class within Germany and yet were themselves subject to the policies of the Third International. The omnipresence and omniscience of the Party found its way into Brecht's early work as a political myth, treated uncritically, and often accompanied by adulation. This is not to say that Brecht followed a party line, for his kind of theatre was, as we shall see, never a direct vehicle for political propaganda. But its aesthetic distance from a fluctuating and volatile party line was compromised by one factor—identification of the Party as the exclusive political instrument of class struggle against capitalism and the simultaneous identification of drama as a weapon in that struggle. The political and the artistic operated for Brecht on separate but parallel lines. The internal aesthetic distance of the early political work such as *The Mother* and *The Measures Taken* comes from the historical and geographical transferences. *The Mother*, adapted from Gorky's novel, is set in pre-revolutionary Russia, and *The Measures Taken* in contemporary China. The shibboleth of the Party, removed in this way from the actual historical struggles of socialism in Germany, contains no comment on the split in social democracy during 1918 nor its consequences. A complex fragmented history is subsumed under the aura of the Party itself and subsequently ignored. As an uncritical adulation of the supremacy of the Party line, *The Measures Taken* has been a potential embarrassment to ruling communist parties throughout Europe. But it turns out to be more than an unintentional vindication of Stalinism. As

Brecht himself acknowledged, the Party could, dramatically speaking, take the place of the classical Gods as the arbiter of human fate. In practice it was beginning to do the very same thing in ways Brecht was publicly loathe to admit, even when he came to know of them. But if the public silence can be held against Brecht as an individual, the artistic silence is a more damaging comment on his status as a political dramatist. That the evasion was calculated rather than naive, may be seen in *The Caucasian Chalk Circle*. The idyllic opening on the Soviet Collective farm is the corruption of an authentic theatrical device to the level of total cynicism. It is not just that such a scene could never historically have taken place—since this in terms of Brecht's own aesthetic is perfectly viable. It is what *has* taken place historically but is never mentioned which is more important, the omission rather than the content. And taking this scene in the context of Brecht's drama right through the thirties and the period of the Soviet–German pact, the omission is unforgiveable.

Brecht's earlier drama, in which he developed new forms for the epic theatre, is at its best when attempting to uncover the nature of everyday life in the capitalist world. Here again, there are historical and geographical forms of transference. But they accord very well with Brecht's idea of a gestural theatre in which a visually multi-faceted performance has the power to astonish its audience and simultaneously unmask the real world.[11] This was Brecht's major theatrical innovation, seen at its best in *The Threepenny Opera, A Man is a Man, Saint Joan of the Stockyards* and *The Seven Deadly Sins of the Lower-Middle-Classes*.

The success of the gestural theatre here lies predominantly in its comic forms, occasioned by the deliberate use of dramatic distance and the encouragement of modes of complex seeing in which, to use Brecht's words, 'thinking *about* the flow of the play is more important than thinking from *within* the flow of the play''.[12] Essentially the epic form compels the audience into a detached critical amusement at the disparity between the aspirations of Brecht's characters and the processes of material life within which they operate. In his explicitly political drama this quality is usually lost. And where, as in *Arturo Ui*, Brecht explicitly depoliticises a political figure, the detached amusement is not critical enough, for the act of transforming a fascist tyrant into a Chicago gangster is a reductive procedure, an evasion of political context which prevents the mechanism of complex seeing from really working at all.

One critical view of Brecht sees in the later work a mature genre of historical tragedy more than compensating for his earlier compromised didacticism. But the later work is just as much a part of the gestural theatre as the earlier, and where the dramatic form does alter, as at the end of *Mother Courage*, tragic catharsis does not replace it. The difficulty of the later historical drama lies in its actual acceptance of aspects of realist convention which are less significant in much of the earlier work. There exists both in text and performance of the later work, a yardstick of historical verisimilitude. In *Mother Courage*, there are the historical contours of the Thirty Years War, and in *Galileo*, the immensely successful dramatisation of the controversy over the solar system. The predominance of these factual aspects unfortunately distorts another significant feature of the two plays—the concern with capitalist relationships of production. As Adorno remarks, Brecht here tries to construct typical capitalist relationships in atypical and pre-capitalist circumstances.[13] The displacement which works so effectively in *The Threepenny Opera* or *The Good Person of Szechwan* operates here as a laboured distortion. To present the patronage of scientists or minor war profiteering as central elements of exchange-value is to reduce their autonomy as complex social relationships and also to evade the issue of portraying the more central elements dramatically onstage. Brecht constantly seeks out a dramatic space in a pre-capitalist world to portray capitalist relationships with a degree of simplicity which the complexity of modern capitalist life visually obscures. The simplicity of the profit motive is chosen, one feels, as an easier alternative to the complexities of commodity production although the moral judgment which he seeks to elicit from his audience is intended to relate to the latter rather than the former. But too much is left to chance. Capitalism *in absentia*, cannot be rationally condemned as a *known* process.

This criticism is not in itself enough to suggest why the fate of Galileo or Mother Courage is not tragic. That question is much wider. For both of Brecht's heroes here commit two different kinds of capitulation which prevents the tragic resolution of the drama, and also subverts the whole process of complex seeing. Each operates initially as the critical lens through which the audience views the action of the play, but then in turn becomes the criticised *persona* placed under the dramatist's spotlight. The audience is then seemingly confronted with one of two choices—either to accept the criticism made of the hero and so reject the hero's critical judgment, or else to reject the criticism of the hero by continually identifying with the hero in the empathic way which Brecht constantly sought to destroy. Brecht clearly wanted the audience to do neither, rather to accept the hero's critical judgment but also accept the playwright's criticism of the hero. In *Mother Courage*, this process of seeing is difficult to operate because identification with the heroine is too great to break down. The identification is not merely a sympathetic response to her plight, but also an acceptance of her judgment. Identification, dramatically conceived, has both emotional *and* rational sources. And the problem here is that the audience identifies with Mother Courage's fate emotionally because they have accepted her judgment rationally. The same can be said, in part, of Galileo. It is asking too much of the audience to criticise Galileo for his recantation after they have identified with his resolutely rational defiance of ecclesiastical and princely authority up to that point, for the result would be cognitive confusion.

Brecht cannot criticise the performance of the play or the inadequacy of the audience's judgment here with any real honesty or self-consistency. There are crucial absences in the text for which the writer himself is solely responsible. One can ask why Mother Courage, having 'seen through' the whole relationship between war and profiteering and realised that neither can satisfy human need, should always be glad about the prospect of the renewal of war. In Galileo's case, one can legimately ask why he succumbed so easily when threatened verbally with torture, and failed to put up any resistance to the Inquisition. In neither play is there anything substantial which enables the audience to make any judgment about either of these things. The matter is not merely one of figural deficiency. It is related to the contradiction in the hero between rational knowing in theory and impulsive capitulation in practice. The contradiction is subsequently frozen into dramatic hiatus in performance. Neither Galileo nor Mother Courage resist at the crucial moment, and thus there is no basis in their predicament for tragic strife. The fate of Mother Courage, often cited as tragic, is gratuitous and degenerates into sentimental pity.

In the light of the familiar forms of transference, Brecht's later work, *The Days of the Commune*, is a rarity. It shows a recent history of revolution, relevant to Brecht's own time, and it shows equally a disengagement from the fetish of the Party. Set in the period prior to the formation of the communist parties of Europe, it poses many of the questions which brought them into being, but not in their official terminology. The epic technique is used here to pose a fundamental dilemma about political action, and the balance that is struck at all levels of the play is a triumph for the theatrical method. It lends itself to

immediate comparison with *Danton's Death*. Büchner's play was literally an attempt to forge historical meaning out of revolution when in
1837, it barely existed. Brecht's play is a dramatic riposte to a historical
work, based on a close reading of Marx's *The Civil War in France*, and
contains an inevitable awareness of the Russian Revolution. Büchner's
quest is more original but his task more difficult. Brecht by
comparison, has written a play whose structure is founded on the prior
analytical articulation of a political dilemma. There is an even greater
divergence in the work of the two writers. The dilemma facing Danton
leads to a tragic climax, but the plight of the Paris Commune is not
posed tragically by Brecht. The key to his play is a political decision on
which the audience is asked to make a distanced judgment, that is,
whether or not the Commune should have started a civil war by
ordering the National Guard to march on Versailles.

The original statement of the question can be found in Marx. But in
Marx's writings there is a sharp bifurcation which has led to much
controversy. The links between the Commune and the First International had been very tenuous and Marx's work was something of a
discreet eulogy, conferring on the commune the myth of political
martyrdom in the cause of working-class struggle. In his more informal
letters to Liebknecht, Kugelmann, and Domela-Niewenhuis, Marx
raises the questions which the official tribute had ignored and the tone
is very different. The contradiction in his work, then, is between a
stated admiration for the new form of social organisation embodied in
the Commune, which is described at some length, and his private
exasperation at the leadership's lack of revolutionary strategy and
their failure to march on Versailles.[16] In Marx the dilemma is never
resolved. The demands of revolutionary strategy contradict the
sociological insight into the significance of the Commune as a social
organisation which could replace the military and bureaucratic organs
of the capitalist state. That the Commune did have an impact on his
thinking is evident in his 1872 preface to the second German edition of
The Communist Manifesto where he concedes that the precedent of the
Commune had now made parts of the *Manifesto* redundant.

Brecht's dramatisation of the Marxian dilemma brought a new kind
of achievement to the stage. He had produced a drama in which the
dialectic between the social and the political was theatrically
realised. The links between Papa, Coco, the Cabet family and the
leaders of the Commune are brilliantly made, in a way which puts
much subsequent political theatre to shame. Thus the circumstances
which drove working-class Parisians to revolt against the government

and support the mutiny of the National Guards is not reified into a preformed political posture on the part of their leadership. Certainly *Danton's Death* had set a kind of precedent, but here the ordinary workers occupy the front of the stage. Unlike Büchner's revolution, Brecht's uprising is a predominantly working-class phenomenon. Historical veracity dictates the change, since this is the first historical occasion of modern revolt in which the proletariat does take the major part. As the Cabet family celebrate the establishment of the Commune there is too the sense of the freedom which it brings:

(*Across the square comes a group of men and women.*)
Ist Man. Ladies and Gentlemen. Come and join us. Monsieur Corbet, the artist is speaking at the Place Vendome. He is proposing we should demolish the Napoleon Column, cast from 1200 cannons captured on his campaigns.
2nd Man. A monument to war. A shrine of militarism and barbarism.
Papa. Thank you very much. We're all in favour.
Coco. Shouldn't we go with them?
Papa. I'm all right sitting here.
Coco. Thanks very much. We're sitting here for a while. (*The group moves on.*)
ist Woman. All right, as you wish.
2nd Man. The Commune invites you and you won't come.
Papa. That's freedom for you.[14]

However, the alternative to the Commune, continued dictatorial rule by the Central Committee of the National Guard and war on Versailles is displayed side by side with the reality. The Commune wants to set itself up as an exemplary model of socialism in defiance of a capitalist state; the alternative is to use dictatorial power to try and destroy that state despite its support in the countryside. Here Brecht uses the method of complex seeing to judge the Commune as a collective hero. He acclaims it for its achievement, but undermines identification with it on the part of the audience by questioning the political validity of its decisions. The movement toward political sympathy is then undercut by an alienation-effect in which the judgment of the Commune's leadership is increasingly questioned. Unity and solidarity are thus replaced by divisiveness and indecision, presented by Brecht not as the fruits of democracy but as forms of obvious political weakness the audience is invited to condemn. The audience begins by thinking from within the flow of the play and is subsequently prompted to think about the flow of the play.

Before the decision to set up the Commune the alternative is starkly presented in the argument between Papa and Langevin:

Papa. There are twenty thousand men waiting outside the Hotel de Ville alone. Bread speared on their bayonets. They've dragged 50 guns with them. You've only got to shout from the window 'To Versailles' and everything will be settled once and for all.

Langevin (*slowly*). Perhaps, but have we the legal right to do it?

Papa. What right? You have the power. You've got 215 battalions at the back of you.

Langevin. Yes, but we need the backing of the Electorate, don't we? We've got to hold elections.

Papa. God, hold elections, or don't hold elections, but destroy the enemy while there's still time. Now.[15]

Later when the delegates of the Commune debate their policy while Paris is under attack, Langevin has switched to Papa's point of view, but the dilemma and the split within the leadership remains:

Varlin. The question of humanity or anti-humanity is decided by the historical question—their regime or ours?

Avrial. We don't want a regime: because we don't want oppression.

Varlin. Their regime or our regime?

Vermoral. If we use the tools of oppression then we cannot keep our hands clean. We fight for freedom.

Langevin. You cannot have freedom unless you fight the oppressors. At the moment we have no freedom other than to fight our enemies.

Vermoral. I cannot understand that men who all their lives have borne the inflictions of oppression on their bodies and have fought passionately against it—I can't understand, I say, that those very same men when they come to power must rush headlong to take over the same criminal practices.

Rigault. Terror against terror; oppress or you will be oppressed. Crush or they will crush you.[16]

The defeat of the Commune, in Brecht's presentation, finally tips the balance of the play in favour of the policy of civil war which was never carried out. At this point Brecht does not merely condemn the Commune's military inaction but attempts theatrically to subvert the principles on which it rests. They are presented to the audience as illusory. One by one Langevin looks at the tablets on which the principles of the Commune are written and one by one he rejects them. In that didactic rejection, intended as the general conclusion to be drawn from the preceding action, Brecht fundamentally contradicts himself. For Langevin reduces all human freedom to one basic principle:

> Langevin. We ought to have only one determining principle before us. The Right to Live.
> Genevieve. Why haven't we done that?
> Langevin. Because we don't know what freedom is. We were not ready, as we should have been, united: fighting for the right to go on breathing, prepared to renounce our personal freedom until we had established universal freedom. The freedom we were fighting for.[17]

The basic impetus for civil war had been the idea that in waging it the Communards would exercise control over their destiny. But Langevin's argument reveals instead the idea that in waging war they would be forfeiting their own freedom. In his terms it would be temporary, but there is again no guarantee of its restoration, or of a dissolution of dictatorial power similar to that performed willingly by the central committee when setting up the Commune in the first place. The revolutionary moment then becomes one, not of freedom, but of bald decisionism. That decisionism replaces the Communard principles Brecht tried unconvincingly to expose as inadequate.

The dramatic difficulty produced by the method of complex seeing remains. The first part of the play is constructed around the Commune as an exemplary model for living. But the conclusion demanding temporary dictatorship and civil war, means holding in abeyance the very freedoms which have already been experienced in the play. The audience is then asked to deny what it has initially acclaimed. The contradiction of course does not rest purely on dramatic practice, but on the real history of the events to which that practice refers.

The same contradiction affects Brecht's relationship to Marx. Although he patterns the play very scrupulously on the argument in *The Civil War in France*, the didactic emphasis is on the conclusions drawn from the private correspondence rather than the lessons emphasised in the analytical statement. Power and dictatorship triumph over right and principle, operating as a kind of dramatic counterfactual where their consequences are never put to the test. But in more recent communist revolutions where they have been put to the test, the concentration of power in the hands of the Central Committee of the Party has never, to date, resulted in 'the self-government of producers' which Marx saw as emerging embryonically out of the Commune, with its elected 'responsible and revocable' councillors.[18] Instead it has resulted in a new form of state power, officially sanctioned by the doctrine of the dictatorship of the proletariat. This ended in Paris in 1871 immediately the Commune was elected, but Brecht's audience is invited to conclude that this was precisely the moment it should have been consolidated.

Rather than using the Commune's dilemma as the basis of tragic experience, Brecht operates the dramatic counterfactual to indicate decisionist tactics. The felt experience of the Commune, the growing isolation, the fear, the starvation, and the agonising self-destruction are there, but drastically minimised. This is not a direct consequence of the alienation-effect, for earlier the collective experience is emphasised. It is a consequence of the gradual movement from a social to a political level in the play, the growing centrality of the political debate which dominates the final stages of the play. Though the dramatic balance between alternative policies is maintained, these scenes show the limitations of Brecht's epic method in political drama. It is successful in objectifying political issues, but falls short in presenting their human consequences. The portrayal of the slaughter of the Communards is absent, just as in *Galileo*, the incident where Galileo recants under the verbal threat of torture, is not presented onstage. The absences are necessary for the Brechtian method, but reveal the limitations which cancel out their other advantages. The relationship of subject and object, the historical dialectic which Büchner had successfully transformed into drama, is lost in Brecht because the political decision is given priority over its consequences.

The epic theatre, as a gestural theatre, had in general marked a decisive advance on the purely didactic theatre of Ervin Piscator from whom Brecht had derived many specific techniques. The alienation-effect is itself a form of aesthetic distance which complements Brecht's theatricalisation of the moral fable. The play as performance has to be judged in its own terms and cannot be reduced to the distinctive message or conclusion it seeks to propagate. This method of judgment is clearly absent from most tragic drama which presupposes the emotional involvement of the audience. While that involvement cannot ever be reduced to empathy or to pity, and in some cases, such as *Hedda Gabler*, relies on its own alienation-effect, the involvement is nonetheless a commitment to the persona or personae onstage, to a specifically human fate which is irrevocable. The epic theatre offers an alternative mode of seeing where this involvement is replaced by the gestural processes of unmasking and realisation. These alternative modes, the figural and the gestural, are the major alternatives of the twentieth-century theatre, each with their decisive advantages and limitations. Brecht's theatre remains, despite the influence of Büchner, the major aesthetic challenge to modern tragedy.

The pattern of Brecht's own career does provide, however, an important autobiographical element which is assimilated into the work and actually hinders his ability to advance his dramatic praxis as much as he would have liked, or as he himself claimed in his theoretical writings. His commitment to communism was never accompanied by the public expression of the private reservations he came to have about the excesses of Stalinism. Nor in any of his works did he tackle the problem of the degeneration of communist rule in the Soviet Union or Eastern Europe. *The Measures Taken* condones the party's cruelty and ruthlessness against its own members. The setting of *The Caucasian Chalk Circle* resembles that of an eighteenth-century fairy tale. The refusal to tackle the shortcomings of communist rule by the master theorist and practitioner of the *Lehrstück* is a major and irreversible defect. A similar question-mark hangs over the treatment of fascism. The unsatisfactory nature of dramatic transference in *Arturo Ui* has already been mentioned, while *Fear and Misery in the Third Reich* presents a set of unmemorable cameos which scarcely figure among his better work. Apart from that, there is very little, and the question-mark that hangs over this evasion cannot be referred back to the pedagogy of dramatic method.

Brecht, after his conversion to communism in the Weimar Republic, shared the false optimism of a communist party which did not recognise the danger of its own sectarian political isolation. After 1933, complete defeat and dispersal meant silence and exile, and an attraction to the virtues of cunning and stoicism. The passage from *The Mother* to *Mother Courage* and from *The Measures Taken* to *Galileo* thus becomes clearer. Equally, Brecht's own career throws light on the ambiguous character of the hero in the work written between 1933 and 1948. Brecht himself never willingly confronted political authority of any sort. His exile from Germany took him to Scandinavia, whose liberal environment proved conducive to prodigious output. He made no attempt to settle in the Soviet Union. When war convulsed Europe he obtained a visa for the United States. His major clash with political authority was in 1947 when he was summoned to hearings of the House Committee on Un-American Activities.[19] The answers he gave at the trial attempted rather abjectly and ingenuously to deny his personal commitment to communism and the didactic character of his drama. He left the United States the following day. When he returned to Germany, it was by invitation of the East German government and he retained his Austrian passport as a safeguard against possible restrictions on travelling from East to West. Patience, stoicism, cunning, the qualities Brecht admired in *The Good Soldier Schweik*, were those of his own life, used to protect his artistic endeavours. When they surface in his major drama, however, they contain decisive limitations of heroic stature—in *Mother Courage* the tendency to acquiesce, and in *Galileo* the tendency to capitulate.

After the defeat of Nazism, Brecht's influence as a dramatist was most strongly felt in that part of a divided Germany he had spurned. The use of epic forms had its greatest impact on Friedrich Dürrenmatt, Max Frisch and Günther Grass, though significantly the first two were Swiss and Grass was from Danzig in the East. The development of epic forms at a level of creative writing in West Germany was matched by the actual performance of Brecht's work by his own company, the Berliner Ensemble in East Berlin. But the division was significant since the respective political systems provided different kinds of advantages and constraints. In the East, the performance of established work was easier than the development of a new politically uncensored drama. In the West, the drama of the fifties and the sixties adapted Brechtianism for liberal political purposes. This, ironically, was proof that Brecht's aesthetic was not politically servile, if such proof was needed. But in adapting the Brechtian use of fable, Frisch and Dürrenmatt distanced themselves significantly from German historical drama and from the realist theatre to which Brecht himself had a much closer attachment.

The relationship of Grass to Brecht is the open one of dependency rather than the indirect one of influence. For in his single major drama, Grass tries not only to incorporate Brecht's praxis but also his first-hand experience of the communism whose virtues he had extolled since the late 1920s. *The Plebeians* is a play of pungent yet intricate self-regarding irony. In it, Grass invites his audience to make a Brechtian judgment on a central dramatic figure clearly based upon Brecht himself. He applies to Brecht's own experience in East Berlin the

Brechtian pronouncement that drama should be judged in political as well as aesthetic terms. The play is then not only about the theatre but also about its relationship to the society in which it operates and the political system to which it is subject.

The plot is based, even more directly than *The Cherry Orchard*, on the meaning of the play within the play. The Boss of a new theatre in East Berlin is rehearsing his own adaptation of Shakespeare's *Coriolanus*, as Brecht himself did, during the period of the workers' uprising in East Berlin in 1953. A group of workers invade the theatre asking for the support of the Boss in their public demonstrations against increased production norms. He and his company equivocate, attempting at first to evade the political issue. But just as theory and practice seem to be coming apart at the seams, the Boss arrives at an ingenious method for ensuring the umbilical cord will not be broken. He tries to persuade the workers to enact their revolt onstage so that he can incorporate the lessons into his version of *Coriolanus*. But this impromptu suggestion contradicts his original political intention of adapting *Coriolanus* in the first place. He had wanted to use the historical example of the Plebeians' Uprising to show the strengths and weaknesses of a particular kind of revolt. But here, instead of drama instructing life, life is used to instruct drama. The link between art and revolution is maintained but the dramatic praxis is reversed. The rehearsals become an artistic response to revolt when in theory the finished drama should be a catalyst to it. Grass stresses the aesthetic distance of the autocratic boss by contrasting his attitude to the workers' invasion with that of the theatre company. Their response is to see the revolt of the Plebeians as a historical instance of what is happening on the streets of Berlin at that very moment. But for the Boss, one stage further removed, the revolt in the streets merely provides him with a contemporary illustration of possible devices he can use in his play. At the end what emerges is the aesthetic distance the Boss has created both from the workers and the bureaucratic state they are opposing. But this distance, which is the price of artistic survival, is also an acknowledgement of political failure.

The most intricate use of self-regarding irony in the play revolves around the celebrated metaphor of 'the belly' which is essential to the Shakespearean play. The Marxist adaptation pointedly omits it, and in the first act the Boss explains why:

To think that wretched limping parable
Has earned itself a world-wide reputation!

Try it, I ask you, on welders or mechanics,
Just try it on a modern cable winder.[20]

But despite the contempt of their Boss, the actors do use the parable
in their rehearsal, not for ideological reasons, but in order to save their
lives. When the workers threaten to lynch them for lack of support,
Erwin turns the metaphor of the belly into a Brechtian parable,
making it the East German state upon which both workers and actors
are in different ways dependent. The very parable the Boss had
rejected as reactionary and irrelevant, is transposed from drama into
life to save his own neck.

The threat of violence to which the workers eventually resort, is not
merely a result of the theatre company's equivocation, or even their
own philistine ignorance of the theatre. It stems directly from mistrust
and a lack of communication. They object to the way in which the Boss
treats their intrusion. Here Grass introduces a further irony: breakdown of communication with the very people the theatre pledged to
instruct. As the Boss persuades them to 'rehearse' their uprising on
stage, he taunts the workers with their timidity, vagueness, and lack of
planned strategy:

All revolutionaries if you please,
Keep off the grass and mind the shrubs and trees.

and:

Kindly shoot above the trees
We want our freedom, but no bloodshed, please.

He damns their inadequacy just as the real Brecht had unmasked the inadequacies of Mother Courage, Galileo and the
Communards.

There is a link here between *The Plebeians* and *The Days of the
Commune*. It arises through similar dramatic statements about revolutionary efficacy. Both the Berlin workers and the Paris Communards eschew the attempt to overthrow the state by force. The Boss
cannot resist the temptation to gloat over the ironic contrast between
the workers' enthusiasm and their refusal to adopt ruthless means of
action. Rather than instructing them in the use of tactics by rehearsing
Coriolanus, he dispenses with drama, and makes a blunt pointed
statement:

Boss. Ask them about the grass. And ask them whether
    They've made a plan and who their leader is.
    (*Jumps up.*) Have you occupied the radio?
    Called a general strike? And what
    About the Vopos? Looking the other way?
    Taken precautions against Western agents?
    And have you reassured the Soviets?
    Have you made it clear that socialism stays?
    And now suppose they send in tanks
    The model you are all familiar with.
Foreman. Tanks? Tanks? Why tanks? We are unarmed.[21]

The advice is politically sound, and shows the Boss as a dramatist
has a greater awareness of what revolution entails than the workers
who are hoping to carry it out. But his role is not to lead them. It can
only be to advise them, and ultimately to demonstrate his advice
theatrically. When he attempts to do this, however, the advice loses its
coherence. Theatricality cannot rival direct political statement. The
Boss persuades them to march onstage with placards attempting to
avoid plots of grass he has put there, the object lesson being to show
them the absurdity of their caution. But the workers feel patronised
and insulted, the mason removes all the signs and denounces the
futility of the whole exercise:

> Grass, grass, all I hear is grass. There isn't any in this town. Nothing
> but rubble, war-damage, weeds. What are we, anyway! Clowns?
> Horsing around with his grass while our people are down
> there . . . [22]

Technically the exercise does work, because in trying to avoid the
grass, the workers are reduced to a state of hopeless confusion. Yet in
proceeding from this to the dramatic counterfactual reminiscent of
The Days, the Boss fails miserably. 'By showing what shouldn't be
done', he claims, 'we make it clear what the revolution demands.' But
the workers irritated by theatrical debut, think the Boss is trying to
distract them from their real tasks in the streets. They are unable to
make the right connections.

At the end, the Boss is a broken and defeated figure, escaping to a
country retreat to write poetry in the knowledge that the revolt will
fail. The letter he writes on the workers' behalf will be censored out of
all recognition and quoted selectively to alter its meaning, just as in

history, Brecht's letter to the Party leaders was selectively quoted and not published in full until a decade after his death. The Boss then is not a tragic hero. Nor are the workers. As the drama is already history we know their revolt must fail, but we do not see it do so, nor do we see the arrests and the trials which followed. Yet the play is a tragedy, and the tragic experience must be sought in the relationship between the Boss and the workers. It lies in the connecting link between the two different kinds of failure, the first artistic, the second political and the sense of loss comes from the failure of the individual and the collective hero to unite. The issue is not the narrow one of political decision but the wider one of human solidarity, which breaks down at the crucial moment. The workers cannot understand the Boss's theatre; the Boss cannot actively identify with the workers' plight. The loss of sympathy, which is part of the deliberate Brechtian strategy in the theatre, is here transformed into the personal weakness of the theatre director himself. His powers of perception allow him no powers of sympathy. The commitment remains purely cerebral and, like Coriolanus, the autocratic Boss lacks any sense of pity.

The most decisive break with Brechtian forms in the play lies in the use of a single stage setting throughout. But since that setting is itself a stage within a stage, we then witness a rather rare phenomenon. The play within the play uses epic forms but the play itself adopts naturalist conventions. In order to show the fluidity of the epic forms and the response of the company to external intrusion, Grass has to use a fixed naturalistic setting. Moreover the fixity suggests a kind of willed imprisonment on the part of the Boss. The stage is his life and he cannot leave it to demonstrate in the streets with the building workers. While Grass diverges with Brecht in this respect, in another he is closer to him than he is to Büchner. The play makes effective use of the alienation-effect. We are distanced from both the Boss and the workers. Moreover 'complex seeing' also operates through the figure of the Boss himself. We can see the limitations of the workers through his eyes, but then in turn his own limitations are unmasked in his response to them. Grass therefore does not reinstate the sympathy for the tragic hero upon which Büchner had insisted and which Brecht discarded. A relationship is established between tragedy and epic forms but it lacks the figural dimensions present in Büchner or Ibsen, O'Casey or O'Neill. And it also begs the question as to whether Grass could write tragic drama outside this uniquely reflexive mode of theatre.

The play of Grass illustrates a more general point. Tragedy has, at best, been tangential to the development of modern German drama.

The promise of Büchner's tragic writing, which linked realist themes and epic forms, was never to be fully realised. Ibsenist tragedy was equally transformed, diluted by the German naturalists into domestic bourgeois drama, only possible in the culturally protected ambience of the pre-war period. The war and its chaotic aftermath in fact changed the nature of German drama radically. The disintegration of the old social order, the development of an unstable and often hated democratic republic under Weimar, made social disaffection into an open and public phenomenon. Expressionist and epic drama echoed that disaffection, but both were responses equally to its social environment. Expressionism immersed itself in the world of the city and the machine; Piscator and Brecht used the theatre as a dramatic forum for unmasking class struggle in all its complex forms. Although both modes used historical drama, they simultaneously severed the link between politics and historical consciousness. Expressionism, enlarging and distorting human emotion, often cultivating a fetish of the machine, was more effective in painting and film than on stage. Here the bloating of individual emotion, the use of social types and anonymous collectivities dwarfed by a technological environment blurred the perspective of history and dissolved its relative clarity. Brecht's gestural theatre reinstated an important criterion of objectivity in a theatre which seemed at times glued to the integument of contemporary life. But Brecht's forms of transference, historically to the late-medieval or early-capitalist period, geographically to peasant societies or to modern America, created a theatre which at times was involuntarily remote. In its comic forms, the use of the *gestus* as a dramatic technique helped to overcome this. Moreover, the purity of fable often overcame the absence of a coherent historical meaning. But in his serious work, there were times when neither *gestus* nor fable could compensate for this absence of historical perspective.

This presents us, in the period from 1914 to 1945, with a very paradoxical circumstance. The German theatre was inextricably bound up with the important events of the time, the revulsion against the war, the 1918 revolution, the establishment of Weimar democracy and finally the rise of fascism. Individual playwrights, producers and actors were often politically committed to socialist or libertarian causes. Yet thematically this period of German life tends to be absent from the German stage. There were exceptions as in the expressionist war drama, Agit-Prop, or Arnolt Bronnen's sensationalist *Vatermord*. But for a country which developed the political theatre to such a degree of artistic achievement and which brought the working classes onto the centre of the modern stage there is little about the historical relationship of the German people to either communism, or, more important, to fascism. While it is an easy exercise to place the German theatre, sociologically speaking, in this kind of political context, it is much less easy to see, dramatically speaking, a direct thematic confrontation with such momentous issues; a kind of confrontation, that is, in which an artistically transformed historical consciousness produced drama of lasting value. The result was work which tended to be too transient and immediate, or too distant and remote. On the other hand, the development of dramatic forms suited to the thematic presentation of modern urban life, and the rhythms of the city and the machine were successfully developed. Moreover, in the German political theatre at its best there is a solution of sorts to one of the major problems of modern drama, the movement back and forth between the social and political levels of dramatic action.

The general formulas and advances made, however, were largely detrimental to historical tragedy, because the dramatic space of tragic alienation was necessarily relinquished. It had become an immensely difficult task to maintain in societies experiencing the advent of a mature industrial capitalism, and new dramatic forms developed in its place. The link between tragedy and urban life developed in Büchner, is however, advanced under different conditions. In Ireland, O'Casey achieved this in a backward society in transition from quasi-colonial status to national independence, and also retained in his dramatic action the important dialectic of the social and the political. In America, O'Neill, using both expressionist and epic forms, developed it in an industrialised country but significantly forfeited the dialectic of the social and the political, writing little in the way of political drama at all. But though the legacy of Büchner was indirectly incorporated into Irish and American drama, the naturalist forms stemming from Ibsen also reasserted themselves. In the first half of the twentieth century, the chance of cementing an organic link between tragedy and epic theatre had vanished.

Part III
The Irish Renaissance

7 Tragic Nobility and National Awakening

The birth of Irish tragedy was hardly an auspicious occasion. The first version of the Deidre myth by George Russell (AE) had its premiere in April 1902 at St Theresa's Hall in Dublin before an audience of no more than twenty-five people. The following year it had its first outdoor performance at Dundrum before a substantially larger following. However, as Joseph Holloway, the eminent diarist of the Irish theatre, remarked, the result was not the tragic catharsis which Aristotle had recommended. The heavy rain put paid to all that:

> When the second act was over and Deidre had finished her lamentation in dumbshow, unfortunately owing to the noisy patter of rain on innumerable umbrellas, the audience stormed the stage (got under the trees I mean) overturning the benches and chairs in the flight to keep themselves dry until the auditorium looked for all the world like a restaurant dining car *en deshabille* in the morning before being swept out for the day's occupation. This was positively the first appearance of many on the stage and they did not make a happy debut huddled closely under the friendly branches of the sheltering foliage.[1]

There was little to suggest the imminent renaissance of Irish drama. But the subsequent history of the Abbey Theatre from its foundation in 1904 to its production of Sean O'Casey's *The Plough and the Stars* in 1926 proved to be one of the most important periods in modern drama as well as one of the most important periods in Irish history.

The two processes, the struggle for national independence and the struggle for an Irish theatre were closely linked. But as in Russia, where similar connections could be made during the same period, the drama was not an exalted expression of a growing political tendency. Nor was it even the elemental statement of Irish patriotism which many Irish patriots wished it to be. The relationship between politics and the theatre was more complex. As in Norway, the new drama in Ireland was part of a national awakening and a national consciousness. The comparison was explicitly made by Gaelic nationalists in *Sinn Fein* confident of discovering 'Irish Bjornsons', and within the dramatic movement itself. W. B. Yeats, the leader of that movement and the founder of the modern Irish theatre, declared that in Ireland the peasant saga would provide the basis for a new drama and poetry as it had already done in Norway. Yet the view of the cultural nationalists in the Gaelic League and the leaders of the new dramatic movement differed significantly. The former made a direct comparison between Anglo-Irish and the King's Norwegian as the respective languages of the ruling classes in both countries. They saw a new literature arising from the spoken Irish of the western peasantry which they compared with the Norwegian peasant dialect *Maal*. Yeats, J. M. Synge and Lady Gregory made similar connections. But they saw the new drama as written in English, not Gaelic, but incorporating the dialect and spoken rhythms of the Irish language. This, as opposed to the Anglo-Irish culture of colonial Dublin, was Hiberno-English, the dialect of a peasantry in the west who thought in Gaelic but now spoke English. While Gaelic dramas came to be written and regularly performed during this period, it was the linguistic form of Hiberno-English which dominated the first phase of the Irish renaissance.

Already then there was a basic cultural tension between the practices of the Abbey Theatre and *Sinn Fein* nationalism. It was to be reinforced by differences over the themes of the new Irish drama. The Abbey Theatre never became the vehicle for expressing exalted patriotic sentiments which Arthur Griffiths and other *Sinn Fein* leaders wished it to be. After Yeats' first important work *Cathleen Ni Houlihan*, there was never again to be stirring patriotic call to arms from amongst the Abbey playwrights. And yet the tension created by the expectations of political militants and critics alike contributed immeasurably to the high productive level of writing for the Irish theatre. As Yeats himself remarked during the bitter controversy over *The Playboy of the Western World:* 'An audience with national feeling is alive; at the worst it is alive enough to quarrel with.[2] The dialectical tension between politics and art which developed up to the formation of the Irish Free State, complemented the more general European dialectic of centre and periphery, already observed in Norway and Russia, from which tragedy for the modern stage emerged.

Despite the historical similarities with Norway, there was no real basis for an Irish Ibsenism. The nearest to it is James Joyce's *Exiles,* and that, in terms of the Irish theatre was a very untypical play, and particularly so because, as the title suggests, it was written in exile. As with Ibsen, its themes lend it a middle-class cosmopolitan appeal not readily characteristic of the Irish dramatic movement as a whole. Irish tragedy, in particular, did not lend itself to the facile cosmopolitanism by which Ibsen's work was often diluted. It depended on a distinctive combination of spoken word and historical context, and found a tragedy rooted in its own people. Here dramatic speech, which Yeats unfortunately erected into an archaic dogma about the nature of theatre itself, has a more specifically colonial aura than the linguistic tensions emerging from Norway. The 'Europeanness' of Ibsen's work was only possible because of Norway's escape from colonial tutelage. The forced English colonisation of Ireland, however, had produced a unique linguistic resonance. The country was formally integrated with Britain by political union yet its western regions remained wild, peripheral and primitive. This contrast was reflected in language itself. 'Ireland is always Connacht to my imagination', Yeats had claimed. The poetic dialect of the Connacht peasantry reminded him of the English of the King James Bible, and lay behind his polemical distinction between a poetic peasant speech and a prosaic provincial Ibsenism.

Yeats and Lady Gregory constantly juxtaposed the oral tradition of the west of Ireland to the Anglo-Irish literary culture in Dublin, which, for Yeats, remained the culture of an alien ruling class. It was in the latter tradition that he placed the Ibsenist legacy. While admiring the work of Wilde, Shaw, George Moore and Edward Martyn, he saw them essentially as 'dramatists of reform' governed by an interest in 'matters of opinion'.[3] Aside from the reform drama of the early realist Ibsen, there was a more fundamental thematic difference between the Norwegian playwright and the leaders of the Irish dramatic movement. Ibsen had sought to create the 'aura' of nobility in a contemporary Norway where no titled aristocracy existed. In Ireland, on the other hand, there was a titled Anglo-Irish aristocracy, but Yeats and his associates chose on the whole to ignore it. Instead they focused on the peasant life of contemporary Ireland, which Ibsen had ignored in his own country, and on an archaic nobility bequeathed by heroic myth. These heroic myths were part of the oral tradition of the western peasantry, tales collected by Lady Gregory and used as a basis for the new drama. The connection between speech and myth in this respect is of immense sociological importance. The sagas of the royal rulers of Ireland's feudal past were preserved as peasant tales in peasant dialect.

In translating them, Lady Gregory used the idiom of her own area of Kiltartan, and it is with this dialect that the royal figures of the saga speak. The link between the peasant and the noble is then maintained in historical drama, inspired by the sagas, and tragic nobility arises out of the strife of tribal chieftains at a time when Ireland was divided into primitive warring kingdoms.

In his fascination for this dialect, Yeats went on to create an impossible mandate for modern Irish tragedy. He called for a poetic speech through which a pure passion could be refined, devoid of Ibsenist conventions of character, and which would then create a compelling 'tragic ecstasy'.[4] But even in his own major works, the figural dimensions he consciously sought to eliminate continued to be present. In the Irish drama of contemporary life the Abbey Theatre was subsequently to produce, they were of central importance. Within this figural framework, Irish drama passes through three separate but related phases, overlapping chronologically. After the heroic drama of Yeats, Russell, Synge and Lady Gregory comes the peasant drama of Synge, Padraic Colum and T. C. Murray, and finally Sean O'Casey's trilogy set in Dublin during the period of national revolution. In this overlapping, often discontinuous movement we find, thematically speaking, a progression from distant history to the contemporary country and thence to the contemporary city.

At the same time, in the development of the Abbey Theatre company as the major centre for the new drama, was to be seen the interpenetration of political and institutional controversies. Under the guidance of Yeats, the Abbey manifested a curious mixture of democratic and élitist practices. The democracy was reflected in the general goals of the Theatre outlined by Yeats and in the way it was run until 1905. The élitism became apparent in the decision-making powers which Yeats, Synge and Lady Gregory assumed as a triumvirate thereafter, mainly as a price of the financial support of an Englishwoman, Annie Horniman, who was unsympathetic to the politics of Irish nationalism. From the beginning Yeats had attempted to promote a people's theatre, and at one stage was confident enough to claim that the Abbey had achieved a remarkable degree of self-awareness amongst the Irish people by effecting a process 'that will be done all over the world and done more and more perfectly: the making articulate of the dumb classes each with its own knowledge of the world, its own dignity, but objective . . .'.[5] Yet the Abbey's audience consisted mainly of educated middle-class Dubliners, Catholic in religion and philistine in taste, who felt their social respectability and cultural pretensions threatened by the most substantial work of the theatre. The reception of Ibsen in Dublin had been nothing short of disastrous, and the Abbey was forced to nurture its more important works through a difficult period by interspersing them with more popular comedies. But the popularity of these peasant comedies of Colum, William Boyle and George Fitzmaurice was not what Yeats had in mind when he spoke of a People's theatre. In his view they were necessary commercial concessions to a debased popular taste which would allow the theatre to survive. By no stretch of the imagination could Yeats have seen in them 'the making articulate of the dumb classes'.

The other major democratic practices lay in the recruitment of lower-class theatre personnel, and the initial policy of allowing all company members a say in the selection of plays. The former policy produced social contrasts between the leadership and its followers which was actually reflected in the development of the Abbey style. The brothers Frank and Willie Fay were as important to the founding of the Abbey as Yeats himself. Their raw makeshift amateur experience, coupled with their relative lack of education or privileged upbringing, made them hostile to Yeats's idea of a 'literary' theatre. Their own feeling for the stage had been based on visiting English companies steeped in popular forms of theatricality. But their major contribution lay not so much in imitating the melodrama they so clearly enjoyed as in linking figural conventions which focused on the individual actor with a naturalist simplicity of setting.[6] It was they, not Yeats, who possessed the necessary feeling and expertise for staging *Riders to the Sea* and ensuring that the more abstract absurdities of Yeats's thinking did not hinder the development of a rudimentary Abbey style. They also had more in common socially with the theatre personnel who were often recruited from the same social background to which Yeats referred, proudly rather than patronisingly, as one of 'clerks and shopkeepers'.

The dilemma created by the democratic procedure of the selection of plays was more centrally related to political controversy. In a period of growing nationalist ferment it led to tendentious debates within the company which Yeats abhorred. In making the Abbey a fully professional company in 1905, the theatre adopted more élitist procedures but in doing so, protected itself in the long term against the volatile pressures of politics. Those in the Abbey who left in protest at this change of policy in 1906 were confronted more squarely with that very dilemma. They helped to set up a nationalist rival, The Theatre of Ireland, staging a variety of peasant plays and works in modern Irish. But the theatre ran for only six years until it dissolved in 1912, when many of its officials, who included Padraic Pearse, became absorbed into the Irish Volunteer Movement and concentrated on purely political activities.[7] The professionalisation and political neutrality of the Abbey, on the other hand, contributed to its endurance, though it could never remove it from the realm of controversy. The refusal of the Abbey to bow before public condemnation of *The Playboy of the Western World*, for example, was due to the strength of the theatre leadership rather than unanimity among the company itself, many of whom were uncertain of the merits of the play. The situation in which the leading playwrights also possessed administrative authority over both producers and actors was rather as if Chekhov and Gorky had come to control the Moscow Arts and treated Stanislavsky and Nemirovitch-Dantchenko as their subordinates. Indeed, it produced the rather unique situation where the Abbey Theatre, more than any other in modern history, developed its artistic policies out of the decisions of its three most performed playwrights, a situation which caused the Fay brothers to leave a few years after the theatre was founded.

The subordinate role of the Abbey producer was a serious problem. *The Playboy* was first performed as a sombre serious drama lacking in comic gusto. The development of a theatrical style for the historical drama was continuously inadequate. Not until Yeats incorporated the masks suggested by Gordon Craig, for example, did *On Baile's Strand* become a theatrical success. Equally the production of Synge's unfinished *Deidre* was disappointing and Lady Gregory's tragedy *Grania* was never performed at all. The great initial success of the theatre, artistically speaking, came with a drama of contemporary life, J. M. Synge's *Riders to the Sea*.

The impact of *Riders to the Sea* was immediate and profound. The response of Holloway to the play's first appearance in 1904 is worth recording in some detail. It was a two-stage response in which initial reaction to the opening night was tempered by the deeper reflection of a second viewing. To Holloway and to the Abbey audience, the play was an intensely *realistic* spectacle and at the same time, a spectacle which shook their conventional notions of reality to their foundations:

Mr. Synge has given us an intensely sad—almost weirdly so— picture of the lives of the humble dwellers on an isle in the West in his *Riders to the Sea*, and from the rise of the curtain the Spirit of Gloom takes possession of the scene and holds sway until the last of Maurya's six sons is brought home to her a corpse . . . The scene is one of intense gloom . . . and it was interpreted with rare natural-ness and sincereity, it held the audience in a marvellous way. This was a triumph of art for the players as well as the dramatist, as the subject was one that the slightest error of judgment would set the audience in a titter. But as the illusion was complete, no titter came and profound impression was created instead.[8]

Holloway's ambivalence deepened the following day. He claimed to like the poetry and glamour of AE's *Deidre* much better than the 'morbidity' of Synge. But for him the morbidity was real, so real that he subsequently thought the eyes of the audience should be shielded from it:

I have come to the conclusion that a more gruesome and horrifying play than *Riders to the Sea* has seldom been staged before. The thoroughly earnest playing of the company made the terribly depressing 'wake' episode so realistic and weirdly doleful that some of the audience could not stand the painful horror of the scene and had to leave the hall during its progress. There are some things too horrible for public representation on stage, and I am strongly of the opinion the final incidents in this direful picture of peasant life . . . are cases in point. The superbly realistic acting made it even more so; and the 'atmosphere' of wind and waves was felt, and the desolation of the lives of the toilers of the sea on the remote parts of these windswept islands made to become very living pictures before us, while the rapidly accumulated calamities to the household . . . become part and parcel of our own misfortune, so natural did all that was taking place on the stage appear to us.[9]

Holloway retained a conventional notion of the tragic as an idealist form, regarding the intense realism of the play as too painful to be tragic. But it is quite clear that the play marks a step forward in the history of modern drama by combining social realism and the tragic vision. The astonishing thing is the direct appeal that the tragic sensibility had for its Dublin audience. Though both characters and audience are Irish, the play depicts a completely remote world governed by natural disaster. The lives of its primitive fishermen are unspoilt yet murderous. The struggle is not that of man against man but man against nature, and nature has not yet been pacified.

Consequently the previous relationship in modern drama between tragic alienation and tragic strife becomes somewhat altered. The alienation is that of an isolated community and its strife with nature, not with its more prosperous and civilised countrymen who never appear in the play. The human dimension of that strife is the expression of loss for nature's victims. In the family where all the menfolk have been taken by drowning, it is simple yet tragic lament. Synge's drama shares with *The Cherry Orchard* an enduring expression of lament which is collectively felt. But in contrast to the Russian tragedy which displays the glitter of upper-class sophistication amidst its joy and melancholy, it is a play of the poor and the humble who exist on the margin of European civilisation. Despite the ritual homage to a Catholic God in the utterances of the family, the play is predominantly pagan in sensibility. No Christian God is expected to have any impact upon the source of external misfortune. The latter is simply there, given as the inexorable fate of nature.

This stoic response to nature, and the sustained image of death and mourning, do suggest the possibility of the Yeatsian tragic formula being applied to contemporary life. But Yeats' idea of tragic ecstacy, where situation gives way to mood, and character to passion, is not really appropriate. The play is socially observed and its figural dimensions retained. The wives and daughters of the western fishermen are substantial figures in their own right, not ciphers of a universal sensibility. This is true above all, of the response to bereavement at the end of the play. The choric expression of lament was based very accurately on the ritual of keening which Synge had observed on his visits to the Aran Isles. The tragic lament is therefore constructed out of the rare cultural practices of the fishing communities of that time. The *caoin* of the Aran Islands, sung as women accompany a coffin to the place of burial, becomes the choral accompaniment to Maurya's climactic speech, a musical embellishment of the spoken word:

> Maurya (*raising her head and speaking as if she did not see the people around her*). They're all gone now, and there isn't anything more the sea can do to me . . . I'll have no call now to up crying and praying when the wind breaks from the south, and you hear the surf is in the east, and surf is in the west, making a great stir with the two noises, and they hitting one upon the other. I'll have no call now to be going down and getting Holy Water in the dark nights after Samhain, and I won't care what way the sea is when the other women will be keening.[10]

The fascination of western life and tradition for the Abbey triumvirate lay partly in their own religious background. Protestant origin
was part of the basis for seeking out an elective affinity with a primitive
way of life not fully absorbed by Catholic custom and culture. It was
not the Protestant connection which mattered here, for southern
middle-class Protestants of the time generally held to philistine and
materialistic values alien to artistic endeavour. It was the freedom,
once these personal ties were broken, from the moral imperatives of the
dominant religious culture. The importance of this break with
Catholicism can be seen negatively, in the adverse reaction of middle-
class audiences at the Abbey to most of Synge's peasant plays. Even
Riders to the Sea, the best received of them, was too 'real' for Holloway.
The breakthrough of the Protestant dramatists was equivalent in
stature to the transformation of modern fiction wrought by a solitary
Irish Catholic novelist. Whereas James Joyce achieved his momentous
feat through the austere discipline of 'silence, cunning and exile',
Synge's work was written under conditions of internal exile. As Joyce
left for Paris, so Synge returned from there on Yeats's advice to find the
themes for his drama in the Aran Isles. Protestant origin became
virtually aligned with the primitive west of Ireland and historically
with heroic pre-Catholic myth.

Much of the success of *Riders to the Sea* is based on the link between its
theme and its brevity. The note of tragic lament is sustained intensely
over a very short period of time. It was complemented, too, by the
dramatic space of the set. In the Abbey productions of 1907, the stage
setting mirrored the exact dimensions of a typical western fisherman's
cottage. Small, enclosed and claustrophobic with its low sloping
ceiling, it formed an appropriate contrast to the surrounding wilderness of sea, and an appropriate focus for the agony of waiting and the
final grief. But the theme had its own kind of historical limitation. The
west of Ireland was changing and the Hiberno-English dialect which
Synge had used so effectively here, was gradually beginning to decline
in usage. Yet, at the same time, as his letters to Mackenna show, Synge
wished to remain a playwright of contemporary life and not to attach
himself to the 'cuchulainoid National Theatre' that Yeats wished to
promote. His problem then became to extend the elliptical image of
the short tragic work into a more sustained vision of contemporary life.
This he tried to do by turning to comedy. Most of his subsequent
dramatic career was taken up with the writing of comic works and he
did not return to tragedy until the end of his life. When he did return,
during a period of illness which finally resulted in his death, he

returned to the tragic myth he had earlier disparaged in private correspondence. It was somewhat ironic that his masterpiece was the unfinished version he wrote of *Deidre of the Sorrows*.

Meanwhile during the middle period of comedy, it soon became clear that his gift for comic writing was at its best when he abandoned the cottage interior for the open roadside, as in *The Well of the Saints*. The play's theme, a blind beggar and his wife fighting the miracle which has restored their sight because it reveals their ugliness, is a masterpiece of comic absurdity. But the better-known works, *The Playboy of the Western World* and *The Shadow of the Glen*, are less successful. The limitation is partly stylistic. In both plays, Synge retains the interior setting and relies more for dramatic effect on the rhetoric and hyperbole of dialogue. Thematically, there is both an advance and a constraint. Synge, in presenting the coarse social underbelly of rural life, the tramps, squatters, and tinkers about whom his middle-class audiences conveniently wished to forget, effectively sabotaged the romantic idealisation of the Irish peasant. But his themes are drawn from peasant myth rather than peasant life. This was not gratuitous. In Aran, Synge had noted the contrast between the frugal existence of the islanders and the imaginative fancy of their tales. The comic absurdity thus comes from making his peasants live out the fantasy that is equivalent to their tales, and the laughter comes from the irreconcilable tension between life and myth.

In *The Playboy*, the tension between life and myth becomes a constraint upon the finished work because Synge attempts to create in the persona of Christy Mahon a thoroughly mythologised heroism. The tension then loses all equilibrium. After the Playboy riots and the avalanche of criticism which deluged the work, Yeats defended his fellow dramatist from the claim of wilful misrepresentation of the Irish peasant by suggesting that the exaggeration came from 'an imaginative delight in energetic characters and extreme types'. But that was an understatement. Synge wanted to resurrect the heroic myths buried in the peasant psyche of the western world, and transmitted orally from generation to generation. But he wanted to do so by displaying that heroism as a phantasmagoric quality of the peasant life itself. Christy Mahon's proud claim to have killed his father is the crystallisation of that heroic conceit, a mythical transgression of the moral code which makes him a hero at the local inn. The resulting action is a comic phantasmagoria closer to Ben Jonson or Molière than to the contemporaneous social comedies of Wilde or Shaw. Yet the naturalistic setting of the play and the Abbey's naturalistic acting were not capable of conveying these qualities. The January performances of 1907 were, ironically, judged in terms of a stereotyped social realism by a hostile audience usually only too happy to forget about any kind of realism. There was, for example, the quackery of George Sigurson who responded to the play by giving 'scientific' lectures to prove the western peasant to be 'chaste, valiant and frugal'.[12] The Catholic middle classes, having greeted previous Abbey productions with a hypocritical moral idealism, now clamoured for an artistically vulgar naturalism.

Beneath the widespread moral indignation, there was, however, a genuine disquiet. The rhetoric of Christy's boasting and the reappearance of his father from the dead raised up the dreaded spectre of the stage Irishman. The speech which Synge insisted 'should be as fully flavoured as a nut or an apple', could be seen as nothing more than Irish wind, its exaggerations permanently disproportionate to the actual achievements of the hero. Instead of acclaiming action, it becomes a substitute for it, and the ability to act heroically is then called into question. What is intended as a comic attribute of the hero sometimes becomes purely perjorative, an expression of contempt.

While Synge's comedies were an often unacknowledged departure from dramatic realism, the historical drama of the Irish Renaissance never approximated to realism at all. Apart from Lorca, it was the most significant point at which tragedy and realism have diverged in modern drama. With Lorca the question is one of dissolution of an ordered reality in the life of contemporary Spain, but for the Irish dramatic movement, it was a question, largely, of the priority of myth over history. The oral myths of a tribal past, handed down over centuries in a colonised country, defied the Lukácsian formula for the substitution of myth by empirical history. The successful resort to myth divides the Irish historical drama quite clearly from its German counterpart of a similar period. But the artistic success can only be understood as part of the more general awakening of national identity, and the artistic function is in many respects similar to Shakespeare's history plays. But the patriotic gloss of Shakespeare is significantly lacking. The best works of the genre, *On Baile's Strand*, *Dervorgilla* and Synge's *Deidre* emphasise the tragic strife of division and betrayal. By going back to a tribal Ireland before the unwelcome advent of the English, we see a country ravaged by the deeds of its own warriors, and subject to the turmoil of perpetual misrule. As tragic myth this was essentially poetic drama with noble heroes, but its link to modern social tragedy lies in two factors—the demotic peasant basis of the dramatic language and the prophetic intuition of future division within Ireland. It is modern in both these senses, even though its figural conceptions are reminiscent of the pre-bourgeois mode of noble tragedy.

Interestingly enough, the two most popular works performed at the Abbey, in a genre that was not always well received, were the two works which most significantly cut across the grain of Irish patriotism—*On Baile's Strand* and *Dervorgilla*. In the former work, Yeats, instead of making Cuchulain an exemplary model of Irish heroism, focused the play on the hero's tragic and unwitting murder of his son. In the latter work, Lady Gregory, choosing as heroine the woman traditionally accused of bringing the English into Ireland, tried to enlist sympathy foe Dervogilla's grief and repentance. She put the conflicting allegiances of her heroine into tragic perspective, placing her passion for Diarmuid above duty to husband and country:

> Dervogilla. O'Rourke was a good man and a brave man, and a kinder man than Diarmuid, but it was with Diarmuid my heart was. It was to him I was promised ever before I saw O'Rourke, and I loved him better than my own lord, and he me also and this was long! I loved him, I loved him! . . . Why must they be throwing and ever throwing sharp reproaches upon his name? Had a man loved by a king's daughter nothing in him to love? A man great of body, hardy in fight, hoarse with shouts of battle. He had liefer be dreaded than loved! It was he cast down the great, it was the dumb poor he served! Every proud man against him and he against every proud man. Oh, Diarmuid, I did not dread you. It was myself led you astray! Let the curse and vengeance fall upon me and me only, for the great wrong and treachery done by both of us to Ireland![13]

The sustained image here is, like *Riders to the Sea*, one of tragic lament. But it is less overpowering, more subdued. By writing in prose without sacrificing her poetic ear for diction, Lady Gregory made her drama more accessible to a modern audience. But her artistic ambition was consequently less. It was left to Yeats and Synge to develop a more powerful poetic speech for historical tragedy.

On Baile's Strand justified the resurrection of poetic speech by a highly striking and original device. It contains a commentary on the life of the noble Cuchulain by a fool and a blind man who enact the scenario of their own lives at the same time. Though the prior example of the Shakespearean fool is indispensable, Yeats goes beyond the traditional separation of styles. The story of the Blind Man and the Fool has its own poignancy, running on separate but parallel lines to that of Cuchulain and Conchubar and based also on the theme of betrayal. The ignorant peasant is the shadow of the mythical king, but even in the stealing of the chickens, has his own destiny. Like Martin and Mary Doul, the Fool and his blind companion are the forerunners of Vladimir and Estragon, Hamm and Clov, and Tom Stoppard's Rosencrantz and Guildenstern. The two-dimensional plot allows Yeats to constantly juxtapose the idealism and sacrifice of war with the materialism of everyday life and the struggle for survival. At the end the two forces are thrust adjacent to each other as Cuchulain learns the identity of the young man he has slain:

Blind Man. None knew whose son he was.
Cuchulain. None knew! Did you know, old listener at doors?
Blind Man. No, no; I knew nothing.
Fool. He has said a while ago that he heard Aoife boast that she'd
    never but the one lover, and he the only man that had overcome
    her in battle. (*Pause.*)
Blind Man. Somebody is trembling, Fool! The bench is shaking.
    Why are you trembling? Is Cuchulain going to hurt us?
    It was not I who told you, Cuchulain.
Fool. It is Cuchulain who is trembling. It is Cuchulain who is
    shaking the bench.
Blind Man. It is his own son he has slain.
Cuchulain. 'Twas they that did it, the pale windy people.
    Where? Where? Where? My sword against the thunder!
    But, no, for they have always been my friends;
    And though they love to blow a smoking coal
    Till it's all flame, the wars they blow aflame
    Are full of glory, and heart uplifting pride
    And are not like this. The wars they love awaken
    Old fingers and the sleepy string of harps.
    Who did it then? Are you afraid? Speak out! . . .
    . . . What is this house? (*Pause.*) Now I remember all.
    (*Comes before Conchubar's chair, and strokes it with his sword as if
    Conchubar was sitting upon it.*)
    Twas you who did it—you who sat up there
    With your rod of kingship, like a magpie,
    A maggot that is eating up the earth!
    Yes, but a magpie, for he's flown away.[14]

Conchubar's betrayal of Cuchulain is mirrored ironically in the treachery of the Blind Man who eats the chicken while the Fool is away. But ultimately the parallel ceases. Cuchulain responds to betrayal by an act of noble madness, while the Fool forgets about it and collaborates with his betrayer. The enraged Cuchulain rushes forth to fight the waves, seeing Conchubar's crown on every crest. But the Blind Man and the Fool take advantage of his tragic madness by stealing chickens from all ovens of all those who have gone down to the strand to witness it. Yeats extends the separation of the base and the noble into the realm of motive. Cuchulain insanely pursues the ideal and loses his sense of material reality. The Blind Man and the Fool exploit his noble madness for reasons of material gain. Each lacks what the other possesses and is trapped by that deficiency into a fate from which they cannot escape. The precarious balance in the work is totally modern, despite the similarities with the Shakespearean fool. The tragic element in the play depends on the mediation of the two peasant figures who lack the capacity for tragedy in their own lives. Yet their own lives are intrinsically important in the play and cannot be reduced to choric function or court dependency. Noble tragedy can only be identified and recognised in contrast to the non-tragic materiality of the poor, struggling with a mixture of cunning and stupidity for everyday survival.

When Yeats came to write the sequel to *On Baile's Strand* in 1939, called *The Death of Cuchulain*, the residual traces of nobility in Irish life seemed to him to have gone for ever. He had witnessed the national revolution and his immediate response to that transformation came in poetry rather than drama, producing *Easter 1916*, *The Second Coming*, and most important of all *Meditations during a Time of Civil War*. It was only when all had 'changed utterly' that he returned to the Irish historical drama, and only at the end of his life that he discovered the creative sequel to the early work. In *The Death of Cuchulain*, the main theme is not the death of the hero but the death of tragic nobility itself. Cuchulain does not die heroically in battle but, wounded and helpless, has his head cut off by the Blind Man for the price of twelve pennies. Humble base materiality finally murders the noble ideal. But in writing the epitaph of the noble ideal, Yeats explicitly made the link between the 'murder' of the ideal and the fateful events which transformed Ireland into a modern nation-state. In the harlot's song to the beggar man, a statue of Cuchulain stands at the post-office to commemorate Ireland's most recent heroes, thus celebrating modern martyrdom by noble ancestry.

I meet them face to face
Conall, Cuchulain, Usna's boys,
All that most ancient race;
Maeve had three in an hour, they say.
I adore those clever eyes,
Those muscular bodies, but can get
No grip upon their thighs.
I meet those long pale faces,
Hear their great horses, then
Recall what centuries have passed
Since they were living men.
That there are some still living
That do my limbs unclothe,
But that the flesh my flesh has gripped
I both adore and loathe.

(Pipe and drum music)

Are those things that men adore and loathe
Their sole reality?
What stood in the Post Office with Pearce and Connelly?
What comes out of the mountain
Where men first shed their blood?
Who thought Cuchulain till it seemed
He stood where they had stood?[15]

The contemporary heroes, Pearce and Connelly, replace the
mythical ones, the heroes of whom the harlot sings that she 'can get/No
grip upon their thighs'. Yeat's epitaph for these heroes was a fitting
one, and came from his increasing feeling that the monuments to a
noble way of life were fast disappearing from modern Ireland. The
noble became increasingly nothing more than a memory. But though
consigned to memory, that memory came to haunt Yeats in his later
life. After Lady Gregory's house at Coole had been pulled down, he
came to have obsessive dreams of ruined noble houses. The living
presence of the aristocracy, now in decline, no longer interested Yeats.
What haunted him was its ruin and its trace. The haunting comes
clearly in *Purgatory*, which Yeats wrote shortly before his death. Setting
aside his weird beliefs in heredity and genetic compulsion, the
haunting theme of the play stresses a major sensibility—the agony of a
past that cannot be altered.

In the play an Old Man, a pedlar, comes upon the ruin of a noble
house with his son. He tells the son his mother once lived there, a noble

lady married to his father, a stable groom who burned the building down in a drunken rage. His mother had died giving birth to him and he later had killed his father to try and destroy the social impurity of his lineage only to find that he in turn fathered a bastard, the son accompanying him, who was 'got/Upon a tinker's daughter in a ditch'. The vicious circle of social impurity, of misbegotten heirs is therefore continued and the bastard of the tinker's daughter is a direct descendent of the noble lady's family. That night is the anniversary of his mother's wedding night and the house is haunted by the ghosts of the past reliving the event which the old man imagines to be the dream of his dead mother's soul in purgatory. It is, in effect, a hallucination in his own mind which he eventually forces his disbelieving son into sharing. The imagined hoofbeats of the drunken stable groom's horse, bearing him to the house in which the pedlar is to be conceived, continue to torment him. He hopes to exorcise the dream, and the social impurity of his lineage, by killing his son—'my father and son on the same jackknife'. But the hoofbeats continue to haunt him after his son has died from the wound. The murder is in vain. Neither the memory of the past, nor the miscegenation destroying the·purity of the noble lineage can be exorcised. Two murders have been committed for nothing and the agony remains. The noble past cannot be forgotten but neither can its betrayal.

The brief, almost transient sense of tragic alienation comes from the arrival of the pedlar at the ruin of his noble place of birth. The landmark is strange yet familiar, its meaning known yet uncertain. And the moment of tragic strife in which he murders his son arises from the desire to resolve the uncertainty by obliterating the past and killing off his own illegitimate line. The noble house his father has 'killed' is seen then from the outside both spatially and thematically, a relic of the past on which he projects his nightmares. In placing the past in the context of Irish myth, and myth in the context of historical tragedy, Yeats succeeds in this short work in achieving something which could never be achieved by writing allegories of the Easter Uprising or the civil war. This brief yet exact response acknowledges the history of modern Ireland yet has its own dramatic world. It succeeds because it is an instant in the history of Irish tragedy just as the passing of the noble after independence was little more than an instant in the history of the Irish people.

One of Yeats' less successful historical tragedies has been his version of the Deidre myth. Synge and Lady Gregory responded to its inadequacy in different ways, Synge rewriting it in the dialect of

Hiberno-English and Lady Gregory creating in the figure of Grania her own tragic heroine, because she felt Deidre to be excessively passive. Her deliberate choice was made because 'sad, lovely Deidre . . . overtaken by sorrow made no good battle to the last', whereas Grania, 'had more power of will, and for good or evil twice took the shaping of her life into her own hands'.[16] Lady Gregory is more interested in the psychology of her heroine than in the myth itself and this interest aligns her work with the modern drama of women in Ibsen and Chekhov. At the same time she consciously chose to write her full-length tragedies in the historical genre, not the contemporary one of *Gaol Gate*. The choice was bold and ambitious and the breadth of that ambition has often been ignored. But the limitations imposed by that choice are also apparent. Grania, as mistress of her own destiny, is at first sight in the modern tradition of Emma Bovary or Hedda Gabler. For she too finds fault with both husband and admirers. But in fact the playwright has returned this modern innovation to the context of medieval romance, and by doing so, unwittingly sabotages the mythic content of the legend she has chosen.

The bold aspect of the play is the way in which Grania outlives the passion of her elopement with Diarmuid, and challenges the motives of husband and lover in desiring her. Here is the condemnation of Diarmuid, her lover:

> Here now is the truth for you. All the years we were with ourselves only you kept apart from me as if I was a shadow-shape or a hag of the valley. And it was not until you saw another man craving my love that a like love was born in yourself. And I will go no more wearing out my time in lonely places, where the martens and hares and badgers run from my path, but it is to the thronged places I will go, where it is not through the eyes of wild startled beasts you will be looking at me, but through the eyes of kings' sons that will be saying: 'It is no wonder Diarmuid to have gone through his crosses for such a wife!'

And here is the subsequent condemnation of Finn, her husband, after he has sought to snatch her back from Diarmuid:

> It is women are said to change and they do not, but it is men that change and turn as often as the wheel of the moon. You filled all Ireland with your outcry wanting me, and now, when I come into your hand, your love is rusted and worn out. It is a pity that I had

two men and three men, killing one another for me an hour ago, to be left as I am and no one having any use for me at all.[17]

She accuses both men of jealousy based upon a desire for sole possession, and her challenge is a threat to that aspect of male domination conventionally part of the fabric of medieval myth. But Grania's consequent disillusion with both men leads to weary resignation and once the myth is tampered with by the attribution of a very modern psychology, the tragic sense diminishes. The implicit criticism of the male-dominated society of Lady Gregory's own time, of the loveless marriage and the widespread neglect of woman demand a contemporary scenario and lose their force by being lost in historical myth. It is as if Lady Gregory had stopped at the bridge which Ibsen had already crossed, and though the intention was radical, the effect is partly retrogressive. In the Irish context, Grania has rejected the keening role of the woman for heroic self-assertion, but weariness eventually turns that self-assertion to resignation.

The failure of such an accomplished piece of work throws into perspective the achievement of Synge in his last unfinished tragedy *Deidre of the Sorrows*. It is the closest work in the Irish theatre to the medieval myth of passion. The inner conflict within Deidre is between passion and love of country. Her resolve to return to Ireland indicates less a resignation to fate than the active willing of it. Deidre's will though finally self-destructive, is stronger than that of Naisi who hesitates to return, fearing Conchubar's treachery. But Deidre faces the tragic dilemma with a greater recognition. The passion of their affair necessitated exile, yet, as she forsees, their homecoming will result in death. The choice is not simply that of passion and exile as against homecoming and death. It is rather that passion, 'the short space' of their life, can thrive only as a temporal form of transgression. It does not grow old. It is shorter and more mortal than life itself:

> Naisi (*his voice broken with distraction*). If a near death is coming what will be my trouble losing the earth and the stars over it, and you, Deidre, are their flame and bright crown? Come away to the safety of the woods.
>
> Deidre (*shaking her head slowly*). There are as many ways to wither love as there are stars in the night of Samhain; but there is no way to keep life, or love it, a short space only . . . It's for that there's nothing lonesome like a love is watching out the time most lovers do be sleeping . . . it's for that we're setting out for Emain Macha when the tide turns on the sand.

Naisi (*giving in*). You're right maybe. It should be a poor thing to see great lovers and they sleepy and old.

Deidre (*with a more tender intensity*). We're seven years without roughness or growing weary; seven years so sweet and shining, the gods would be hard set to give us seven days the like of them. It's for that we're going to Emain, where there'll be a rest for ever, of a place for forgetting, in great crowds, and they making a stir.

Naisi (*very softly*). We'll go surely, in place of keeping a watch on a love had no match and it wasting away.[18]

The link between patriotism and betrayal is similar to *On Baile's Strand*. The return to Ireland is followed by the treachery of Conchubar and this element of betrayal is common to all three great historical tragedies, to *Dervorgilla, On Baile's Strand* and to *Deidre*. It enables Synge to successfully transfer the language and the sensibility of *Riders to the Sea* into Irish history. It has been suggested that the Hiberno-English dialect is inappropriate for noble grandeur.[19] But given the historical circumstances of that speech, its growing disappearance from the life of Western Ireland, then the transference is an important and successful one. *Deidre* succeeds at the level of dialogue where *Playboy* fails, because it takes a poetic and preserved dialect back into history as myth. And it retains the tragic sensibility which Synge had created in his first play. This is the element of lament. Here it is not keening at the misfortune of nature but at the horror of human betrayal, particularly the betrayal of passion. The latter achievement goes beyond Yeats and makes Synge's *Deidre* possibly the greatest love story of the twentieth century in the English language, rendering Naisi and Deidre figures equivalent in stature to Tristan and Iseult. At the beginning of the twentieth century, it could not have emerged in any other country except Ireland, in a peripheral colonial country with its own language, where there still remained a residual immunity to the embourgeoisement of passion which had taken place in the romantic·fiction of eighteenth and nineteenth-century Europe.

The transformation of the fate of Deidre and Naisi into contemporary terms comes later with O'Casey's story of Jack and Nora Clitheroe in *The Plough and the Stars*. Without the precedent of Synge, it is unlikely that O'Casey could have created them. Moreover he was unable to create the same intense passion of noble lovers in his own working-class couple. But that was clearly an impossible task. The keening of Deidre after Naisi's treacherous murder is one of the most moving passages of Irish drama. Synge had finally managed to create tragic nobility out of a poetic peasant dialect, and in doing so, linked it back to the great literary sensibility which had earlier sprung up in medieval Western Europe. It was an accomplishment not achieved by the artificial creation of an archaic noble speech but by the use of a vital and living speech among the poor and the primitive. Without the latter the achievement would not have been possible. This then is Deidre's lament:

> Deidre. I have pity surely . . . It's the way pity has me this night, when I think of Naisi, that I could set my teeth into the heart of a king.
> Conchubar. I know well pity's cruel, when it was my pity for my own self destroyed Naisi.
> Deidre (*more wildly*). It was my own words without pity gave Naisi a death will have no match until the ends of life and time. (*Breaking out into a keen.*) But who'll pity Deidre has lost the lips of Naisi from her neck and from her cheek for ever? Who'll pity Deidre has lost the twilight in the woods with Naisi, when beech trees were silver and copper, and ash-trees were fine gold?
> Conchubar (*bewildered*). It's I'll know the way to pity and care you, and I with a share of troubles has me thinking this night it would be a good bargain if it was I was in the grave, and Deidre crying over me, and it was Naisi who was old and desolate. (*Keen heard.*)
> Deidre (*wild with sorrow*). It is I who am desolate; I Deidre, that will not live till I am old.[20]

Synge's play is a major individual achievement. For it consummates an alternative tradition in European literature, in which the conceit of passion is handed down directly from a medieval to a modern society. The major tradition is of course that of the troubadours and the code of chivalry developed in medieval France, transformed into Shakespearean and Racinian tragedy and culminating in the nineteenth-century novel of tragic realism. But the Irish tradition was different because it was sustained orally through the telling of epic myth among primitive peasant communities and only transformed into literature after its European equivalent, the major novel of Stendhal and Flaubert, had already passed into history. It was not merely the accomplishment of transforming the heroic saga of the oral peasant tradition into modern art. While Yeats and Lady Gregory were also part of this accomplishment, it was Synge alone who sustained it at the level of that transformed sensibility we can call passion, and in so doing made the development of modern Irish drama something quite unique in the history of world literature.

Synge's *Riders to the Sea*, the most acclaimed and accepted work of his own lifetime was a spur to many younger writers of the period who, without the Abbey's existence, would not have considered playwriting as a serious career. The most important of these were Padraic Colum, T. C. Murray and George Fitzmaurice. Both Colum and Murray introduced to the Irish stage the more typical and recognisable peasant of central Ireland. But of the two, it was Murray alone who developed a viable tragic drama out of this material. Colum's main attempt at tragedy *Thomas Muskerry* was not a peasant play, and instead suffered from a kind of sentimental and provincial Ibsenism which seriously flawed it. Murray, on the other hand, established a consistency of theme, narrow in nature and execution, which nonetheless captured the pulse of contemporary rural life in Ireland. Unjustifiably neglected since the twenties, he remains the major Catholic playwright in Irish drama. Dramatically speaking, he is a mediating element between Synge and O'Casey, between the primitive life of the Western coast and the tenements of North Dublin, and provides, chronologically and thematically, a crucial connecting link. His first two major works *Maurice Harte* and *Birthright* were written about the time of Synge's death. His last major play *Autumn Fire* was contemporary with *Shadow of a Gunman*.

Because a number of the playwrights with whom he was associated came, like Murray, from County Cork they were referred to as 'The Cork Realists'. But none had the artistic coherence of Murray, nor the instant acclaim for their serious drama.[21] *Maurice Harte* and *Birthright* were probably the two most popular plays on serious themes the Abbey produced. The reasons were clear. Murray's plays dealt with the major concerns of the Catholic peasantry in the Ireland of the period. They were particularly concerned with the major problems of land at that time—inheritance. This is not to say that Murray's plays mirrored the social predicament of the small farmer in Ireland. In many ways he idealised it. His self-sufficient, successful and civilised farmer is the ideal with which a middle-class and lower-middle class audience could easily identify in mythologising the rural life of Ireland. This was all the easier because his Irish audiences in Dublin and Cork, in London and Boston, would themselves have known through personal experiences or the experience of their families, the dilemma of living on the land or leaving it. At a time of mass mobility and migration, both from land to city, and from homeland to England or the United States, the appeal was there. Murray crystallised a social predicament which struck a chord of personal experience. And at the same time he subtly glamourised it.

This can be shown in the stage setting for *Autumn Fire* which confronts his audience with their own ideal of how an Irish farmhouse should be, and offers it as living reality.

> An observant stranger with a feeling for the beauty which lies in homely simplicity looking through the open door of Owen Keegan's farmhouse would be moved to something of admiration. The table is laid for tea and the kitchen is fresh and clean, everything indicating skilful housewifery. The dressers, the chairs and tables have been scoured to an ivory whiteness. The brass candlesticks on the shelf over the fireplace catch the sunlight and flash. A curio-hunter would drop reverently before the collection of lustre jugs and willow pattern plates on the dresser and the pewter dishes on the walls— survivals which express the careful habits of the women folk who have successively managed the farmhouse.[22]

The household is to be seen as tasteful and immaculate even though Owen Keegan's wife is no longer there. A stage setting identical with the prosperous and cared-for farmhouse came to be a trademark of Murray's theatre . Its importance can be seen more clearly when contrasted with the farmhouse of Eugene O'Neill in *Beyond the Horizon*. O'Neill had been strongly influenced by seeing Murray's early work during the Abbey tour of Boston but his evocation of a farmhouse gone to seed in the stage directions for the Third Act is unthinkable in Murray's work:

> The room, seen by the light of a shadeless oil lamp with a smokey chimney which stands on the table, presents an appearance of decay, of dissolution. The curtains at the window are torn and dirty and one of them is missing . . . Blotches of dampness disfigure the wallpaper. Threadbare trails, leading to the kitchen and outer doors, show in the faded carpet. The top of the coverless table is stained with imprints of hot dishes and spilt food.[23]

It was precisely because he had rejected the images of rural squalor offered earlier by Synge, that Murray gained his instant popularity. For this idealisation was linked to a genuine predicament in the small-farmer proprietorship of southern and central Ireland—the question of succession. The ethos of individual ownership is never questioned, but at the same time its personal consequences were deeply felt. And Murray's drama is of the sufferings imposed by such consequences. In *Birthright*, Hugh and Shawe fight to the death over who will inherit the farm, and who emigrate across the Atlantic. In *Maurice Harte*, the son who is encouraged to enter the priesthood to find a career eventually resists the solution his mother attempts to impose on him. And in *Autumn Fire* Owen Keegan drives his son from his house after finding him in mutual embrace with his young step-mother. Murray's tragic vision arises from this widespread destruction in the continuity of generations which individual proprietorship and primogeniture had given rise to. But it is drastically limited by the very source from which it arises.

Against the suffering which Murray graphically portrays there is always a rebellion by the younger generation. But it is a muted rebellion and never fully challenges the twin pillars of Catholic authority in Irish rural life—that of the local clergy and the patriarchal proprietor. Maurice Harte goes steadily mad but his refusal to take up Orders becomes a silent withdrawal into self. There is no rage against Church or theology but only a despairing and fatalistic refusal. The refusal itself is genuine and Murray does not cloud the simplicity of it by trying to overwhelm the drama with theological issues. But Maurice is not granted heroic stature by his author. He becomes a silent and withdrawn object of concern and the anxiety expressed and accepted by a middle-class Catholic audience is that of the mother who has set her heart on a career in the Church for him. In his other play of the period, *Birthright*, there is a different but complementary failure to challenge authority—the authority of the tyrannical father. In it the father lays down the fate of his two sons only to reverse it at the last moment. Yet in the crucial final act where the two brothers fight over the fate he has arbitrarily given them, he is conspicuous by his absence. Having dominated the family household with his oppressiveness, the brothers fight in his absence against one another but not against their father. Only by artificially removing the father from that last scene can Murray permit the tragic denouement to unfold.

In *Autumn Fire*, written in 1923, there is embedded a valedictory lament for the kind of drama which Murray had been writing. One of his great qualities had been to evoke sympathy for all his characters despite and through their frailties. He did it with a simplicity and delicacy in some ways superior to that of Synge and O'Casey, and this is true of the portrait of Owen Keegan, a widowed farmer who attempts to rejuvenate himself through marriage to a woman half his age. Not only is the fire autumnal but also the sensibility. The fading of that fire, the injury after being thrown from his horse, and the attraction of his young wife for her stepson, signify not only the hero's demise but also the demise of the genre which Murray had done so much to sustain. Keegan's loss of power and of pride presents us with a wider symbolic loss. At the same time the poignancy of the play, and its power to evoke sympathy, provides a stark contrast to O'Neill's ugly and brutal *Desire under the Elms* written at the same time and with a similar plot. The loss is deeply felt but the tragedy at the same time contained, for the loss is not irreparable. 'They've broken me', Keegan murmurs at the end, 'son—wife—daughter. . . . (*He pauses, looking intently on the cross.*) I've no one now but the Son of God.' The Catholic consolation is unshakeable and holds steady against the assault of the tragic impulse.

Murray's deterioration as a playwright occurs about the same time as that of O'Casey. There were other talented writers in a similar vein to follow, notably Lennox Robinson and Brinsley Macnamara but they were minor talents and the vitality of the rural drama had evaporated by this time. Moreover, Murray's work after the political stabilisation of the Free State exhibited a greater tendency to compromise with the existing social fabric than his previous work. In *Michaelmas Eve*, written in 1932, he promised much only to achieve little. The character of Moll Garvey as a fiery servant maid who challenges her social position and the bourgeois aspirations of her lover, is finally made to look ridiculous. failing in an attempt to prevent his marriage to the mistress of the household, and failing in her ludicrous attempt to poison him. She is made to swear the truth of her sin and her passion on the cross but cannot do so, and leaves the household 'a figure of tragic defeat'. But her rebellion is abortive and she is not tragic. Her gratuitous crime, of attempted poisoning, vindicates the existing order of things and the marriage of mistress and household servant, the symbolic marriage of different rural classes. In challenging this, the potential heroine is clumsily transformed into a villain and pays the price before a devout Catholic community and its God. The intermarriage of classes here has precisely the opposite meaning to that of Yeats' *Purgatory*. In Yeats' parable about a dying aristocracy, that union is seen as miscegenation and social impurity. In Murray it is a victory for reconciliation and common sense. More than any other play, Murray's work presents thematically the artistic accommodation to the new bourgeois theocratic order of the Irish Republic, and he involuntarily played into the hands of the new cultural philistinism which attempted in the next three decades and more to smother the country's artistic heritage.

8 Sean O'Casey:
The Shadow of a City

Sean O'Casey's trilogy about the Irish Uprising, written between 1922 and 1926, is a landmark in the history of modern drama. It has remained the most sustained work in the medium of the theatre dealing with the process of political upheaval. But it has been more than that. O'Casey was the first major *working-class* dramatist writing of working-class life. While Hauptmann's similarity is to Zola, O'Casey is closer in terms of background and achievement to Jack London or Robert Tressell. But his artistic accomplishment is much greater than either. While *The Weavers* cannot begin to rival *Germinal*, the reverse relationship between drama and the novel obtains here. The novels of London and Tressell cannot rival the Dublin trilogy. O'Casey produced the major political drama set in a modern city, on a par with the work of Büchner and Brecht, while reproducing at the same time, the immediate concern with contemporary life characteristic of Ibsen and Chekhov. The personal background to this accomplishment is remarkable. Born into a Protestant lower-middle class family, O'Casey experienced the gradual proletarianisation of the family after the early death of his father. He came to live in the riverside East Wall district of Dublin, a working-class industrial suburb where, however, his living standards were far higher than many thousands of Dublin slum dwellers. After leaving school at fourteen he abandoned the Unionist prejudices of his Protestant environment and joined the Irish Republican Brotherhood. Subsequently, while working as a railwayman, he began to develop the working-class sympathies and socialist aspirations instrumental in his involvement with the Irish Citizen Army. His drama is the outcome of a complex fusion between this double transformation, first Republican, later socialist, and the literary renaissance to which he was fortunate enough to become heir. O'Casey drew much of his strength from immediate predecessors and contemporaries, particularly from Shaw, Synge and Murray. But he surpassed them in writing the two outstanding contemporary plays of the Irish renaissance, *Shadow of a Gunman* and *The Plough and the Stars*.

His initial success at the Abbey was due in no small way to the cultural attitudes which enabled artistic communication to cut across class boundaries, a situation largely unthinkable in English theatre at the same time. His appeal to Yeats and Lady Gregory, as a working-class writer of promise, was closely aligned with their previous thinking about a People's theatre performing work by actors and producers who were devoid of social privilege. O'Casey was aided in addition by the personal concern of Lady Gregory. We can find in her journals, as opposed to O'Casey's misleading and indulgent autobiography, a graphic and moving account of the mutual artistic sympathy which developed between the aristocratic gentlewoman and the former stone-breaker from North Dublin.[1] The artistic and cultural tendencies of the Abbey had of course been anti-bourgeois from its inception. But O'Casey brought with him a much more substantial basis for that opposition than had previously been available, for it was based on his own experience of reversed social fortune and later, from 1913 onwards, his witnessing at first hand of the terrible squalors of Dublin slum life.

In the context of O'Casey's political commitment, his membership of the Irish Citizen Army is of complex significance, Through his trade union experience, he switched from a strongly nationalistic position to a strongly proletarian one in which, however, he hoped for a spontaneous fusion of working-class and Republican aspirations. While James Connolly, with his greater political experience and depth of perspective, thought that separate socialist and Republican movements could be linked through tactical alliance, O'Casey felt that an 'either/or' situation prevailed. The ICA had to supersede the larger Irish Volunteers or else go under. The two-fold wrench of his own life, from Unionism to Republicanism and thence to socialism, produced a utopian – almost messianic – impatience with the practical difficulties facing the ICA in 1913 and 1914. For him its success depended upon whether it could effectively become *the* mass army of Irish workers almost immediately. From the first O'Casey's vision had been glowing and euphoric. 'Like the loud rolling of a multitude of drums, the cheers broke out again', he wrote, describing the inaugural meeting.

> This was what was long wanted—a Citizen Army! What could not Labour accomplish by an army trained and disciplined by officers who held the affection and confidence of workers! Now they would

get some of their own back; and vivid visions of 'Red-coats and Black-coats flying before them' floated before the imaginative eyes of the Dublin workers filled with and almost intoxicated by the wine of enthusiasm.[2]

The intoxication was *in* O'Casey, optimistically imputing his own feelings to the assembled audience. The style of writing, its inflated rhetoric, shows clearly the danger of exaggeration. The momentum behind it was a utopian one in which O'Casey envisaged an irresistible effloresence of working-class enthusiasm for the cause. Yet disillusionment was there soon after the start, strangely co-existing for a time with the euphoria. The failure of the Dublin strike of 1913–14 had halted the momentum towards recruitment among workers. In a country which, outside Dublin and Belfast, was predominantly rural, the appeal of nation remained greater than that of class. And even in Dublin itself O'Casey's organisation was overshadowed by the formation of the National Volunteers. Explaining the defection of thousands of workers from the Army to the Volunteers, he wrote:

Many, no doubt, preferred Caithlin ni Houlihan in a respectable dress than a Caithlin in the garb of a working woman. Many also realised that the governing body of the Volunteers was eminently influential, and that the ban which was over the Citizen Army, like a dark cloud, because of its arterial connection with the Transport Union was not to be chosen as a shelter, when they could radiantly enjoy the National halo that glittered around the whole structure of the National Volunteers.[3]

From then on O'Casey's utopia fervour was undermined by growing disenchantment. Once his formal ties with Irish Socialism lapsed, the conflict between hope and disenchantment formed the basis of his artistic sensibility. It added a further dimension to the dialectic of art and rebellion in Ireland. His aversion to literary patriotism fitted into the Abbey tradition but had been developed from a radically different perspective. O'Casey could not view the Irish people as a unified and indivisible entity as long as there remained a class division between labour and capital, a division he saw at its most antagonistic in industrial Dublin. Through him the focus of Irish drama thus shifted from the periphery of western Ireland to its metropolitan centre at a time when the country was poised to shed its colonial heritage. But the dialect of country and city actually confounded O'Casey's premature hopes for the establishment of socialism. In a largely rural society, opposition to the British was based on feelings of nationality and religion rather than those of class. Out of O'Casey's premature hope and the knowledge that even during the period of national rebellion such hope could never find fulfilment came the inner contradiction indispensable to the tragic vision.

It was a tragic vision from which, like Chekhov, comedy could never be absent. The vision itself was one which O'Casey often consciously tried to repudiate. On witnessing the Abbey performance of *Maurice Harte* for example, he had confided to Holloway that Murray's play 'took too much out of him'. He expressed a preference for Shaw instead because 'in the very kernel of tragedy he can introduce something to laugh its sting away'.[4] But in his attempt to consciously emulate Shaw, O'Casey usually failed to laugh the sting away. Comedy is there in abundance but it is not the cerebral and rational wit of Shaw. It is closer to Synge's comic hyperbole, transformed from the dialogue of Hiberno-English into the slang of the Dublin tenement dweller, but its function was to humanise tragedy rather than exorcise it.

One device which O'Casey also took from Synge was the rhetorical illusion of personal success. In *Playboy* Christy Mahon boasts of a parricide which it turns out, he has failed to commit. He becomes a hero by living off the false reputation the deed has gained him. In *Juno and the Paycock*, Boyle thrives on the false reputation of having acquired a small fortune, and in *Shadow of a Gunman*, Donal Davoren thrives on the false reputation of being a 'gunman on the run'. While the latter device is a successful transformation of Synge's theme into a contemporary political context, the figure of Boyle is much more traditional and restricted. The theme of the inheritance is one O'Casey acquired from the well-made play and sits uneasily with the political context of the Civil War between Free Staters and Die-Hards. By using traditional devices to superimpose a comic situation on a tragic one, O'Casey ends up by cleaving the play in two.

It is ironic then that both the comic *and* the tragic modes in the play are inspired by Synge. The lament for the dead son of Mrs Tancred, repeated by the later lament of Juno Boyle for her own son, is strongly reminiscent of the keening at the end of *Riders to the Sea*. It places the same aura of tragic lament into a different social context. And the transformation is indeed remarkable. While Synge's play was about the strife of man and nature, O'Casey's was about the strife of man and man, specifically Irishman and Irishman. At both funerals the same lament is heard, repeated almost word for word. But the second victim,

Johnny Boyle has been shot as the betrayer of the first, commandant Tancred of the Die-Hards. The sexual division follows exactly the pattern of Synge and Lady Gregory's short play *The Gaol Gate*. The men are the victims of tragic strife, the women the poetic yet passive voices of tragic lament, mourning the suffering of their departed men. Juno Boyle echoes the earlier lament of Tancred's mother and earlier still, in Synge's play, that of Maurya for her husband and six sons taken by the sea:

> Maybe I didn't feel sorry enough for Mrs. Tancred when her poor son was found as Johnny's been found now—because he was a Diehard! Ah, why didn't I remember that then he wasn't a Diehard or a Stater, but only a poor dead son! It's well I remember all she said—an' it's my turn to say it now: what was the pain I suffered, Johnny, bringing you into the world to carry you to your cradle, to the pains I'll suffer carryin' you out o' the world to bring you to your grave! Mother o' God, Mother o' God, have pity on us all! Blessed Virgin, where were you when me darlin' son was riddled with bullets, when me darlin' son was riddled with bullets? Sacred Heart o' Jesus, take away our hearts o' stone, and give us hearts o' flesh! Take away this murderin' hate, an' give us Thine own eternal love![5]

This is the climatic moment of the play, and the ensuing scene, where Boyle and Joxer enter drunk and incapable, thick-skinned and oblivious, ends up as bathos. The fate of his children and the grief of their mother is something which Boyle's own comic misfortune cannot rival. Instead the spectre afflicting Christy Mahon rears its ugly head. At times Paycock and Joxer Daly appear as updated versions of the stage Irishman. They are laughable and lack menace, but they are also laughable *because* they lack menace. And this lack of menace, the absence of brutality and malice, the incapacity to be cruel, means that the trials of Juno with regard to her skiving husband are nothing compared with the tribulations of her hunted crippled son. The fate of Johnny Boyle, purely through force of circumstances, clearly outdoes that of his father, despite the contrived plot of the botched will. And the political sub-plot unwittingly dominates the main action instead of being its accompaniment.

The comic and tragic elements in the play thus fall apart. The background of the Troubles outweighs the plot relating to the will. And the treatment of the daughter's failed love-affair with the conniving theosophist lawyer is a social and artistic disaster. The traditional forms of comic exaggeration which lie at the root of the well-made farce do not translate into tragic terms and the true test of this failure is the character of Juno herself. As the mother of a murdered son, her grief is a tragic affliction but as the wife of an idle drunkard, her anger is that of a comic harridan. One feels that O'Casey's imitation of traditional comic devices hinders the expression of a social truth. He cannot convince the spectator that a trade unionist like Mary should reject a fellow socialist worker in favour of a vapid middle-class lawyer. In many ways O'Casey had merely transposed the eighteenth-century conceit of the aristocratic scoundrel and the virtuous middle-class woman he seduces and abandons, into a class context where it makes no sense at all. And while he may personally have confessed to crying over *Tess* his anaemic Bentham hardly convinces as a bourgeois version of Alec d'Urberville. And the sufferings of a working-class woman in a demoralised tenement household are lost in the second-rate comic scheming of Boyle and his sidekick. Here the sting *is* almost laughed away and the damage is almost, though never quite, irreversible.

Previously, in *Shadow of a Gunman*, O'Casey *had* achieved the integration of the comic into tragic drama, in fact the most outstanding example since Chekov's *The Cherry Orchard*. Here the tautness of the action and the power of his dramatic irony allow him to extract humour out of a set of accidents and misunderstandings which carry with them a tragic power. We immediately see the advantage of this work over that of Murray, especially *Maurice Harte*. O'Casey uses humour to relieve the possibility of a monotonal gloom. But it is a temporary relief which cannot stem the eventual flow of tragic experience. The theme concerns the false identity ascribed to Donal Davoren, an anonymous poet, when he is mistaken for a gunman on the run. The mistake arises out of the zealous measures with which he safeguards his privacy to write romantic poems. The social context of the rebellion and the personal predicament of Davoren are harmonised from the outset, intertwined so that any development in one precipitates a change in the other. In this lies the beautiful and comic confusion which threads its way through the play until it results in real tragedy. The desired privacy of the poet is portrayed as the surrogate for the necessary secrecy of the gunman. The play's title acts as an ironic echo of Trotsky's arrogant claim that in time of revolution the literary word is the mere shadow of the militant deed. Tragedy arises from a conventional stage device of mistaken identity, but the relationship between the confused identities is highly original and dramatically explosive.

Davoren cannot and does not want to shed the aura of heroism conferred on him by the tenement dwellers. But only Minnie Powell knows of his poetry and it is she who weaves a dream out of the confusion of identities. For her, Davoren is both poet *and* gunman. They are fused and romanticised in her vivid imagination while in reality, the desired fusion cannot be sustained:

> Minnie. . . . Poetry is a grand thing, Mr. Davoren. I'd love to be able to write a poem—a lovely poem on Ireland an' the men of '98.
>
> Davoren. Oh, we've had enough of poems, Minnie, about '98, and of Ireland too.
>
> Minnie. Oh, there's a fine thing for a Republican to say! But I know what you mean: it's time to give up the writing an' take to the gun.[6]

Davoren's heroism possesses a double irony. He is passive towards the cause, yet also passive towards his false reputation. The latter passivity effectively conceals the former. Davoren becomes a hero by default, his glory clinched by the chance discovery of the Mills' bombs he did not know had been left in his room. And at the end Minnie dies heroically, converted to the cause by a man who never believed in it, ignorant to the last of the cowardice with which Davoren berates himself.

The centrality of false reputation, as we have seen, follows the format of *The Playboy of the Western World*. But the tautness of contradiction, its compelling realism of enactment, here places it in a different world. The possibility of militant Republicanism is a real possibility, the mistake a genuine one. O'Casey, himself subject to police and military searches at the time because of his previous affiliations, knew that from personal experience. He had discovered a social and a political correlative where Synge had not. Moreover Davoren is in some respects the antithesis of the stage Irishman. His stoic acidity is precisely the sensibility required of the detached poet in the midst of political chaos. But O'Casey creates this distance in order to show that detachment is finally impossible, that everyone, whether they wish it or not, will finally be involved. In this play Irish tragedy is transformed from tragic lament into a fully realised tragic strife—strife, that is to say, in a contemporary and realistic setting. And Davoren's craving for detachment, expressed as a precious aesthetic conceit, heightens the impact of that strife when it finally comes.

The relationship between Minnie Powell and Donal Davoren is not a genuine passion, precisely because it is based on mistaken identity. At best it is a romantic and sentimental attachment. But the inversion of heroism at the end, portraying female bravery and male cowardice, is often overlooked as one of the play's major achievements. But it is the central theme constructed on the basis of a cumulative dramatic irony. Thus when Davoren accepts the identity of a gunman, he immediately begins to play the part:

> Minnie. . . . Do you never be afraid?
> Davoren. Afraid! Afraid of what?
> Minnie. Why the ambushes of course; *I'm* all of a tremble when I hear a shot go off, an' what it must be in the middle of the firin'?
> Davoren (*Delighted at Minnie's obvious admiration; leaning back in the chair, and lighting a cigarette with placid affectation*). I'll admit one does get a bit nervous at first, but a fellow gets used to it after a bit, till, at last, a gunman throws a bomb as carelessly as a schoolboy throws a snowball.[7]

Yet later when Davoren and Shields hear a volley of shots in the lane, they both shrink back in 'violent fear'. When the prospect of a visit from the Tans is imminent that fear changes into sheer terror. At this point the relationship between Adolphus Grigson and his wife throws into relief the special attachment of Minnie and Davoren. Grigson, the arch Orangeman, propogates the lie of the man as brave and the woman as panic-stricken. Having grovelled to the sadistic Tans during the house search, he boasts openly of his own coolness and his wife's fear:

> Excitin' few moments, Mr. Davoren; Mrs. G. lost her head completely—panic-stricken. But that's only natural, all women is very nervous. The only thing to do is show them they can't put the wind up you; show the least sign of fright and they'd walk on you, simply walk on you.[8]

The tragic ending of the play repudiates Grigson's philosphy. It is Davoren who is afraid and Minnie who is totally without fear. Davoren realises that after Minnie's tragic slaughter he no longer deserves to be alive. His final speech not only records his anguish at her death and disgust at his own cowardice, it mimics the conceit of the romantic poet he has aspired to be; the conceit that suffering is a purely personal emotion to be inwardly cherished:

Davoren. Ah me, alas! Pain, pain, pain for ever, for ever! It's terrible to think that little Minnie is dead, but it's still more terrible to think that Davoren and Shields are alive! Oh, Donal Davoren, shame is your portion now till the silver cord is loosened and the golden bow broken. Oh, Davoren, Donal Davoren, poet and poltroon, poltroon and poet.[9]

Like the heroic tragedies of the previous decades, O'Casey's play is a statement on a conflict engulfing the whole of Ireland. But it is specific to time and place. The anomalous figure of Grigson shows us an Ireland disunited, and the British auxiliaries treat Republican and Unionist, Protestant and Catholic alike with cruel contempt. There is not here the sectarian hatred later to flare up in the North, but the triangular nature of the Irish dilemma is shown in detailed terms. In this sense, O'Casey's play is truer to the Belfast of the 1970s than most of the recent drama which has been written about it.

In *Juno and the Paycock* and *Shadow of a Gunman*, the violence of the Irish Rebellion operates at the periphery of the drama, only to appear suddenly and unexpectedly at its centre in the final act. *The Plough and the Stars* differs markedly because the political issue is there, in the foreground, right from the outset. Yet the play cannot be totally separated from the earlier work. Nora Clitheroe has to be seen in the context of Minnie Powell: the uprising of the later play in the context of the wider rebellion and civil war portrayed in the earlier ones. The uprising was the work of a committed few, at first ignored or despised by many. Only later with the death and execution of its leaders did it gain the status of heroic martyrdom. The aura of the 'gunman' did not yet exist. As a result O'Casey's later play was closer to the actual sensibility of 1916 than the response of his 1926 audience whose attitude had been transformed by subsequent events. For many, O'Casey had, in his earlier work, taken 'the sting out of tragedy' by his ability to portray the comic aspects of Dublin working-class life. More than this, he had extracted comedy from the confused working-class response to the reality of rebellion, a confusion which enabled Yeats for one, to laugh his way heartily through *Shadow of a Gunman*. But *The Plough and the Stars* offered no such possibility. It was more throughly uncompromising, and by virtue of this, offended many of the Republicans personally involved in the Uprising. As a result, it brought back to the Abbey riots and a general commotion unparalleled since the *Playboy* incident nearly twenty years previously.

O'Casey had without doubt written the major military version of the Uprising. But he had failed to glorify it in terms acceptable to its supporters. Mrs Skeehy-Sheffington, wife of the well-known martyr of 1916 shot by a British officer while unarmed and defenceless, saw it as a deliberate attempt to debase an event of momentous historical importance. Her objections voiced a wider current of feeling:

> A play that deals with Easter Week, and what led up to it, that finds in Pearse's words . . . a theme merely for the drunken jibe of 'dope', in which every character connected with the Citizen army is a coward, slacker, or worse, that omits no details of squalid slumdom, the looting, the squabbling, the disease and degeneracy, yet that omits any revelation of the glory and inspiration of Easter Week, is a Hamlet shown without the Prince of Denmark.[10]

As in the case of Synge, the detractors' vituperation totally confused moral and patriotic sentiments. But equally it showed a fastidious bourgeois distaste for those elements of working-class life and of the Uprising which the respectable patriotic leadership preferred forgotten. O'Casey's reply, however, was only partly convincing. He claimed to have faithfully rendered 'the fear in the eyes of the fighters', a fear he assumed ten years later to be generally forgotten. While possibly true, this was still a superficial justification for the play, and there were more profound ones which he failed to articulate.

In the first instance he seemed to have insulted the patriotism of Irish women. And the predominance of Irish women among the demonstrators who interrpted the play with stink bombs illustrated the importance of the gender distinction. But the response of Nora Clitheroe to the Rising which many of them detested, can only be understood in the context of the play's concern with social class. O'Casey wanted to portray active working-class participation in the Uprising, and the sensibility stems from the predicament of a minor proletarian involvement. The uprising in this respect is both near and far, familiar and strange, and it is this predicament which explains Nora's eventual madness. The romantic aura of the gunman and the glory of heroic martyrdom did not yet exist. Unlike Minnie Powell, who can find glory in mass rebellion a few years later, Nora sees the onset of the Uprising as just another affliction she has to bear in addition to the oppressive forms of everyday slum life from which she desperately wants to escape. And when her husband dies a hero in battle, she cannot offer that basic recognition which others expect of her, since her whole life is in ruins.

By contrast with all the histories of working-class movements in the twentieth century, especially those which glorify them, parts of O'Casey's drama seem homely and parochial. There is the scene for instance where Clitheroe first finds out about his new appointment as Commandant:

> Clitheroe. I don't understand this. Why does General Connolly call me Commandant?
> Capt. Brennan. Th' Staff appointed you Commandant, and th' General agreed with your selection.
> Clitheroe. When did this happen?
> Capt. Brennan. A fortnight ago.
> Clitheroe. How was it word was never sent to me?
> Capt. Brennan. Word was sent to you . . . I meself brought it.
> Clitheroe. Who did you give it to then?
> Capt. Brennan (*after a pause*). I think I gave it to Mrs. Clitheroe, there.
> Clitheroe. Nora, d'ye hear that?[11]

At first Nora does not answer but then confesses all:

> Nora (*flaming up*). I burned it, I burned it! That's what I did with it! Is General Connolly and th' Citizen Army goin' to be your only care? Is your home goin' to be only a place to rest in? Am I goin' to be only somethin' to provide merrymakin' at night for you? Your vanity'll be the ruin of you and me yet.[12]

There are two things which need to be noticed here. In the first place, O'Casey adopts naturalist forms reminiscent of Ibsen. Whereas the Norwegian introduced social taboos into the middle-class drawing room, O'Casey in like manner, imports revolution into the working-class parlour. He makes the contradiction between public and domestic life explicit, even to the point of dramatic clumsiness. The earlier eulogies to the Irish Citizen Army are gone. Instead it is portrayed as slapdash and unsure of itself. Secondly, the domestic tension between Jack and Nora has its dramatic precedent in Yeats's patriotic piece *Cathleen ni Houlihan*. Like Michael Gillane in Yeats's patriotic drama, Jack Clitheroe is called on to abandon domestic happiness to fight his country's cause. But O'Casey presents us with a more substantial figural conception than Yeats of the domestic ties his hero must temporarily abandon, and equally of the desperation with which Nora clings to him. What is remarkable here is the ability of O'Casey to move back and forwards between the social and political levels of the play with a dramatic effectiveness rivalled only by Büchner and Brecht. Moreover while the Germans used epic forms to achieve this fluidity, O'Casey retained traditional naturalist devices, even in the setting of the public house which evoked so much hostility from his puritanical middle-class audience at the time. The question then remains to be asked why it was that O'Casey was able to achieve a political drama, using naturalist forms, as effective in its own way as Hauptmann's *The Weavers* but also conceived at a level of tragic intensity which the German dramatist was unable to attain?

The answer lies in the unique mode of tragic alienation which O'Casey created in his treatment of working-class politics and life. There is a double alienation here which is both overlapping yet based on incompatible division. There is first the alienation *of* a whole class, an alienation made substantial by the predicament of Jack Clitheroe and made explicit by the demotic comic preaching of 'The Covey'. There is equally alienation *within* that class, an alienation *from* working-class life most deeply felt by Nora who experiences the life of a poor and degraded tenement community as a prison from which she desires to escape. The extent to which Jack wishes to participate in resolving the alienation of his own class conflicts with Nora's wish for domesticity and escape from a demoralised environment. The experience of both forms of alienation is equally valid. But the bonds of love and marriage, which O'Casey at times sentimentalises, cannot hold in check these fissiparous tendencies. The case of Nora actually highlights the inconsistency of O'Casey's outraged critics. They objected both to the lack of patriotism *and* the portrayed squalor of slum life. But Nora is indifferent to any form of patriotism precisely because she is more concerned to escape from the squalor of slum life. It is the primacy of *this* concern which explains, though it does not justify, her failure to acknowledge Jack's heroism.

In the second act, O'Casey produces a direct theatrical confrontation between the apolitical life of the working-class community he knew and the patriotic ideals of the Irish Volunteer Movement. Inside the pub are its working-class clientele: outside the voice and silhouetted figure of Padraic Pearse extolling his listeners to a redemptive blood-sacrifice. While it was clearly O'Casey's intention to show the disparity between Pearce's idealism and the grim reality of Dublin working-class life, the balance between noble exhortation and mundane existence is never lost. There is a compulsion in Pearce's voice which will not dissolve despite the ridicle that can be heaped upon it from inside. The call to action is unshakeable. The Voice will not go away, and finally Clitheroe, Brennan and Langdon, entering the pub at the end of the act, solemnly pledge themselves to its sacrificial demands.

Where O'Casey goes beyond *Shadow of the Gunman* here is in the power and intensity of his tragic heroine. The relationship of Minnie and Donal Davoren is reversed. It is Jack who is brave, Nora frightened. But she is a more substantial heroine than Minnie because she suffers quite centrally the full anguish of political strife rather than romanticising it from the position of an impassioned onlooker. The consequence is madness, taken derivatively perhaps from Shakespeare's Ophelia, but closer in sensibility to her twentieth-century contemporaries, Ella Downey of *All God's Chillun got Wings* and Blanche Dubois of *A Streetcar Named Desire*. The sustained development of madness and despair provide the dramaturgical link between the initial alienation and the tragic climax. In that climax are fused, remarkably, the modalities of lament and strife which generally have been *alternative* outcomes of modern tragic drama. The element of keening present in *Riders to the Sea* and *Juno and the Paycock* is preserved here in a climatic strife where Nora is first the subject then latterly the object of that lament. Initially she laments Jack's decision to take his place in the Uprising. Subsequently the lament by her neighbours is for Nora herself when her senses have deserted her. Finally, in lamenting the loss of her past life with Jack, she becomes the subject once more, but sings Jack's affectionate serenade to herself as if, so deranged, she were trying to appropriate the voice of her dead husband to her lament without acknowledging his death. The interrelationship of madness, lament and strife is complex and brilliant, Shakespearean in its grandeur and intensity. There is no other modern play about working-class life which has the same figural power in the creation of both its male and its female hero.

In retrospect, Nora seems to represent at first sight a perverse resistance to the onward march of history, an anguished denial of the 'terrible beauty' which Yeats considered to have been born in that fateful work. But her desperate struggle for possession of her husband involves an implicit recognition of the power of that fate. Her madness expresses not only her personal loss, but also the depth of sacrifice demanded in the political struggle which she consciously rejects. This complex involuntary response can, in the circumstances, only be that of a respectable working-class woman. Nora is not amoral enough to loot like the parasites who move in to take advantage of the Uprising. Nor can she afford the noble and patriotic sentiments of her middle-class compatriots who can accord recognition to the noble sacrifice of their men. She is stranded between two worlds, and without her husband, drifting helplessly. Her personal flaw is possessiveness. She tries to dictate terms of absolute devotion which prove unacceptable. Jack must in the end reject her ruthlessly and go to his death. The scene where Nora clings to him while Langdon, the Volunteer officer is dying agonisingly in a pool of his own blood is one of the most moving in all of O'Casey's work. What emerges is the way her instinct for survival overcomes her power of pity, upon which her original pleas to Jack were based, and her wish to get back her husband is so intense that she is totally numb to the dying officer's fate.

Because the flaw of possessiveness is so explicit early in the play, it is the final act alone which establishes the tragic stature of Nora. Here the anguished and false response has been transformed into a permanent affliction. Significantly, Nora has turned insane before Jack's death, as if in her deranged mind he has already been taken from her. The actual news of his death in action, conveyed by Brennan, can no longer mean anything to her for madness has pre-empted its significance. Here is Brennan recounting Clitheroe's last moment, followed moments later by Nora's unexpected entry.

> Capt. Brennan. He took it like a man. His last whisper was 'Tell Nora to be brave; that I'm ready to meet my God an' that I'm proud to die for Ireland'. An' when our General heard it he said that 'Commandant Clitheroe's end was a gleam of glory'. Mrs. Clitheroe's grief will be a joy when she realises that she has had a hero for a husband.[13]

But Bessie retorts that 'if you only seen her, you know to the differ'. The sentimental relationship Nora had wished to create for them, rural, idyllic and free from their material world, comes back as the fragment of an insane dream. The dream dominates her walking life. The real Jack who has just died, has been replaced prior to his death by the imaginary Jack who never existed:

> Nora (*in a quiet and monotonous tone*). No . . . Not there, Jack . . . I feel comfortable only in our own familiar place beneath th' bramble tree . . . We must be walking for a long time; I feel very, very tired . . . Have we to go further or have we passed it by?

(*Passing her hand across her eyes.*) Curious mist on my eyes . . . Why do you hold my hand, Jack? (*Excitedly*). No, no, Jack, it's not. Can't you see it's a goldfinch. Look at th' black satiny wings with the gold bars and the splash of crimson on his head . . . (*wearily*). Something ails me, something ails me . . . Don't kiss me like that; you take my breath away, Jack . . . Why do you frown at me? . . . You're going away, and (*frightened*) I can't follow you. Something's keeping me from moving . . . (*crying out*). Jack, Jack, Jack![14]

Even at this point when Nora has removed herself entirely from the real world, the real world still has the tragic power to intervene. Her madness reacts with the slaughter Pearce had regarded as a necessary redemption. She rushes to the window calling for Jack at the sound of machine-gun fire, and Bessie, trying to pull her away, is killed by British soldiers looking for snipers. Not only does Nora have no sense of responsibility, she no longer has the power to pity the dying woman who tried to save her. She is instead an uncomprehending spectator at the murder she unwittingly helped to instigate. This simultaneous involvement and deranged detachment confirms O'Casey's fusion of tragic lament and tragic strife. The traditional passive role of the woman who laments catastrophe is changed into a lamenting heroine who tries simultaneously to intervene in it – with tragic results. Sane, Nora has failed to prevent murderous strife: mad, she has unwittingly aided it. But the element of lament is still retained. In the mad fragments of her memory the tone of lament is sustained amidst the strife which surrounds her. And O'Casey, whether he intended it or not, had taken his revenge on Cathleen ni Houlihan.

To use Adorno's important distinction, O'Casey's tragic drama belongs to the theatre of commitment but not to that of political tendency. He had written the major literary work concerning the Easter Uprising, but he had not written a work which glorified its actions or exalted the sentiments behind those actions. Rather he had juxtaposed political ideal and human experience, political aspiration and human loss. Revolution as an impersonal process with extraordinary personal consequences had taken over the role of the retributive Gods of classical tragedy. But revolution is neither a mystical fate nor a *deus ex machina*. It is rooted in time and place. Its terms of reference are social and political in the modern sense of both words. This is the supreme truth which O'Casey had captured in the shadow of a city. But the life which conventionally remained concealed and unspoken, was shorn of its anonymity and openly brought out into the light of day. What had lain in shadow was the city's true substance. In its power of illumination O'Casey's trilogy can truly be said to rival the indisputable achievement of Joyce's *Ulysses*, reaching a level of dramatic creation which O'Casey was never again to attain.

It was ironic therefore that he should have regarded his next play, *The Silver Tassie*, as a major advance on his previous work. It certainly was more experimental in its use of expressionist forms and consequently very daring in the context of the Irish theatre. But the much-maligned judgment of Yeats, accepted with much heart-searching and embarrassment by Lady Gregory, was fundamentally correct. The Abbey Theatre's rejection of the play, though obviously a bitter blow for O'Casey, cannot be regarded as the major reason for his subsequent decline as a playwright. His retreat into exile in England was an exaggerated response, in no way comparable to the earlier departure of Joyce for Paris. Part of the exaggeration was due to O'Casey's optimism about the stylistic and didactic qualities of his play. By comparison with Denis Johnston his use of the Expressionist chorus was woefully derivative and the open expression of his pacifist beliefs led him quite unintentionally to reverse a longstanding cultural practice. His martinet trench Tommies of the second act showed an Irish playwright in the process of creating stage Englishmen. At a more serious level, there was a deep-seated historical basis for the deterioration of O'Casey's talent. Like Murray, O'Casey had been unwittingly seduced by the aura of suburban respectability to be found in the new bourgeois republic. The ending of the play, which is supposedly tragic, takes place in the suburban dance hall of the Avondale Football Club, a setting hardly suited to expressing the pathos of the predicament in which O'Casey's young crippled ex-soldier finds himself. Whatever the institutional rights and wrongs of the situation in which O'Casey felt himself to be rejected and betrayed, his spontaneous bitterness certainly concealed from his own mind any true insight into the sudden death of Irish tragedy.

In its compressed form, the sudden transition from tragic to comic writing in the Irish theatre of the twenties provokes comparisons with the more extensive change in seventeenth-century England from Jacobean tragedy to Restoration comedy. The rebuilding of a new nation-state after a revolution, a process long retarded by the complexities of Ireland's colonial history, has usually been inimical to the tragic vision. The contrast is all the greater here because of the tragic drama which immediately preceded the transformation and the tragic poetry of Yeats and plays of O'Casey's which then accompanied it. And though comedy had co-existed with this tragic renaissance, the major comic genius of the Irish theatre only emerged when tragedy was in eclipse. This was Denis Johnston whose two early plays, *The Old Lady Says No* and *The Moon in the Yellow River*, represent the peak of comic dramatic writing after Oscar Wilde. Equally and embarrassingly, they reveal the limitation of theatrical technique within the Abbey. The title of the first play, wittily amended to acknowledge Lady Gregory's rejection of it, also recalls that other famous lady, Cathleen ni Houlihan in whose spirit it was definitely not written!

The play's theme is similar to those of the early O'Casey. But seen from the perspective of the politically secure Free State, the immediacy has gone and the distancing in time provokes a distancing in subject matter. When Robert Emmet, as romantic as ever, returns from the dead to the urban Dublin of the twenties, the myths of Irish romanticism are subject to deadly forms of comic laceration. And *The Moon in the Yellow River* is *the* play of the new Free State just as *The Plough and the Stars* was *the* play of the Easter Uprising. While the Abbey could reject *The Silver Tassie* for failing to combine naturalist and expressionist methods, *The Old Lady Says No* had to be rejected because of its technical success. Johnston's expressionism was technically too advanced for the traditional naturalist methods of the theatre and thought to be unstageable there. *The Moon and the Yellow River*, less advanced in this respect, was produced by the Abbey. But it actually contains a superb parody of Abbey stagecraft and acting including identical sets for the first and third acts—which made it easier for the Abbey to stage!

The similarity in the literary careers of O'Casey and Johnston, an early flourishing and later decline, cannot be explained purely in terms of the institutional features of the Irish theatre. Irish culture itself was undergoing an unexpected transformation. With the founding of the Irish Free State, the cultural and political power of the Catholic church increased considerably and had a distinctly repressive effect upon the development of Irish art and culture. The Censorship Bill of 1928, which Yeats as an Irish Senator opposed in vain, was one important manifestation of this. From then until the late 1950s when the Republic began to reverse its policy of cultural and political isolationism, many great Irish writers were either suppressed or deliberately forgotten. For the theatre the irony was this. The policy of theatrical 'Irishness' in the Abbey only worked in the context of artistic freedom and links with European developments. But once these freedoms were constricted and the links severed then cultural isolation turned Ireland into a parochial backwater. Yeats, who had seen independence as the basis for new forms of cultural expression in Ireland, retreated in the twenties into his Protestant Anglo-Irish identity. As a senator, however, he was soon to find the Protestant upper class in the south too materialistic and philistine to be interested in aiding his fight against Catholic hegemony.

The Senate to which he belonged, though containing twenty-four non-Catholics and fifteen titled people, was an alien assembly of merchants, bankers and lawyers, more keen to talk about Irish lace or stained glass than to consider the importance of a new national theatre.[15] This traumatic experience explains in part at least Yeats' disenchantment with Irish politics and his brief flirtation with fascism. He mixed socially with a reactionary caste of Southern unionists and identified the Catholic masses with the policies of the Church he abhorred. His consequent anti-democratic turn was fuelled by the experience of fighting on the issues of Divorce and Censorship as part of a meagre minority which had Church and public opinion ranged against it. He thus justified his élitism through the practice of fighting for basic human rights which were widely unpopular at the time. And yet too much can be made of his foolish connection with O'Duffy's short-lived Blueshirts. There were other rival forms of fascism in Ireland—the IRA was soon to form ties with Nazi Germany and some of the higher ranks of the Irish clergy were very attracted by the clerical fascism of Salazar's corporatist state in Portugal.

It must be said, however, that the quality of Yeats' writing *did* suffer to some extent from the brief and dubious obsession with finding an Irish Mussolini; his drama more so than his poetry. Only when he was finished with practical politics did he write *The Death of Cuchulain* and *Purgatory*, thus re-establishing artistic contact with his work of the pre-independence period. The one-act play *Purgatory* remains the last major tragic piece ever written in Ireland. But the sensibility of the Renaissance was maintained in exile under a different guise, or rather disguise. Samuel Beckett had seen many of the Abbey productions during his days as student and teacher at Trinity College. His work cannot be understood without consideration of this formative experience. His indebtedness to the later Joyce is undeniable but what is often forgotten is the imprint of Yeats and Synge. In Beckett we see a process of effacement at work—the repudiation of time and place, the refusal to name names, the quest for a universality which surpasses all forms of conventional signifying. But in this process of effacement few have bothered to ask precisely what is being effaced. This, unmistakeably, is the Irish dimension and the writer's Irish heritage. The relationship of Hamm and Clov in *Endgame*, of Pozzo and Lucky, Vladimir and Estragon in *Waiting for Godot* echo the relationship of the base and the noble which Yeats had established in his heroic tragedies. Yet in Beckett, the reference to country and cause, time and rank is gone. Heroism itself has been extinguished and what is left is a disguised residue, a domination of man over man without formal authority and without reason, leading nowhere. Beckett pushed the lesson of *Purgatory* to its furthest point. The noble as the only authentic form of authority, and the only true basis of the heroic, is no longer recognisable. Where in the later Yeats it is still a dim memory, in Beckett it is frozen in permanent amnesia. But the tragic poignancy of Beckett derives precisely from what cannot be remembered, what can no longer be felt or known. If Beckett is taken as a prime exemplar of what Roland Barthes has called 'white writing', we must add the necessary proviso. It is Irish white writing, in which the process of effacement cannot ultimately be separated from what is being effaced.

Exile and the loss of signification seem inextricably linked. The tragic pathos in Beckett of the constant movement towards death expresses a universal predicament, yet at the same time recalls the words of Synge's Deidre: 'It's a lonesome thing to be away from Ireland always'. Beckett's universal darkness is forged out of that specific reference, that country, that name. His drama bears no trace of it, yet the trace is indelible. This is not only a paradox for Beckett, but for Irish theatre as a whole. It has the mark of national identity stamped on it more clearly than any other theatre in the Western world and the temptation always is to indulge in a metaphysics of 'Irishness'. But this creative body of writing, and the theatre which actualised it, must be understood in terms of a special and peripheral relationship to modern Europe. This is not a static sociological attribute but a changing predicament subject to gradual historical dissolution. Ireland during this period when it had thrown off British rule to become an independent yet truncated nation-state, moved away from the social and political conditions which clearly helped to produce the literary Renaissance. And the drama itself—from *Riders to the Sea* through to *The Plough and the Stars*—captures that movement, the movement away from the original sources, which for Irish tragedy at least, brings eventual dissolution.

This is not an argument for decay in modern tragic drama since the focus after this point shifts to America where the work of O'Neill had already demonstrated continuity with the European tradition. More recently the Abbey has produced the great works of the Renaissance as classics in repertory. Successful revivals such as *The Plough and the Stars* and first productions, such as *The Old Lady Says No*, have maintained the continuity. But the talent of dramatists since the thirties has been comparatively minor, and strictly incomparable with that of its predecessors. Occasionally there has been a distinct echo of the earlier greatness, and one of the most unusual of these was Heno Magee's *Hatchet*, successfully staged by the Abbey in 1972. Written by a working-class Dublin playwright and highly biographical, the echo is of O'Casey. But the drama, of the internecine family feuds of working-class Dublin, is depoliticised. The violence is turned inwards, endemic and cyclical. The raw brutality of a dehumanised working-class possesses at times a naturalistic clumsiness but it is dramatically powerful, and free of tendentious constraint. By comparison O'Casey appears almost sentimental. Although the play lacks the figural and political dimensions of O'Casey, the most significant expression of its brutality lies in the role of the mother. Hatchet's mother cajoles her son into action against their local enemies by accusing him of cowardice, and finally follows him into a street to fight with a broken bottle in her hand. She is the ultimate negation of the passive lamenting mother, of Maurya and Juno, of Mary Cahel and Mrs Tancred. While the play could not have been written without O'Casey's legacy, the changed social circumstance produces a raw Oedipal relationship running counter to the Irish dramatic tradition. But it offers no escape to its battling hero from the demoralising trap of the working-class community constantly fighting its own kind. Staged at a time when civil strife had reached its height in the North, it makes no comment on it, for it is too self-contained. Instead *Shadow of a Gunman*, written fifty years earlier, still casts its shadow over the whole of Northern Ireland.

For the direction of tragic drama after the Irish Renaissance we have to look west to the New World. It is perhaps significant that of the migrants to the New World, most had come from Norway and Ireland during the nineteenth century. And the later passage of tragic drama followed the seaward passage of millions who had seldom if ever been to a theatre in their native country. It is significant too that the major tragedian of the American theatre was himself a second generation Irishman called Eugene O'Neill. The Irish connection proved vital but, as it turned out, not in the way O'Neill himself saw it.

Part IV

American Tragedy and the American Dream

Part IV

American Tragedy and the American Dream

9 Eugene O'Neill I: The Living Tragedy

The tragic drama of Eugene O'Neill has two distinct phases. The first is the period of his early work between 1919 and 1925 and the second that of his two great masterpieces, *The Iceman Cometh* and *Long Day's Journey into Night*, written between 1939 and 1941. In the long passage of time between these two brief periods lies the historical dramatisation of the Electra myth *Mourning Becomes Electra*. But it was in these two distinct phases that he created new heights in the writing of modern tragedy. The distinctiveness is sometimes obscured by the sheer continuous output and prolific energy of a writer who had managed to produce volumes of near mediocrity during his life. The unevenness of O'Neill's writing testifies not so much to his weakness as to his strength, his immense flair for artistic renewal when all seemed lost. In that sense, the bad does not detract from the good, as many of his critics like to suggest. In his early days he produced what no other American playwright of his time was able to—the living tragedy of contemporary American life. In his final years that same life was recalled as history in a vision at once matured and more profound—the tragic vision of the life remembered.

Both phases of his work have, as part of their context, vital connections with the European countries of tragic drama. O'Neill was a second-generation Irishman from a Catholic family which had known poverty on both sides of the Atlantic. The most explicit influences on his work were those of Strindberg and Ibsen, and he came to possess, as they had done, the same grandeur of artistic isolation, outpacing in stature and sheer volume of work the indigenous theatres which attempted to do justice to his plays. But despite the importance of the European connections, O'Neill was distinctively an American playwright writing about his own life and times. His work has to be understood in the context of the second wave of immigration which took place in the latter half of the nineteenth century, the influx of those poor immigrants whose cheap labour helped to make the

United States the most powerful industrial nation in the world. His work therefore offers profound comment upon the tension between the myth of the frontier society and its freedoms, and the reality of life for the new Americans who settled largely in the growing industrial cities of the mid-west and the Eastern seaboard. It embodies and expresses the reality of the newcomer, not the pioneer. The dialectic between wilderness and civilisation, so important in Irish and Scandinavian tragedy, is totally transformed.

The myth of the American frontier had already been expressed in fiction before O'Neill's family ever reached the New World. Through the work of Fenimore Cooper the idea of the wilderness as a source of moral rejuvenation was to be handed down to the writers of popular western fiction, reaching the height of their popularity during the period when O'Neill was embarking upon his own career. The epic narrative of the novel offered scope for the depiction of the monumental scenery of the West, plain and mountain, river and canyon, forest and desert. The Westerner was the hero facing a lawless frontier who found self-rejuvenation through constant danger, a lone figure of strength on an open landscape with limitless horizons.[1] The myth of wilderness made possible by Cooper thus became a familiar stereotype in the work of Owen Wister and Zane Grey, later to be taken over by movies and television.

O'Neill, starting to write plays at about the time the 'old West' had disappeared and the 'Western' became a genre of popular fiction, never really responded to the myth at all. The dramatic space of the theatre never suggested it to him, and indeed he used that space to achieve a rather opposite effect.[2] The mythical space of the American Dream co-exists theatrically with a sense of imprisonment. The low ceiling of the stokehold in *The Hairy Ape*, the suffocating boughs of *Desire under the Elms*, present stage images of radical closure where both overall settings, the sea and the country, seem to offer limitless space. To a lesser degree other early works, *Bound East for Cardiff*, *Anna Christie* and *Beyond the Horizon*, express the same limits. O'Neill in his drama thus inverts the theme of the new popular novel genre of his time. His plays close the avenues to freedom and prepare the way in his mature works for what can truly be called the full-scale dramaturgical destruction of the American Dream.

The contrast with the peripheral nature of tragic drama in Europe also becomes apparent. While based in the new immigrant society with its culture of individualism and its spirit of optimism, the freedom suggested by the country and the sea is banished from O'Neill's stage.

The tragic universe is transferred, as in O'Casey, to the bars and tenements of the city or linked organically to the productive energies of the new industrial world. Settings of sea and wilderness are still maintained. In *The Hairy Ape* and *Anna Christie* the dialectic of country and city is replaced by the dialectic of city and sea. In *The Emperor Jones* the black hero from the 'jungle' of Harlem is cast adrift in the real primitive jungle of Honduras. But neither jungle nor sea are part of the official mythology of the frontier, nor, as in Ibsen, Chekhov and Synge, is the sense of wilderness infinite. It is part of the fabric of closure, not of the space beyond. Ibsen's demonic trolls and Synge's pitiless sea which takes men by drowning are replaced here by fog and steam, the recurrent modalities of the early work. Menacing and oppressive, the fog obliterates the horizon while steam is part of the new technology linking the human conquest of the sea to the industrial age. The dynamic and volatile world of the city, of industrial energy and physical labour, is never far from the centre of O'Neill's stage.

This thematic contrast with the European tragedians is reinforced by changes in dramatic form. O'Neill used the expressionist idioms of the German theatre in his bid to find a dynamism in theatrical action pertinent to his choice of themes. But a division of his drama into an early expressionist canon and a later naturalist one is arbitrary and false: O'Neill used expressionist and naturalist forms simultaneously in the early work and his commitment to figural drama was never in doubt. What Expressionism allowed him to do, and what the drawing-room dramatist could not, was to polarise images of openness and closure, and to accelerate the pace of movement on the stage. The wedding ceremony, for example, in *All God's Chillun Got Wings* is an open spectacle set outside the church and showing the mass movements of racially segregated crowds staring at each other in mutual hostility. But unlike Ernst Toller and the other German Expressionists whose example O'Neill followed, the choral function of the crowd, expressed spatially and kinetically, was part of a social setting intended to dramatise individual fate rather than to obliterate it. Unlike his American contemporaries Elmer Rice and John Howard Lawson, O'Neill retained the figural commitment and refused the Expressionist temptation of using individual personae as social stereotypes.

The change in form also complemented another major thematic change, which in turn merged with the transformation from periphery to centre. This was the dramatic breakthrough into lower-class life, accomplished more thoroughly and convincingly by O'Neill than by any other modern playwright. O'Neill's naturalism here consisted in creating poetic rhythms out of the demotic speech of the new northern ethnic Americans—Irish, Scandinavian, black and that hybrid which rapidly emerged from all of them, the Brooklynese of Yank, the stoker in *The Hairy Ape*. The vitality of the demotic language complements the vitality of the new Expressionist forms, but the playwright's figural powers were still at an embryonic stage. In *The Hairy Ape* and *The Emperor Jones* is to be witnessed the creative struggle for the figural construction of the solitary proletarian hero. The struggle was the necessary antecedent for the multiple characterisation in subsequent works, but it also explains the brevity of the earlier plays, since they focus on a solitary, tragic fate. Any consideration of O'Neill as tragedian must begin with them because they initially incorporate the changes in theme and form which come to be the fundament of all his major drama.

In *The Hairy Ape*, the setting of the play below decks directly recalls Gorky's *The Lower Depths*. But the environment, however degrading, is a moving, working one, in which the sea can no longer be a source of adventure or freedom. Paddy, Yank's Irish companion, sets the scene with a nostalgic lament for the days of schooners and sailing ships:

> And there was the days too. A warm sun on the clean decks. Sun warming the blood of you and wind over the miles of shiny green ocean like strong drink to your lungs. Work—aye, hard work—but who's mind that at all? Sure, you worked under the sky, and 'twas done wid skill and daring to it. And wid the day done, in the dowatch, smoking me pipe at ease, the lookout would be rasing land maybe, and we'd see the mountains of South Americy wid the red fire of the setting sun and the clouds floating by them! . . . 'Twas them days a ship was part of the sea, and a man was part of the ship and the sea joined all together and made it one.[3]

The tone is one of Irish lament, but the tone of Yank in reply, is one of American exaltation. He acclaims the infernal vision of steel and steam and expresses a perverse sense of triumph at being its centre, its enslaved prive mover:

> Sure, on'y for me everything stops. It all goes dead, get me? De noise and de smoke and all de engines movin' de woild, dey stop. Dere ain't nothin' no more! Dat's what I'm sayin'. Everything else dat makes de woild move, somep'n makes it move. It can't move without somep'n else, see? Den yuh get down to me. I'm at de

bottom get me! . . . I start somep'n and de woild moves! It—dat's
me—de new dat's moiderin' de old! I'm de ting in coal makes it
boin; I'm steam and oil for de engines; I'm de ting in noise dat makes
yuh hear it; I'm smoke and express trains and steamers and factory
whistles; I'm de ting in gold makes it money! And I'm what makes
iron into steel! Steel, dat stands for de whole ting! And I'm steel—
steel—steel! . . . Slaves, hell! We run de whole woiks. All de rich
guys dat t'ink dey're somep'n, dey ain't nothin'. Dey don't belong.
But us guys, we're in de move, we're at de bottom, de whole ting is
us![4]

As Yank's speech reaches its climax all the other men in the hold
copy his example and pound their fists against the steel bunks until
there is a deafening metallic roar. The celebration is total, the
solidarity uncompromising. Paddy the nostalgic dreamer becomes an
outsider who does not belong.

The drunken ceremony is a brief and transitory triumph over the
collective alienation of work. But O'Neill's real concern is to show his
hero's brief experience of the alien world of the privileged for whom he
sweats and slaves, and here the alienation is portrayed as an individual
estrangement, an estrangement of the authentically primitive from the
falsely civilised. Although the conditions are there to make the
alienation tragic, O'Neill is nonetheless unable to raise that alienation
to the plane of tragic strife. The main reason for the failure lies in the
sustained metaphor of animality which charts an alternative course of
action. Yank systematically divests himself of all human qualities as a
response to the conferred attribute of animality which starts when
Mildred Douglas, on seeing him at the boiler of the stokehole
brandishing his shovel and cursing violently, deems him 'a filthy beast'
before fainting. The response of the industrialist's daughter,
'slumming' in the inferno of the ship's stokehole, is pathetic and
unconvincing. But it sets the course for Yank's future estrangement in
which he systematically attempts to destroy any redeeming human
qualities.

The play thus seems to vindicate the modish sociological theory of
labelling. The girl does not actually call Yank 'a hairy ape' but
Paddy's suggestion that when she fainted, ' 'Twas as if she'd seen a
hairy ape escape from the zoo', is enough for the image to stick in
Yank's mind as a description of his animal nature. 'Hairy ape, huh?
Sure! Dat's de way she looked at me, aw right. Hairy ape! So dat's me,
huh?' The catalyst has an erotic echo, the dramatically convincing

sense of Yank being caught out by the girl at his most primitive. But ultimately that echo is trapped in the Strindbergian conceit of the woman as pampered and privileged, and man as indispensable yet exploited. The figural failure of the play is not to place the sense of privilege any higher, theatrically speaking, than Mildred Douglas and her aunt bitching each other on the promenade deck. Femininity, in any form, is reduced to a leisured conceit of the upper classes. The other scene where Yank confronts the respectable sector of society, as he insults churchgoers on the corner of Fifth Avenue, is equally a failure because O'Neill's Expressionist devices actually mar his dramatic intention. The churchgoers are marionettes who do not seem to see or hear him and only answer with a 'mechanical affected politeness'. Thus the burden of representing the exploiting class figurally rests on Mildred, who then appears as a stereotyped symbol. The absence of confrontation with any other class enemies (who are also real people) is a defect highlighted even more by the superb political cameo in which Yank tries to join the I.W.W. but because of his terrorist fantasies is mistaken for an *agent provocateur*.

The descent to pure animality, therefore, is an alternative to tragic strife. It is an alternative made inevitable by the immature nature of the figural creation. The bourgeois churchgoers are puppets because O'Neill cannot yet make them real. The lack of figural dimension also affects Yank's own misfortune. Pity or sympathy are withheld from the audience by the unintentionally comic exaggeration of the gorilla-like qualities which were deliberately intended to shock. The final and fatal embrace with the gorilla in the zoo puts Yank beyond human fate and makes the audience external to his doom. The problem is that the audience can identify O'Neill's hero as just plain stupid, a grotesque parody of Rodin's thinker in whose pose the playwright at one point deliberately places him.

Nevertheless the play was the most important proletarian drama after *The Lower Depths* and more stark and uncompromising than Jack London's novel of the same period, *Martin Eden*, which degenerates into sentimentality. The biographical background to the work was also important. O'Neill had discovered the hardships of the sea and of sailors at first hand, and his own life generally during this earlier period skirted the intersection of proletarian and bohemian life on the eastern seaboard. His life at sea, his abortive gold-prospecting in Honduras, his prolonged bouts of drinking in run-down New York bars like the 'Hell Hole' and 'Jimmy the Priests' were a form of temporary proletarianisation during the time spent away from his family and before he had a family of his own. The bohemian milieu provided him with a means of bringing his talent to fruition while the proletarian one actively inspired the themes of his early work. His early work in turn had an instant success which meant that he was able to devote the rest of his life to writing as a professional career, having no need, like Ibsen, for the stimulus of exile or, like Hawthorne, the security of a government job. Yet whether the Provincetown Players who produced O'Neill's earlier work, were really capable of doing justice to his work is another matter. The initial production of *The Hairy Ape* was one in which the director was unable to cope with the demands of the play,[5] and subsequent productions of O'Neill's work were never as alert to its potential as the Moscow Arts had been to Chekhov or the Abbey to Synge or O'Casey. But the themes in his drama were sufficiently broad and powerful to create a theatrical impact in a country where theatre had as often as not been confined to the kind of melodrama in which O'Neill's father was such an expert actor. O'Neill stood out as a genuine answer to Europeans who accused American culture of sterility and philistinism, and his stature grew over the decades. The prolific nature of his drama seemed like a remarkable single-handed response to the vast diversity of American experience.

In the early period, one particular theme in his lower-class drama cannot easily be attributed to the purely biographical. This is the theme of racial conflict and suffering. Two of the most publicly controversial of his plays, *The Emperor Jones* and *All God's Chillun Got Wings*, had black heroes in what was still, at the time, an explicitly racist society. *The Emperor Jones* was written before *The Hairy Ape* and, socially and dramatically, is a less complex play. But it is also more powerful and successful in its tragic climax. Both plays chart a mythical return to source on the part of their heroes. In the case of Yank Smith, it is to his brute animal nature. In the case of Brutus Jones, it is to the jungle of his ancestors. In theatrical and figural terms, however, the journey of Jones is more convincing. For the journey to source is a flight from real enemies and becomes a journey of fear, evoking horror and hallucination from the deposed Emperor.

The example of *Heart of Darkness* was clearly before O'Neill's mind in writing the play. His innovation is to make a black hero discover that darkness yet fail to recognise it as part of his roots. Jones plays upon the superstitions of the 'bush-niggers' with his silver bullets, but their superstition of modern technology is nothing to his of the primitive jungle. When he flees the roles are reversed and his capacity for survival as an urban sophisticate possessed of urban cunning is markedly less than theirs. The silver bullet he saves, if need be for his own suicide, is wasted in shooting at the Crocodile-God he sees in hallucination. The natives meanwhile, who have been taught by Jones that only a silver bullet can kill their emperor, ingeniously start making them for that very purpose. They harness cunning to superstition whereas all his cunning eventually gives way to super-stition when he is confronted by the phantoms of his dreams in the jungle.

The phantoms, however, are usually not arbitrary. Despite one or two uneven episodes such as the fairy tale scene with the Little Formless Fears, there is a logic to Jones's serial nightmare. For the hallucinations, perfectly suited to a variety of expressionist techniques, are all based on previous incidents in the life of the hero or the history of his race. The murder of his gambling partner, his escape from a chain gang, the auction of slaves, and finally the witch-doctor and the crocodile-God, represent a backward chronological descent into the horror of suffering and of origin. It is a mimed wordless history which, specific to the descendants of black slaves, has a remarkable universality. The nightmares actually redeem Jones as he moves inexorably towards his tragic doom, for they remind us what, in his wish for absolute power, he has tried to escape from. The often wordless experience of suffering purifies him and throws into relief his capacity for corruption and cruel arrogance. They then reveal, with increasing intensity, the true nature of his tragic alienation.

His initial cynicism is correspondingly thrown into perspective. Jones's empire over superstitious 'bush-niggers' has been achieved only by copying the corruption he has learned from white men, that is, through his enforced contact with white civilised living. An early exchange between Jones and Smithers, the crooked trader and cockney acolyte, makes the point in an acidly amusing manner:

> Jones. . . . Ain't I pertected you and winked at all de crooked tradin' you been doin' right out in de broad day. Sho' I has—and me makin' laws to stop it at de same time! (*He chuckles.*)
>
> Smithers. But meanin' no 'arm, you been grabbin' left and right yourself, ain't yer? Look at the taxes you put on 'em . . . And as for me breakin' laws, you've broke 'em all yourself just as fast as yer made 'em.
>
> Jones. Ain't I de Emperor? De laws don't go for him. (*Judicially.*) You heah what I tells you, Smithers. Dere's little stealin' like you does, and dere's big stealin' like I does. For de little stealin' dey

gets you in jail soon or late. For de big stealin' dey makes you
Emperor and puts you in de Hall of Fame when you croaks.
(*Reminiscently.*) If dey's one thing I learns in ten years on de
Pullman ca's listenin' to de white quality talk, it's dat same fact.
And when I gets a chance to use it, I winds up Emperor in two
years.[6]

Jones successfully displaces the corruption learnt from whites from
the economic into the political sphere, tearing it adrift from a white
society in which he has only a menial status and transporting it to a
primitive society of blacks. His rule is in many ways an echo and
parody of white colonialism, but it is more than this. There is also an
echo of John Gabriel Borkman's mythical kingdom. Branded elsewhere as a member of an inferior race, Jones can here dream of self-
aggrandisement and personal power but only at the expense of his own
race. His empire is a fraud made possible by the racial similarity he has
with his subjects, and conversely, his cultural alienation from them.
The urban cunning of the black American from Harlem derides all
native superstition yet exploits it ruthlessly. The sense of extravagant
aggrandisement is that of a bubble which must ultimately burst, of a
confidence man eventually to be exposed. 'I'se good for six months yit
'fore dey gets sick of my game. Den, when I sees trouble comin', I
makes a move.' Even this candid confession is out of date by the time it
is made for the revolution has started, the tom-tom beats incessantly
and Jones's rule is at an end. The pattern in the recent history of the
Third World makes O'Neill's play highly prophetic. The neo-
colonialism of our times has spawned black dictators governing even
more ruthlessly than Jones, and aided by sycophantic white capitalists
in a situation of mutual interdependence which is often soured by
mutual contempt. It is very much the world of 'Papa Doc' Duvalier, of
Bokassa and Mobutu and of Idi Amin.

The tragic alienation of the hero is only revealed through the strife
between the fleeing Jones and his primitive environment. As fraudu-
lent Emperor, there is of course no real possibility of alienation. But as
the flight reveals the vulnerability of the man, the legacy of oppression
which his life embodies, he becomes paradoxically more human.
While the movement of Yank Smith is to animality, that of Jones is
towards the oppressed history of his race. While the strife is never with
the pursuers who seek to overthrow him, it is with a primitive
environment he cannot, as a man of the city, ever hope to master. His
silver bullets, fired in panic, cannot destroy the phantoms produced in

his imagination through fear. Nor can they prevent the hallucinations from continually tormenting him. O'Neill's effective theatricalisation of the nightmare widens the figural dimensions of his tragic hero, extending the real to the verge of the fantastic but never mistakenly overbalancing into fantasy.

The expressionist portrayal of hallucination marked a similar kind of advance to that of the stream of consciousness in the novel. The boldly imaginative theme enabled O'Neill to explore the unconscious more effectively here than later when he deliberately experimented with theatrical techniques of Freudianism. The play was also the first major work on the American stage with a black American hero. With Charles Gilpin, a small-time black actor and lift operator at Macy's brought in to play the lead on a majority decision of the Provincetown Players, its performance became a landmark in the American theatre. O'Neill himself maintained that Gilpin was one of the three great actors to play a major role in one of his plays, and near the end of his life the playwright conceded that Gilpin was probably the best of all.[7] But as the play did successful re-runs throughout the early twenties, it soon became clear that Gilpin was limited to that one play. As a black there were no others in which he could perform major roles and out of which he could make a professional career. O'Neill's writing about black Americans was an exception, not a precedent in the theatre of the time, and Gilpin returned to obscurity and poverty, claiming that the play was his and that 'that Irishman only wrote it'. As a last ironic gloss on the pertinence of the theme to contemporary America, Gilpin's short-lived fame enabled him to play the 'Emperor' up in Harlem in real life, where he could flaunt among fellow blacks his unexpected success in a white world. His life was a poignant but horrifying exemplar of Oscar Wilde's dictum that life imitates art.

O'Neill's dramatic use of the racial dimension revealed the limit of the impact that one person's writing for the theatre could have on social life as a whole. *The Emperor Jones* and *All God's Chillun Got Wings*, though generating social and racial controversy at the time, did little to foster immediate social change. Yet no other white playwright of the time had the boldness or the courage to attempt it, nor endure the imbalance it caused in his literary reputation. *All God's Chillun*, largely forgotten during O'Neill's lifetime because of racial embarrassment, never received the critical acclaim it deserved. Despite the intense controversy which preceded its opening in New York, it was subsequently buried. It remains however one of the major works of O'Neill's tragic drama, in which he proceeded from the tragedy of the solitary hero to the tragic portrayal of social relationships. It is instructive for that reason to see how and why this was achieved and to compare it with *Anna Christie*, written three years earlier in 1920, where the promise of a similar breakthrough was suggested but never materialised.

Anna Christie became one of the most universally popular of O'Neill's early dramas, largely because of its optimism and sentimentality. The play was about the overcoming of potential tragedy, and as such produced a kind of formula easily vulgarised in the Hollywood films of the next decade—the resolution of social problems by true romance. But O'Neill, in his portrayal of Anna Christie as a prostitute deceiving her father about her true occupation, had initially produced something tough and uncompromising. A recent American revival of the play illustrated the point when it received a favourable reception from feminist audiences. Anna sets the tone at the beginning when she remarks to Martha, another prostitute, that her hatred of men could easily include the doting father she is about to meet for the first time in fifteen years: 'Give you a kick when you're down, that's what all men do. (*With sudden passion.*) Men, I hate 'em – all of 'em! And I don't expect he'll turn out no better than the rest.' Yet her hatred, though fierce and hardened through the bitter experience of being a twenty-year-old prostitute, finally does soften through her romance with Mat Burke, the Irish stoker with whom she eventually falls in love. In *Anna Christie* one experiences an almost complete reversal of the dramatic sequence in *A Doll's House*. Nora Helmer, an unbearable petit-bourgeois for most of the play, partially exonerates herself at the end. Anna, credible and heroic for most of O'Neill's work, capitulates at the end to a sentimentality she abhors. The unconvincing liberation of Nora provides a total contrast with the barely credible enslavement of Anna. Yet both plays express a similar kind of artistic betrayal, in which the play's potential is never fully realised.

Since *Anna Christie* is a powerful play which sustains its power through the first three of its four acts, we have to look for how this betrayal occurs. In the relationship of father and daughter, a relationship based on myopia and deception, O'Neill had perhaps created the most powerful relationship in his drama to date. The two salient motifs of his early work, the country and the sea, are combined here in a truly remarkable way. Father and daughter each look to the opposite motif for the ideal their actual life could never give them. A veteran sailor who has come to hate 'dat ole devil sea', Cris Christopherson hopes his daughter will set up a farm back west. The rural idyll dominated his thinking and is part of his self-delusion: 'Ay bet you', he tells Martha, 'some day she marry good steady land fallar py golly'! But Anna's account of her life on a farm is different: 'The old man of the family, his wife and four sons—I had to slave for all of 'em. I was only a poor relation, and they treated me worse than they dare treat a hired girl.'[9] And later, Anna comes to express a yearning for the sea Christopherson so despises. 'I'd rather have one drop of ocean than all the farms in the world!' Yet the terms of that commitment are not Those her father can offer her. He belongs to the sea, she tells him, 'but not a coal barge. You belong on a real ship sailing all over the world.'

Christopherson's constant failure to guess at his daughter's true occupation, and the uneasiness with which Anna tries to play the role of virtuous daughter conspire to create a potentially tragic situation, where each looks in the other's life vainly for some ideal to sustain them. But within this relationship alone there is no room for tragic denouement. Instead O'Neill has to introduce the element of a love relationship and so the play becomes triangular. But this development actually conspires to destroy the situation O'Neill has created. Mat Burke whom Christopherson saves from drowning after the collision in the fog, is in many ways a caricature, an Americanised stage Irishman whose appearance turns potential tragedy into sentimental pathos. The influence of Synge, both in the rhetoric of Burke's speech and his exaggerated swagger, is very evident.[10] But the ease with which Anna falls for his stage rhetoric belies the toughness and coarseness of her life until that point, and her previous immunity to male blandishment. Excessive rhetoric, it appears, or just plain overwritten Irish blarney can overcome anything.

Anna's 'falling in love' is a major artistic compromise. But it cannot be divorced from the context of motif and language. She never finds a 'real ship sailing round the world' but only a coal barge shrouded in fog. The fog creates the accident through which she encounters Burke, and the rhetoric of his courting overcomes the reality of her hatred of men. Instead of the open sea she finds the enclosing fog, instead of the sailing ship a coal barge, and instead of passion, rhetoric. The betrayals are all interlocking. Although her relationship with Burke is a stormy one, full of bitter conflict, and although the confessions of her previous life are highly moving, it all operates from a bedrock of sentimentality. In the play Anna is a true representative of a corrupt urban life, but the pain and bitterness that corruption brings are dissipated in the fog of O'Neill's creation. The similarity of the play's ending with *In the Shadow of the Glen* has often been noted. Equally artificial perhaps, is Christopherson's change of heart towards Burke when he learns of Anna's true profession. His idealism is compromised too, and being so, loses any strength it might have had. Marriage is accepted as the only solution, the only true reform for the whore with the heart of gold.

The public approval for O'Neill's play, especially from Irish-American Catholics, derived naturally enough from this affirmative ending. The drama can be read as a parable of social integration, of the personal relationship (i.e. marriage) overcoming the debased substance of the past lives of the prospective partners. Yet in reality, nothing is changed. Both Anna's father and her prospective husband are still tied to the sea. Christopherson's last sombre lament suggests this exactly: 'Fog, fog, fog, all bloody time. You can't see where you was going, no. Only dat ole davil, sea—she knows!' Despite the apparently beneficial impact of Mat Burke on Anna, the Irish of O'Neill's plays do not generally have this kind of healing power nor a distinctly heroic status. He did not portray Irish-Americans either as the saviours of America or as its most oppressed. Indeed his early Irishmen, like Mat Burke or Bill Carmody in *The Straw*, are often caricatures and only when he descended the ethnic scale even further was he able to create a true sense of social oppression, and equally a tragic vision of modern America.

All God's Chillun Got Wings received little public approval anywhere, either before or after its first performance. Apart from W. E. B. Dubois, few blacks condoned it, and the popular press tried to create a scandal around its racial theme. Many saw it as an attempt to create a black and white love story and little else. But the play goes much deeper than this, challenging conventions of race, sex and class in America in a way which at that time was totally unparalleled. It is impossible to reduce the play to any single one of these dimensions or, equally, to consider any one of them in isolation from the others. The mere creation and performance of the play at the time was a challenge to white racist attitudes. Equally, though not as apparent at first sight, the play challenged two more sophisticated kinds of myth about relations between black and white in America during the period. The first, held by a fraction of what Franklin Frazier has called the black bourgeoisie, was the myth of black advancement: the second, held by progressive white liberals of the time was that of harmonious racial integration. Both these myths were products of an earlier period of American life where racial inequality and segration—*de jure* or *de facto*—were the order of the day. The black middle-class myth held that advancement was possible through social conformity within a segregated world, where blacks had to reproduce with greater moral rectitude the respectable manners of the white bourgeoisie. The white-liberal myth held that sympathy for blacks was a noble altruistic act ultimately bound to promote greater racial justice and harmony. Both myths gathered strength during the period of O'Neill's own lifetime, but were to be exploded quite devastatingly by the civil rights protests, the ghetto riots and the Black Power movements of the sixties. While O'Neill never challenged these myths didactically in his work, at a deeper artistic level his tragic vision constantly undermines them. That tragic vision has since shown itself to be utterly prophetic.

By comparison with *Anna Christie*, this work still showed the strong influence of Expressionism. But since it was a tragedy of social relationships and not of the solitary hero, the expressionist forms were modified accordingly. In part they still compensated for the elliptical nature of the dialogue, which at times is too compressed to convey the sensibility O'Neill wished to express. Short episodic scenes are used to convey the sense of life over time. Street settings and the use of crowds convey vivid images of working-class city life. The two essentially complement one another, enabling O'Neill to effectively dispense with the simultaneous use of the domestic interior and the unity of time so typical of Ibsen. The breakthrough permitted by the Expressionist technique is exhilarating yet the figural design is never sacrificed. The wedding scene conveys, above all, the newly-married couple's awareness of the intransigent racial hostility surrounding them. The extensive use of street noises and street crowds in the opening scene is the prelude to the meeting of the black boy, Jim Harris and the white girl, Ella Downey at the point where the white and coloured districts of that part of New York intersect. The gradual lowering of the ceiling and the shrinking of the walls in the successive scenes of the last act parallel the growing claustrophobia and disintegration of the marriage.

The sense of tragic alienation in this play is as great as anywhere in O'Neill's work. As in *The Plough and the Stars*, it is intensified by the different situation of husband and wife and the resulting conflict. Jim Harris and Ella Downey are childhood sweethearts, but their adolescence is largely spent apart because of the difference in the colour of their skin. Their social advantages and setbacks cross-cut each other. Jim's father has built up a successful haulier business enabling him to give his son a good education to partially compensate for the racial stigma of being black. Ella Downey on the other hand is a working-class girl exploited by Jim's white contemporaries, who treat her with casual contempt. She becomes the unwanted mother of an illegitimate child whose father is the most brutal member of the gang. Both then have rather different social stigmas attached to their lives, and both have different means of partially though never wholly redeeming them. When the child dies, Ella turns to Jim precisely because his personal attributes are so different from the men who have used her. He is caring, gentle and devoted, the antithesis of Yank Smith, and O'Neill explores in this play a complex interpersonal relationship lacking in the brief confrontation of Yank and Mildred Douglas. One of the great virtues of the play is to show the precise social circumstances under which rigid racial conventions can break down, yet still produce a socially unacceptable intermarriage.

As O'Neill makes clear, it is not just a mutual sense of rejection which attracts them, but also the memory of their childhood together, taunted by the other children as 'Painty Face' and 'Jim Crow', but still preserving in their memory a sense of innocence and joyous idyllic play. But play and innocence cannot be reproduced in adult life, because the transgression of racial taboo has more serious consequences. Moreover no marriage can be based purely on the make-believe of childhood, and the attempt to invest it with a deeper and lasting feeling eventually fails. Jim and Ella cannot transcend racial barriers, as Othello and Desdemona did, with uncompromising passion. Their marriage is based instead on caring affection, and the memory of childhood. The sensibility which evolves out of this is, however, destroyed by the fact of racial inequality. Despite her social failure and Jim's modest social success, Ella can still be dominant by virtue of being white. The positive qualities of the relationship are ruined by the racial imbalance created by society and cannot be redeemed by a passion of which neither is capable.

O'Neill captures the sense of mutual affection, and how it is marred, in the scene where Jim's devotion reveals a loss of racial pride. The most caring moment in the whole play then becomes a prelude to tragedy:

Ella. . . . (*Affectionately.*) Don't I know how fine you've been to me! You're the only person in the world who's stood by me—the only understanding person—and all after the rotten way I used to treat you.

Jim. But before that—way back so high—you treated me good. (*He smiles.*)

Ella. You've been white to me, Jim. (*She takes his hand.*)

Jim. White—to you!
Ella. Yes.
Jim. All love is white. I always loved you. (*This with the deepest humanity.*)
Ella. Even now—after all that's happened!
Jim. Always.
Ella. I like you, Jim—better than anyone else in the world.[11]

What follows is a predictable proposal of marriage on Jim's part. But this in turn is accompanied by an unpredictable expression of racial self-abasement. 'I don't want nothing . . . only to become your slave!—Yes, be your slave—your black slave that adores you as sacred!' Jim's genuine care for her is thus based on a false humility. Ella's response to that false humility is an equal if not greater betrayal of self. It leads her to regard her husband with a racist contempt. In her case too, virtue and self-betrayal are inseparable. Her critical questioning of the dominant role of the husband in marriage shows an important independence of will, but it only arises from the weakness of the particular man to whom she is married, and results in an unstable hatred which drives her slowly mad. So while she rejects the traditional role of the respectable middle-class wife, which is to encourage the social advancement of her husband, the rejection is never a matter of principle but only of personal hatred developing out of a complete sense of insecurity. Living in a black district, married to a black man and ostracised by her white friends, her husband becomes the convenient target to compensate for her growing sense of isolation, even though he is, ironically, the only person with the power to allay it.

The Uncle Tomism of Jim Harris effectively negates his heroic potential. And while it seems at times to be a structural weakness in the play, the alternative attitudes to racist oppression provide a necessary sense of balance. Early in the play his black friend Joe physically threatens him for attempting to become respectable and 'white':

Joe. What's all dis dressin' up and graduatin' and sayin' you gwine study be a lawyer? What's all dis denying you's a nigger—an wid de white boys listenin' to you say it! . . . Tell me before I wrecks yo' face in! Is you a nigger or isn't you? (*Shaking him.*)
   Is you a nigger, Nigger? Nigger, is you a nigger?
Jim (*Looking into his eyes quietly*). Yes. I'm a nigger.
   We're both niggers.[12]

A more positive and perceptive rejection of Jim's desire to conform comes from his sister, Hattie, who possesses a defiant and uncompromising racial pride. In a way, it is the two women who are the true protagonists in the play. Hattie's refusal to be intimidated by Ella's insulting behaviour acts as a dramatic yardstick of Jim's abandonment of racial pride. In the end her defiance is not decisive for she fails to break up the marriage. But the totally abject nature of her brother's tolerance prompts her into a response which evokes the horror of the chasm between the races, and shows her own feelings to be part of it. Sane where Ella is gradually going mad, the sense of total separation is equally deep in both women:

> Hattie. . . . Today she raved on about "Black! Black!" and cried because her skin was turning black—that you had poisoned her—
> Jim (*in anguish*). That's only when's she out of her mind.
> Hattie. And then suddenly she called me a dirty nigger . . .
> Jim (*torturedly*). She don't mean it! She isn't responsible for what she's saying!
> Hattie. I know she isn't—yet she is just the same. It's deep down in her or it wouldn't come out.
> Jim. Deep down in her people—not deep down in her.
> Hattie. I can't make such distinctions. The race in me, deep in me, can't stand it.[13]

The tragic experience of the play, of which Ella's madness is the major focus, is the recognition of the racial impasse which cannot be bridged. The response of Harris to his sister, with its emphasis on the universal, undoubtedly reflected O'Neill's own feelings. 'You with your fool talk of the black race and the white race!' he accuses her. 'Where does the human race get a chance to come in?' But the reasonableness of the sentiment is undermined by the tragic outcome of the action. The racial dimension has contributed to Ella's madness which in turn increases the impasse by the virulence of its racist sentiments. She is, in her madness, veering constantly from total contempt to total fear. This is conveyed most effectively in her response to the Congo mask which stares down at her from the shrinking walls of the apartment and appears to grow to a grotesquely horrifying size. The mask is as important to the play as the seagull in Chekhov or the wild duck in Ibsen. It is simultaneously a thing of beauty and a thing of terror, an aesthetic object which can be admired by a more distanced culture, but whose original intention was to stimulate fear and terror among those who saw it. The more her racial contempt grows the more the mask enhances her fear. Trying vainly to exorcise its demon, she lays the mask down, stabs through and pins it to the table, thus attempting to destroy its terror and only managing to destroy its beauty. The demon cannot be exorcised from her imagination.

There is only one last hope, to revert to the world of innocence before all involvement began, to the world of childhood where they can play at swapping racial identities, of being turn and turn about Painty Face and Jim Crow. There is the first echo here of Mary Tyrone and her wish to reject all relationships of her adult life. But for Ella the reversal to an idyllic and mythical innocence is no longer possible. The dream of it remains part of her madness, the impossible dream of transforming the past, where the difficult task of transforming the future has already been rejected through fear and terror. The sharp, focused intensity of this experience was never to be recaptured by O'Neill until the last two major works where he finds and develops themes of comparable, and so it proved, even greater stature. During the early twenties Ella Downey was the furthest point he reached in the living tragedy of contemporary America. From then on he sought it, first in the American past, and later, as a mature writer in the past of his own life. Meanwhile his concern with contemporary America led into a vogue for bewildering dramatic experiments over which he exercised little artistic control and which ended up as clumsy and self-conscious innovation. During this period the two historical tragedies *Desire under the Elms* and *Mourning Becomes Electra* retained the kernel of the tragic experience at a time when experimentalism led him into indifferent forays to uncover the new middle-class suburban world of contemporary America.

10 Eugene O'Neill II: The Life Remembered

After the contemporary drama of the sea and the city, O'Neill's work took two alternative directions. A new corpus of experimental work developed set in middle-class New England, a setting both suburban and contemporary. A more formulaic historical drama, tragic in nature, came with two major works *Desire under the Elms* and *Mourning Becomes Electra*. The experimental work was largely a failure. The uncertainty of writing about middle-class or academic life was interwoven with the uncertainty of handling unwieldy theatrical devices such as the experiments with masks in *The Great God Brown* and the prolonged dramatic aside in *Strange Interlude*. *Strange Interlude* took Freud too seriously and tried to create the dramatic equivalent of the stream of consciousness emerging in the novel. *The Great God Brown* took theatricality too literally as O'Neill experimented with the idea of having his personae exchange masks and identities at will. In the lesser works where there was less experimentation; *The First Man, Diff'rent* and *Welded*, the resulting bourgeois dramas were extremely banal. The crisis occurred because O'Neill wanted to extend the stylistic range of his work, but in doing so, he often sacrificed cogency of theme.

It is quite clear that the two historical works, *Desire under the Elms* and the *Electra* trilogy stand apart from all the others of this period. The use of historical perspective is part of a bolder attempt to understand the puritanical roots of modern America, and to come to terms with the Protestant culture of New England in which O'Neill's own family were considered social upstarts and Catholic outsiders. But given these concerns, the social potential for tragedy is limited. The Puritan heritage is presented as grim, joyless and authoritarian. It has the same suffocating grip on much of the New England drama as does Catholicism in Murray's drama of rural Ireland. But whereas the Catholic ambience was something Murray absorbed almost completely, O'Neill's attitude to puritanism was detached and critical. His drama has a dimension inconceivable in the Irish circumspection of the same period—the dimension of a repressed sexuality.

The cultural context of this critical portrait of puritanism can be found in the bohemian culture of New York up to and during the Great War when the sexual mores of middle-class Protestantism were being openly denounced and replaced by alternative styles of life. O'Neill's historical tragedies explore in rather different ways the strength of the puritanical roots of America. They were a sharp antidote to the counter-cultural presumption that traditional forms of constraint can be overthrown without undue effort once they are identified and mocked. In *Desire under the Elms* there is a very bold, striking presentation of the polarity between familial repression and sexual desire. Here the forms of religious and psychological constraint are intertwined and the trees of the title become a visual symbol of their suffocating effect. Both the father and the stepmother in the play, though in conflict with one another, represent two alternative sources of domination over Eben Cabot, and he can free himself from neither. The 'two enormous elms' which 'bend their trailing branches down over the roof' are intended to possess what O'Neill openly calls 'a sinister maternity, a crushing jealous absorption'. Alongside familial enslavement to the grim patriarch of the rural household Eben experiences all the murderous vicissitudes of the Oedipal trap.

The capacity for tragic alienation, and genuine heroism, is subsequently lost. He can only truly hate his father by loving his surrogate mother and falling victim to her form of domination instead. The affair between Eben and Abbie, though it is a transgression and a violation of Ephraim Cabot's authority, never presents a fundamental challenge to it. There is a scene near the end of the play where Abbie explains to Eben that she has killed their illegitimate son. For a moment Eben misunderstands her to mean Ephraim instead. Abbie's reply is one of the most revealing moments of the play: 'No! No! Not him! (*Laughing distractedly*.) But that's what I ought t' done, hain't it? I oughte killed him instead! Why didn't you tell me?'[1] The authority of the patriarch remains too formidable to be challenged in this way, and the desire to murder him is transient and impulsive. It cannot psychologically take root. Having conducted their illicit affair in the family household, neither Eben nor Abbie can free themselves from the guilt that ensues. Eben is subject not only to the greater physical strength of his father and the psychological domination of his stepmother, but also to the guilt at his own actions, a guilt which eventually causes his downfall.

At this point, O'Neill rejoins Strindberg. It is the patriarch who is the victim of wrongdoing, who, injured and affronted, has to bear his own 'lonesomeness'. But in the social and historical context of the play the lonesomeness of Cabot is not tragic, nor the estrangement irreparable, for instead he becomes the instrument of puritan retribution. When Abbie confesses the killing of the child and the affair which has preceded it, he changes from rural tyrant into self-righteous avenger. Stiffening his body 'into a rigid line' and hardening 'his face into a stony mask', he declares: 'I got t' be—like a stone—a rock o' judgment!' While the lovers accept their guilt and punishment, Cabot's own behaviour is exonerated. The play thus moves from criticism of the father toward a position of increasing sympathy, and as it does so, the potential for tragedy evaporates. The sense of Cabot's moral injury is contrived, the passion of the two lovers compromised by ultimate acceptance of the structure of familial authority even though the personal hatred is real. Intentionally or not, O'Neill leaves us with a triumphant male puritanism inimical to tragedy.

The case of *Mourning Becomes Electra* is more complex. Broadly speaking the plot follows the Orestian trilogy, but since it takes place in nineteenth-century New England and is for the most part a social drama, it departs from the version of Aeschylus at several key points. Ezra Mannon (Agamemnon) returns from the American Civil War to his New England mansion, to be rejected by his wife Christine (Clytemnestra) who is having a secret affair with a ship's captain, Adam Bryant (Aegisthus), currently working for one of the Mannon shipping lines. Bryant offers to kill Mannon for Christine, but Christine decides instead to discreetly poison her husband and confess her infidelity to him before he dies. Her daughter Lavinia (Electra) becomes suspicious and confesses her misgivings to her brother Orin (Orestes) who has himself just returned from the war, disillusioned with bloodshed and brutality. She finds the box containing the poison administered by Christine and uses it to convince Orin of the need to murder Bryant, whom she suspects of being the instigator. Orin murders Bryant on board his ship then returns to the mansion to confess the murder to his mother. On hearing of Bryant's fate, Christine shoots herself in despair. In the third part of the trilogy, Orin and Lavinia return from an ocean trip on one of the Mannon ships, in which they have visited the idyllic islands of the South Seas. They are haunted by their past actions. Orin has adopted the austere manner and expression of his dead father, while Lavinia, previously repressed in her desires has taken on the dress and the sensuality of her dead mother, her spirit set free by the islands they visited. The murder, and the incestuous nature of their relationship on the Islands, prevents them from readjusting to New England life and to the prospect of marriage. Orin kills himself and Lavinia stays behind the shutters of the mansion to live alone with the Mannon dead.

In the Greek tragedy, killing and retribution are the reflection of a pattern of divine will, the will of Zeus and Apollo, and the tragic human figures of the drama are the instruments of their will, their fate beyond human control. O'Neill, in secularising the drama has to release human will and action from the chains of divine necessity. It is no longer divinely but humanly ordained by the individual yearnings of his tragic personae. Here the dialectic of human freedom and divine necessity is replaced by a dialectic O'Neill saw as socially and historically appropriate to the period and its setting, the dialectic of puritanism and sensuality. The Mannon household is one of repressed desire, whose eventual fulfilment means violation of the moral order upon which it is based. Christine's adultery is the first violation and the catalyst to catastrophe. The Mannon children feel they have to uphold the moral order by avenging their father's death, but their own desires lead them to a further violation of the moral order, incestuous desire, transforming the murder of Bryant and their mother's suicide into a source of recurrent guilt which can never be expiated.

The dialectic of puritanism and sensuality is thus superimposed on the structure of the Greek myth. It presents us with a forced marriage of classical tragedy and puritan sensibility which is ultimately unworkable. Or rather, each works spasmodically at the expense of the other throughout the play. The dilemma is captured by one of the drama's recurrent images, the exterior of the family mansion, described by Christine Mannon as a 'pagan temple struck like a mask on puritan grey ugliness'. Figurally speaking, the New England persona of each character is also stuck like a mask onto its Greek original, limited by the extremely formulaic nature of the plot. Without the use of the Greek myth, any tragedy would have been unthinkable. But with it, the tragedy is decisively limited. It is not merely the limitations imposed by the action, where there is an intensive sequence of violent action and emotional response to that action. It is O'Neill's alternative figural conception which is at fault. There are contrived symmetries of possession, jealousy and desire which act like a straightjacket on the dramatic development of the individual personae. Lavinia's hatred of her mother is enhanced by her own repressed desire for Bryant, Orin's anger at his mother's adultery by his own repressed Oedipal attraction. As brother and sister, incestuous attraction becomes a surrogate for respective attractions towards mother and father, and at the same time, the experience and guilt of going away together forces brother and sister to adopt the manners and physical characteristics of their parents, and even to undergo an identical emotional confrontation with each other. The metaphor of incest then acts as a constraint on the individual development and freewill of the children. The family, even in its dissolution, is an emotional and psychological trap, from which they cannot escape. The symmetry of sinful desire, the staged exchanging of identities as if they were no more than masks, gives the play a certain camp quality which makes it border upon melodrama. Action, deprived of its divine and noble context, is no longer sustained by motive. The motivation O'Neill offers in its place, though boldly conceived, cannot totally succeed.

The Mannon family are not, like their Greek counterparts, a family of noble warriors. Instead they are a family of puritan businessmen. O'Neill is thus able to convey a contemporary notion of fate through their economic importance. But it is not accompanied by any conception of nobility. Their capitalist undertaking is monumental, but it is not a heroic undertaking, for they are not true warriors. The point is made by the appearance of Bryant the paramour as a romantic adventurer 'dressed with an almost foppish extravagance with touches of studied carelessness, as if a romantic Byronic appearance were the ideal in mind'. But Bryant, though a maverick is still a loyal servant of the shipping line and an illegitimate son of an earlier Mannon into the bargain. He is in no sense a truly independent alternative to the Mannon way of life.

The play thus reveals O'Neill's failure to forge genuine links between tragic nobility and dynastic capitalism. Though it does incorporate the real division between the puritanical and adventurous components of nineteenth-century American capitalism, this is super-imposed rather than organic. Indeed the social modalities of the drama are subordinate to the compressed dramatic action which has more in common with the melodrama of the popular theatre O'Neill knew so well through the acting of his father, and which he detested so much. That it never actually degenerates into melodrama is a testament to O'Neill's achievement. But the formula he presents lends itself to easy vulgarisation. The social melodrama of popular fiction in our own age can be seen as a vulgarisation of O'Neill's formula. The formulaic novel of Harold Robbins, Irving Shaw, Irving Wallace and Jacqueline Suzanne is, as often as not, an exotic variation on the lurid melodrama of dynastic capitalism. Its main theme is the diluted guilt eating away at the conscience of those who have ruthlessly and successfully pursued sex, wealth, status and power. But deprived of the puritanical context with which O'Neill originally invested it, its cosmetic confections cannot hope to convey the same horror of violation and retribution.

These two plays proved that in moving to an extended historical form, O'Neill had in part dissipated his sense of the tragic. The puritan tradition was too deeply ingrained into the nation-building process of the United States to convey that sense of social alienation necessary for modern tragedy. The sense of historical perspective was clearly something which O'Neill felt to be lacking from the early work, but it was not until the end of his life that he finally struck what for him was to be the perfect balance between the life of the moment and the life past. He did this, as a mature artist, through the life remembered. But until the period between 1939 and 1941 when the two late master-pieces were written, a whole epoch of American history seemed to have passed the dramatist by. Why had O'Neill, the most contemporary of dramatists after the war made no artistic response whatsoever to the crisis of the Great Depression?

The question is exceptionally difficult to answer. But the formative social and political experiences of O'Neill's life did belong to a different decade. His own sensibility was nurtured during a time when the American trade unions were more socialist than they had ever been, or were ever to be again, and when the flowering of a radical counter-culture which produced writers like John Dos Passos, Upton Sinclair, Edmund Wilson and John Reed, created a direct intellectual challenge to the American political system. The end of the war, however, saw the collapse of the socialist dream, the disintegration of the I.W.W. and the emergence of a brutal and populist anti-socialism portrayed so well by Scott Fitzgerald in his short story *May Day*. The cultural and political stimulus to O'Neill's early writing came from the crest of a wave which had already broken. There was to be no further elective affinity between O'Neill, the dramatist, and the social crises of America. Lawson and Clifford Odets were the playwrights who fashioned the social experience of the Depression era into live theatre. Significantly the Electra trilogy, written between 1929 and 1931, was completed while O'Neill was away from the United States in France. His sense of contemporary crisis only returned to him when Hitler invaded Europe and by then the last phase of his writing was already well under way. He was already writing *The Iceman Cometh* and planning *Long Day's Journey into Night*.

It is altogether too facile to accuse O'Neill of being insensitive to the social upheavals of the thirties. Despite the high level of unemployment, social dislocation and personal ruin, the New Deal was able to contain and dilute the mass expression of political discontent. Moreover much of the socialist politics of the thirties was compromised by its Soviet connections, and many of the mandates for proletarian literature and art were sterile formulas based on the new Soviet doctrine of socialist realism. O'Neill himself, though now politically agnostic, had not been mellowed by commercial success. His intense dislike of the profit motive and of American capitalism was to last all his life. In this basic disaffection lies part of the reason for the continuity of his work and his desire to go back to an earlier period of his life. True, the biographical impulse to return was very great, but that impulse cannot be extrapolated from its social context. It was what the period meant to O'Neill, in so many different ways, that made him set both the major plays in the same year, 1912, a short time before he had been forced to enter a sanitorium for treatment of tuberculosis and subsequently decided to embark on a writing career. The threshold of transition in his own life as a writer is linked to the promise of transformation in American life as a whole, a promise which, in his own eyes, was never fulfilled.

The two plays present a dual study in contrast. First, there is the familiar division between New York and New England, but, in addition, an important cleavage in the use of autobiographical data. *Long Day's Journey into Night* is specifically based on O'Neill's family and includes no one else. *The Iceman Cometh* borrows from his bar acquaintances in the seedier areas of West Side New York and no direct portrayal of himself or his family is to be found. The latter play is the longest of O'Neill's major works and as a result, one of the least-performed masterpieces of the twentieth century. This famine of performance was inaugurated by his own refusal of artistic compromise. While he had been willing to cut earlier plays like *Strange Interlude* for commercial purposes, he was adamant that in its first production *The Iceman* should run its full length of nearly four and a half hours. For most directors, the temptation to cut it must be very great. The play is deliberately repetitive and rhetorical and at times restatement seems to add little to what has already been expressed. But the strength of the play is cumulative like a musical symphony. The restatement and recurrence are progressive. Taken together action and dialogue have an almost operatic impact upon the eye and the ear. Out of this cumulative strength the immense power of the play's tragic climax unfolds. It is *The Iceman*, not *Mourning Becomes Electra*, which approximates most closely to the lyrical and auratic power of Greek tragedy.

One thing which stands out, and makes the play a masterpiece of its own age, is the extraordinary use of the choric device. The inhabitants of Harry Hope's backroom bar are not merely a choral appendage to Hickey, the salesman, but have their own collective destiny. They are both collective hero and dissonant chorus to their own fate. The final euphoric chant of the play is shouted in 'enthusiastic jeering chorus':

The days grow hot, O Babylon!
'Tis cool beneath the willow trees!

Out of dissonance and chaos, it reaffirms the collective identity and the collective experience of the ensemble. The musical harmonies here and throughout recall Chekhov, and by contrast the one play with which *The Iceman* has been systematically compared, Gorky's *The Lower Depths*, seems chaotically ill-composed.

There is no doubt that the Russian play had been a formative influence on O'Neill's writing. He saw it as the outstanding example of revolutionary proletarian drama in the twentieth century, and the borrowing of the play's theme is obvious. But merely to see the difference between the two plays in terms of their ending, contrasting Gorky's optimism and O'Neill's pessimism, is rather myopic. The more central difference lies in the role of the major protagonist in each play. Whereas Luka mysteriously disappears after having set into motion the actions and suspicions leading to the breakdown of community, Hickey himself is the tragic figure of O'Neill's drama remaining at the centre of the dramatic action until his fate is sealed. Both are redeemers but the crucial shift of role is clearly apparent. While Luka is a mere catalyst, Hickey is a tragic protagonist. Because the link between the redeemer and the collective is more organic, it is also more tragic. In this respect, Hickey is closer in sensibility and enactment to Gregers Werle. Though it appears deceptively simple at times, the salesman's idealism is equally complex, and its appropriate dramatic expression is integral to the success of the play.

This complexity is sometimes obscured by the performance of Hickey as a frantic evangelical salesman obsessed by his own powers of exhortation. His extended speeches are then delivered one-dimension-ally in an exhortatory manner with little variation in rhythm or tone. But vary they must, as sharply in places as the mood of Ella Downey or Mary Tyrone. This complexity can be just as easily obscured by critical references to the religious model upon which the confrontation of Hickey and the drunken roomers is based—that of Christ and his disciples at the Last Supper. For Hickey is more than a failed Christ figure come to visit his twelve reluctant disciples, and offer them salvation. The whole play should be seen more as a Nietzschean negation of the New Testament myth in which the redeemer himself is insane and actively attempts to deny the redemption he offers. On a metaphysical level, the denial of redemption leads to the hero's madness. Hickey is both Christ and Antichrist, saving no one, yet finally himself crucified.

The dramatic context of the denial of redemption, is not, however, metaphysical. It is social. In the relationship between the expectant barflies and the magnanimous salesman, O'Neill establishes a social correlative fundamental to the United States of his own lifetime. It is the relationship between the purgatory of social failure and the promise of the American Dream. The sense of squalor and degradation is perhaps not as great as in Gorky. But the sense of social downfall is correspondingly stronger, and the feel of that downward movement is preserved in Larry Slade's pronouncement to Parritt, the young newcomer to the bar:

> What is it? It's the No Chance Saloon. It's Bedrock Bar, the End of the Line Café, the Bottom of the Sea Rathskeller. Don't you notice the beautiful calm in the atmosphere? That's because it's the last harbour. No one here has to worry about where they're going next because there is no farther they can go.[2]

Yet there is an important addendum to this grim image of finality. Even at the lowest level of spiritual and material existence, it remains impossible to live without some residual hope: '. . . Even here they keep up the appearance of life with a few harmless pipe-dreams about their yesterdays and tomorrows . . .'. The keyword is 'pipe-dream'. It occurs a myriad of times during the course of the play from the mouth of almost every figure even when, as is usually the case, its existence is being vehemently denied.

At the beginning of the play the arrival of Hickey is awaited with great eagerness, not only because he has the money to buy round after round of drinks, but because he has the knack of encouraging a drunken camaraderie that the inmates of the saloon are too demoralised to generate of their own accord. The reform of his character, announced soon after his arrival, comes as a complete shock to them and suggests an imminent confrontation. The hard-drinking narrator of dirty jokes appears to have turned into a moral crusader exhorting them to give up their alcoholic ways and make the effort to return to their former more productive lives. To this extent Hickey does resemble Luka in Gorky's play. But the resemblance is only superficial. Beneath Hickey's evangelism is a hidden dimension which makes it apparent that the crusade is part of a strategy, at best a ruse to help reveal to the inmates a more fundamental aspect of their existence. For Hickey expects each of them in turn to fail to come to terms with the outside world, and to return one by one to the backroom bar, dejected and defeated. It then becomes clear that Hickey is not the reformed salesman of the American Dream but something more sinister. The prophet of the ideology of individual self-help and success emerges as the very opposite, a harbinger of destruction who by his action unmasks the very ideology to which he appears to bear allegiance.

His idealism is not, like that of Gregers, based purely on a fundamental misreading of the lives of others, but on the false connection he makes between his own experience and what he is demanding of them. He wants them to kill off their pipe-dreams of a better tomorrow because he himself has already been forced to do so:

> I've been through the mill and had to face a worse bastard in myself than any of you will have to in yourselves. I know you become such a coward you'll grab at any excuse to get out of killing your pipe dreams. And yet, as I've told you over and over, it's exactly those same damned tomorrow dreams which keep you from making peace with yourself. So you've got to kill them like I did mine.[3]

Like Gregers, Hickey is attempting the impossible. But whereas Gregers can blithely ignore the accusation of his failure at the end of the play, Hickey's very life depends on the possibility of success in his enterprise. His attempt to reveal to the roomers their fundamental inadequacy is the prelude to an even more extraordinary revelation of his own failure. His self-confession is not an intentional unmasking, but an unintended result of his failure to unmask and exorcise the pipe-dreams of others. Once doubt begins to creep into the whole enterprise, the mask begins to slip from his face. Slade, the ex-anarchist

philosopher, the most intellectual of the roomers and the one with the
most to lose, first recognises the weakness. The process of counter-
exposure then begins. After Harry Hope, venturing outside the saloon
for the first time in twenty years, stops dead in the middle of the street
and scurries back like a frightened rabbit, the peace which Hickey
promised him by exorcising his pipe-dream seems as far away as ever:

> Hope (*dully*). What's wrong with this booze? There's no kick in it.
> Rocky (*worriedly*). Jees, Larry, Hugo had it right. He does look like
> he'd croaked.
> Hickey (*annoyed*). Dont't be a damned fool! Give him time. He's
> coming along all right. (*He calls to Hope with a first trace of underlying
> uneasiness.*) You're all right aren't you, Harry?
> Hope (*dully*). I want to pass out like Hugo.
> Larry (*turns to Hickey with bitter anger*). It's the peace of death you've
> brought him!
> Hickey (*for the first time loses his temper*).That's a lie! (*But he controls this
> instantly and grins.*) Well, well you did manage to get a rise out of
> me that time.[4]

Slade has at last come to understand the extreme nihilism of
Hickey's vision. The alternative to the alcoholic pipe-dream, the
residue of the ideal as O'Neill conceives it, is death. The illusory peace
of which Hickey has spoken is permanent oblivion. Hickey's vision also
has repercussions for the dramatic action itself. What it entails is a total
destruction of the last elements of figural prophecy. The pipe-dreams
of the roomers are the essential base condition for that figural sense to
be conveyed as dramatic action. The dramatic space of the play
depends on them and is paradoxically enlarged by Hickey's attempt to
destroy them, for the drunken choric elements of the action, whether as
rambling reminiscence or absurd aspiration are both thematically and
aesthetically indestructible. Inevitably, Hickey must fail. There is then
a dual basis for the creation of Hickey as a tragic figure. Not only is his
dream a dream to end all human dreams, his destructiveness, if
successful, would annihilate tragedy itself. The general failure to
destroy tragedy turns him into a tragic hero. O'Neill has explored in
his play the bedrock conditions for the figural dramatisation of human
life and the *figura* is vindicated.

Thematically speaking, the tragic nature of Hickey's failure arises
from his own involvement in the life he preaches for others. He tries to
mould the inmates after the pattern of his own concealed destiny, and

when that fails, has to reveal on the point of madness his own failure—
the murder of his wife. Unlike Melville's confidence man who is the
sum of all his ingenious disguises with no basic self, it is Hickey's
intractable self which is his own undoing. The confession to
murder turns the inspired crusader into a helpless crazed victim,
waiting to be led away by detectives to trial and to the electric chair
while the inmates of the 'No Chance Saloon' are made aware in
amazement of a worse fate than their own which they have managed to
avoid. In a wider context, Hickey's crusade *against* the American
Dream is similar to Nietzsche's incestuous revolt against Christian
redemption. It mirrors the pattern of the redemptive crusade by
turning bitterly and uncompromisingly against it. Yet it retains the
style and the pattern while forsaking the substance, and disintegrates
into insanity.

The relevance of the subplot to the main action is not always
apparent because of its dramatic looseness, but in the last act is helps to
throw into focus both the power of Hickey's vision and its relation to
revolutionary idealism. The subplot hinges upon a particular kind of
absence crucial to the play—that of women except as prostitutes. Both
Hickey's murdered wife and Parritt's betrayed mother have a white
purity of absent virtue, a virtue in fact which sometimes strains
credibility, but at the same time exempts their sex from the self-
betrayals which brought their menfolk to the 'No Chance Saloon'.
Parritt's guilt at betraying his mother and the Movement to the
authorities, and Slade's subsequent refusal to recognise Parritt as his
son, are often clumsy diversions from the main dramatic development.
But ultimately they dovetail with the main plot since Larry combines a
growing recognition of Hickey's dementia with a stubborn refusal to
face the truth about Parritt, and in so doing reveals the link between
the insight of intellect and the weakness of personality.

Slade's growing awareness of Hickey's role as a messenger of death is
connected with the years of political activism he has spent and now
rejected in disillusionment. Because of this political connection, he is
the most ideologically resistant to Hickey and yet in the end, the only
one who is really seduced. His vulnerability can only be understood in
the context of his earlier rejection of the movement, a rejection he
makes explicit to Parritt at great length:

One was myself, and another was my comrades and the last was the
breed of swine called men in general. For myself I was forced to
admit, at the end of thirty years' devotion to the Cause, that I was

never made for it. I was born condemned to be one of those who had to see all sides of a question. When you're damned like that, the questions multiply for you until in the end it's all question and no answer! As history proves, to be a worldly success at anything, especially revolution, you have to wear blinkers like a horse and see only straight in front of you. You have to see, too, that this is all black, and that is all white. As for my comrades in the Great Cause, I felt as Horace Walpole did about England that he could love it if it weren't for the people in it. The material the ideal free society must be constructed from is men themselves and you can't build a marble temple out of a mixture of mud and manure. When a man's soul isn't a sow's ear, it will be time enough to dream of silk purses.[5]

His ability to see through the pretensions of the Movement gives him the resources to resist Hickey's crusade, but his disenchantment with the Movement and the apathy that disenchantment engenders make him vulnerable to Hickey's message of lasting peace with oneself. The peace Hickey offers eliminates the political contradiction which has always haunted Slade. As he remarks at the end, death is the only real alternative to his basic weakness, 'the fool looking with pity at two sides of everything till the day I die!' He is, in his own words, 'the only real convert to death Hickey ever made'.

Why does Slade lack the power of the other roomers to survive? The answer is that his past failures are more haunting and absolute. While the play cannot be seen as a parable about the failure of American socialism—especially since Slade, Hugo and Parritt represent a more anarchistic faction—it does transmit a deep sense of opportunity lost and never again to be offered. The life remembered joins the political failure to the social and the personal and it was the nearest that O'Neill ever came to writing full-length political drama. But the tragic alienation he engenders derives precisely from an absolute with-drawal. Harry Hope's saloon is a refuge for the apolitical and the antisocial, and there can be no possibility of reabsorption. Even Hickey, though he pretends not to, realises this. The saloon represents a residual but invincible affront to the ideals of American life, not by casting them into oblivion but by clinging to them with a stubborn perversity and at the same time, distorting them out of all recognition. The transformation from alienation to strife occurs with Hickey's failure to annihilate the grotesquerie of the ideal, the bar-room pipe-dream, and the horrified recognition of what that quest for annihilation means in normal social life. What Hickey demands of the inmates is exemplified in a normal respectable social context by the murder of his devoted and forgiving wife. The tragic horror conveyed to them as outcast chorus is the transgression of the normal by their would-be redeemer, and this transgression is greater than anything they themselves have managed to accomplish.

O'Neill's work here goes beyond questions of political idealism and disenchantment. It expresses a profound concern with the impact of capitalism on the American way of life, an impact which has persisted throughout the century despite, and sometimes because of, the vagaries of political opposition. While revolutionary idealism has been volatile and at times perfidious, the system to which it is a response has prevailed permanently in all areas of life. In O'Neill's mature work this was the guarantor of tragic alienation and its transformation to a full realised tragic strife. But the work was historical within the span of O'Neill's lifetime since the constancy of his opposition to the American way of life was tempered by the sense of lost promise. The latter gives the vital historical dimension to the former which is both historical and contemporary, a part of time past and time present and also of our own age, time future, when the themes of the play strike a chord of instant recognition through their profoundly prophetic qualities.

This holds equally of *Long Day's Journey into Night* which is usually seen as a profoundly personal statement about personal matters because of its immense autobiographical content. The concentration on the nuclear family and the use of the family living-room as the single setting could easily be seen as a relapse into traditional naturalism after the bold experimentation of the earlier plays. But this reversion to the classical Unities, accomplished by O'Neill with a remarkable rigour, expresses with an even greater intensity than *Iceman* the alienation from bourgeois life so necessary to modern tragedy. Such an alienation could not be created if the audience merely witnessed the personalised disintegration of the bourgeois family. There has to be something more. What this is, remains at first sight difficult to pin down. It is not enough to say the Tyrones are not a typical bourgeois family. There is a more profound sense of displacement at the centre of middle-class life and family life in general which is built up as the drama progresses to the point of tragic climax, where O'Neill shows that there is no real centre to family life at all.

The opening scene starts on a deceptive note of casual domestic happiness. James Tyrone affectionately teases his wife, Mary, about her putting on weight. From the dining room the voices of their two sons Jamie and Edmund can be heard in laughter. But soon the image of domestic contentment has all but evaporated. In its place there is quarrel and recrimination, wounding and suffering, accusation and confession. These are as much the consequence of tragic alienation as its cause, and in themselves do not lead to irreparable breakdown. No one deserts the household, no one is murdered within its walls. The conflict is cyclical and recurrent, an echo of old wounds and grievances and a renewal of them. In modern theatre, this recycled animosity usually derives from the sense of imprisonment it engenders in the household's three-walled room. But in O'Neill the household is not a bourgeois prison and recriminations do not achieve pathos by being bounced off the walls. The Tyrone's house is a rented summer house which they will soon leave, and while the action never leaves it, that action bespeaks a deep rootlessness. The trapped family does not belong there, and never has.

The life of the family has always been based on the theatre, constantly travelling from one town to another, and from one hotel to another, its head an ageing matinée idol whose hour of glory is past. The two sons have inherited the same restlessness. The location provides only a provisional unity, a temporary homecoming, and the domestic setting has no domestic spirit. The mother, who as a typical middle-class woman is expected to provide the aura of domesticity and homeliness, pays ritual homage to her expected role and condemns her family for failing to support her. They have, it is true, all the material possessions—servants, car and chauffeur, and even investments in property. But Mary Tyrone pinpoints the anguished lack in a tirade against her husband:

> . . . Oh, I'm so sick and tired of pretending that this is a home! You won't help me! You won't put yourself out the least bit! You really don't know how to act in a home! You don't really want one! You never have wanted one! —never since the day we were married! You should have remained a bachelor and lived in second-rate hotels and entertained your friends in bar-rooms! (*She adds rather strangely as if she were talking aloud to herself rather than to Tyrone.*) Then nothing would ever have happened.[6]

Yet her accusation concluded in the last line is followed by an even more disturbing statement. It then becomes clear, despite her periodic protestations, her concern over Edmund's health and her bitter attacks on her husband, that she has abdicated from her conventional family role and long ceased trying to create a 'home'.

In the dramatic development of the play a remarkable switch takes place. Ostensibly the main plot concerns the fate of Edmund and the consequences of his tubercular illness. But as concern with his illness intensifies within the family, so gradually the focus switches to his mother and the deeper illness which has already destroyed her. As her entreaties of 'maternal solicitude' toward her son increase, it becomes increasingly clear that her anxiety for his welfare is an attempt to ignore the seriousness of the illness. She wishes no external source of anxiety to impinge upon her. The more she protests her maternal and conjugal caring, the more she tries to wrap herself in a cocoon of her own making, and to seek out protective oblivion. Through her opium addiction she has fled household and family into the interior of her imagination, and she can no longer be called upon as the necessary anchor for family life. The void is terrifying because it underlies the recognisable male vices—the drinking of father and sons alike, the whoring of Jamie, the meanness of James Tyrone, and the introverted agonies of Edmund. All show a greater rootedness in the world than the tragic withdrawals of Mary.

Edmund's bohemian decadence, his fragile sensibility, and his contempt for bourgeois normality give him all the credentials of a tragic hero, a candidate for death through fatal illness in a family which can neither truly care nor understand. In this respect, Mary's rebuke to him is like that of an outraged mother to an overgrown child. But when Edmund jokes about the possibility of his death, the outrage turns into panic, revealing in her the malaise she attributes to her son:

> Mary (*suddenly turns to them in a confused panic of frightened anger*). I won't have it! (*She stamps her foot.*) Do you hear, Edmund! Such morbid nonsense! Saying you're going to die! It's the books you read! Nothing but sadness and death! Your father shouldn't allow you to have them! And some of the poems you've written yourself are even worse! You'd think you didn't want to live! A boy of your age with everything before him! It's just a pose you get out of books! You're not really sick at all.[7]

The next minute she will be teasing Edmund affectionately telling him he wants 'to be petted and spoiled and made a fuss over'. But the focus has switched in that moment from the iconoclastic poet to the mother who acts out the role of motherhood while rejecting it in its totality, devoutly wishing that it had never happened to her.

The family loyalty which underlies the family conflicts is in some senses remarkable. Jamie and Edmund are both grown men, both old enough to have broken all family ties if such ties should interfere with their personal ambitions. The loyalty cannot just be explained by compassion, which is so often betrayed, nor by conventional forms of dependence. The family stays together because of the connecting links between the different forms of alienation which each of them suffer, forms which also link the two generations, some present at the family's inception and others developing through its prodigal sons. The dramatic development of the play must therefore move in the direction of the past, of what underlies the present predicament. Here the figure of James Tyrone is significantly different from the Strindbergian patriarch O'Neill created in a number of his earlier plays. He is certainly head of the household, and certainly the most socially conventional member of the family, his investments in property clearly intended as a means of attaining greater wealth and respectability. But his family background and acting career separate him from bourgeois convention in ways which have a lasting and irreversible impact upon the Tyrone family.

The mode of dramatic revelation works toward establishing a truer identity for the respectable head of the household. Tyrone is a combination of his Irish background and its peasant origins and his successful acting career. According to O'Neill's stage directions he should be 'a simple unpretentious man whose inclinations are still close to his humble beginnings and his Irish farmer forebears'. Yet at the same time 'the actor shows in all his unconscious habits of speech, movement and gesture. These have the quality of belonging to a studied technique.'[8] The physicality of the man embodies directly the two main aspects of his life, and both belie his middle-class persona even when both at times are used to express the most conventional and moralistic of attitudes. Of key importance here is Mary's account of her first meeting with Tyrone, as a great matinée idol playing Shakespeare and French melodrama. The description comes in the form of a reverie, recounted to Cathleen the servant girl when the opium begins to take effect:

> My father took me to see him at first. It was a play about the French Revolution and the leading part was a nobleman. I couldn't take my eyes off him. I wept when he was thrown into prison—and then was so mad at myself because I was afraid my eyes and nose would be red. My father had said we would go backstage to his dressing room after the play and we did . . . And he was handsomer than my

wildest dream, in his make-up and his nobleman's costume that was so becoming to him. He was different from all ordinary men, like someone from another world.[9]

This of course portrays the romantic infatuation of a young girl. But it is more. It is an image held and fixed in Mary's mind for the rest of her life, and intensified by the resort to opium. In her withdrawn world where as she claims 'only the past when you were happy is real', the image has more power over her than any of the difficulties of her present life. She must make it immune from the meanness of her husband, the drunkenness and whoring of Jamie, and the illness of Edmund. The source of the image is itself of vital social importance. The performance which so captivates her is that of a doomed aristocratic hero. The aura of nobility absent from the drama of American life in O'Neill's own plays, is captured reflexively through the grand roles from which James Tyrone derived his acting reputation. Only the theatre in America, by importing plays from Europe, can recreate the aura of nobility which the New World cannot propagate of its own accord. But the theatrical aura of the noble which captures Mary's heart is far removed from the reality of the actor's life, the sordid existence of 'week after week of one-night stands, in dirty rooms of filthy hotels, eating bad food'. Far from domesticating that aura, marriage and family life take second place to the debilitating means of producing it. There is no stable family life and no fixed abode. The romanticism of living with a famous actor is dissipated with Edmund's difficult birth and the subsequent addiction to opium, recommended to Mary by a quack doctor to alleviate her pain. As Tyrone aspires from his rigid Catholic standpoint to the wealth and material success promised by the American Dream, Mary Tyrone becomes the victim of the arduous and unconventional means through which alone he has any chance of attaining it.

The theatrical image of the doomed nobleman cannot be reduced to a cosmetic product of Tyrone's acting ability. The melodrama at which Tyrone was so powerfully adept, and which O'Neill in real life hated so much, drew its strength from another social source which went far beyond theatrical skill. That strength came from the desperation of poverty in a first-generation Irishman who knew the exploitation of his class and race at first hand. That he has to remind Edmund of it, shows how far it can be overlooked within the space of a single generation. But its significance is still with all of them:

There was no damned romance in our poverty. Twice we were evicted from the miserable hovel we call home, with my mother's few sticks of furniture thrown out into the street, and my mother and sisters crying. I cried, too, though I tried hard not to. At ten years old. There was no more school for me. I worked twelve hours a day in a machine shop learning to make files. A dirty barn of a place where rain dripped through the roof, where you roasted in summer, and there was no stove in winter and your hands got numb with cold, where the only light came through two small filthy windows, so on grey days I'd have to sit bent over with my eyes almost touching the files in order to see! . . . It was in those days I learned to be a miser. A dollar was worth so much then. And once you've learned a lesson it's hard to unlearn. You have to look for bargains and if I took this state farm for a bargain you have to forgive me.[10]

His speech is a defence of the attempt to find Edmund a cheap sanitorium and so gravely risk his son's health. But the emphasis on poverty also strikes an appropriate balance with Mary's drugged reminiscence, showing the material basis upon which the future matinée idol had managed to survive before his acting career. The dialectic of the noble and the proletarian is thus revealed in the contrast between the acting persona which captivates his female admirers and the grinding poverty of an exploited child immigrant desperately trying to support his fatherless family. It is only when this dual background is in focus that Tyrone's grotesque maladaptation to the role of man of property makes any sense. Tyrone's thrift is not that of the Protestant Ethic, and in a strictly capitalistic sense he has never come to realise the value of money at all. At different stages in the life of the family, its two tragic figures, Edmund and Mary have suffered immeasurably from his meanness and miscalculation, not because he is a ruthless capitalist but because he is hardly a capitalist at all.

The intense emphasis on individual and family predicament enabled O'Neill to transcend the Shavian drama of social reform and to make personal affliction universally tragic. Such affliction, though it can be labelled in conventional sociological terms as alcoholism, anomie, drug addiction, etc., is ultimately immune to the ethos of Welfare Statism even though superficially the drama can be misread as a series of connected social problems. For the personal predicament of each family member is too powerful for existing society to alter. Rational enlightenment, concocted as a formula for moral reform of self, has no place. Instead O'Neill creates the most intense figural dimension of loss to be found in modern tragedy. It is conveyed in the memorable words of Mary, lost in drugged reminiscence:

> None of us can help the things life has done to us. They're done before you realise it, and once they're done they make you do other things until at last everything comes between you and what you'd like to be, and you've lost your true self for ever.[11]

In fact, the dramatic and figural development of the play are inseparable. They both move simultaneously toward a sense of ultimate closure, the closure of darkness and night. The natural coming of darkness is complemented by the withdrawal of Mary Tyrone into the recesses of dream where she dwells on the life she has lost for ever and condemns without exception the life she is obliged to live.

The dual movement is of course also a movement from alienation to climactic strife, and here a crucial mediating element in the composition of the drama's tragic space interposes itself. This is the enshrouding fog which in Act Three, at half-past six in the evening, has rolled in from the Sound like 'a white curtain drawn down outside the windows'. The apparent freedom of setting and space is suddenly removed. The vista onto the ocean is blotted out, and the freedom of the New World which O'Neill had embraced so subversively with polar images of openness and closure, is finally negated. The process of negation is continuous with the earlier work but the openness of dramatic space is finally relinquished. The effect of closure is greater than in *The Iceman* because in the latter the closure is static, whereas in *Long Day's Journey* the effect is progressive. By the beginning of the fourth act, at midnight, the fog appears 'denser than ever'. There is no outside source of light, the only sound to be heard that of the foghorn operating in the harbour. The setting and substance of the last act are phantasmogorical. The figural sensibility is integrated with the closure of dramatic space. Edmund, who has walked back drunkenly to the house through the fog, links the imprisoning effect of nature to his spiritual yearning for insubstantiality:

> Everything looked and sounded unreal. Nothing was what it is. That's what I wanted—to be alone with myself in another world where truth is untrue and life can hide from itself. Out beyond the harbour where the road runs along the beach, I even lost the feeling

of being on land. The fog and the sea seemed part of each other. It was like walking on the bottom of the sea. As if I had drowned long ago. As if I was a ghost beckoning to the fog, and the fog was the ghost of the sea.[12]

This feeling of a trapped alienation containing within it a metaphor of the dispersion of self into nothingness, is a prelude to the entry of a real ghost whose insubstantiality is more real. It is fitting that Edmund should use the metaphor because he both understands it and is at the same time its main victim. The real ghost is his mother who in her world of dreams has rejected him. As he and his father listen to her moving upstairs, he puts it explicitly: ' . . . She'll be nothing but a ghost haunting the past by this time. (*He pauses—then miserably.*) Back before I was born.'[13] The past she haunts is an alternative fate which excludes all of her family, a haunting dream of girlish innocence and chastity in which she can recall her ambition to become a nun in the days before meeting James Tyrone. The alternative *figura* is realised theatrically with Mary's momentous entry into the room, one of the most powerful moments in all of O'Neill's work. With her wedding gown over her arm and trailing on the floor, her girlish innocence appears as 'a marble mask'. The entrance is the climax to tragic strife. But the strife is not violent and does not result in death. Her entrance shows her alienation not only from life in general but from her family, and rises above the dissonant chorus of internecine strife in which her menfolk are drunkenly indulging. Jamie sardonically recalls the mad scene with Ophelia. But the reference cannot detract from the emotional intensity of the scene. There is a tragic horror about her remoteness which they and the audience finally recognise. For the father and the two sons, it is a remoteness which annihilates all of them. Mary Tyrone has rolled back the years to a chaste girlhood devoid of the cares of courtship, marriage and childbirth, and only by excluding them from her dream world can she continue to cherish any fragment of human hope.

The contrast with Hedda Gabler and Nora Clitheroe is strong and apt. Whereas Hedda attempts to manipulate the men around her, Mary tries to repudiate their very existence. While Nora's madness arises from the feeling that her husband has deserted her, Mary Tyrone's madness and addiction arises from the fact of never being able to escape husband and family. Opium replaces the loved one she cannot find in her own family, though under the spell of it she is no longer able to give it a name: 'Something I need terribly. I remember when I had it I was never lonely or afraid. I can't have lost it for ever. I would die if I thought that. Because then there would be no hope.'[14] The hope continues in the dream of a life she could have led which only opium can sustain and which induces an absolute withdrawal into self. Watching her, her family feel not only pity but at the same time the horror of being liquidated themselves by the process which removes her from them.

With the completion of this play, O'Neill's major work, there is a movement full circle in modern tragedy to the radical closure of the tragic space within. The darkness is deeper than any other twentieth-century play, and has the intensity of Lear. The glimpse of hope which is necessarily allowed to remain, becomes no more than a transient moment of the life remembered. The lost promise is retained in the haunting memory, but the price of re-establishing it as an imaginary universe is insanity. For the sane, no matter how disaffected, how alienated, it can only be a very brief moment of revelation. Confronted by the madness of his mother, Edmund's Nietzschean vision of a fusion of soul and cosmos is eloquent and far reaching, but when all is told, merely a fragment. He recalls the experience of sailing on a square rigger bound for Buenos Aires:

> I lay on the bowsprit, facing astern, with the water foaming into spume under me, the masts with every sail white in the moonlight towering above me. I became drunk with the beauty and singing rhythm of it, and for a moment I lost myself—actually lost my life. I was set free! I dissolved in the sea, became white sails and flying spray, became beauty and rhythm, became moonlight and the ship and the dim-starred sky! I belonged without past or future, within peace and unity and a wild joy, within something greater than my own life, or the life of Man, to life itself![15]

But each of these moments is transitory:

> For a second you see—and seeing the secret, you are the secret. For a second there is meaning! And then the hand lets the veil fall and you are alone, lost in the fog again, and you stumble on towards nowhere for no good reason.[16]

The brief moment of hope becomes wider and more universal but the darkness which soon envelops it is also more powerful. Without mentioning it explicitly anywhere, O'Neill among all modern writers has produced the most prophetic vision of human extinction on a scale made possible by nuclear war. The personal darkness is also the darkness of the universe as a whole. It is a darkness more intense and resounding than anything Beckett subsequently created during a period when the possibility became widely known, and it ranges back and forth without constraint from the personal to the social and from the social to the universal. The night of O'Neill's play is the darkness of the twentieth century fully brought to light. Concentrated in the life of one family, it explodes outwards to embrace the whole of modern civilisation.

11 Williams and Miller: the Cold War and the Renewal of Tragedy

The major impetus to the development of a distinctly American theatre with its own contribution to twentieth-century drama came from the visit of the Moscow Arts in 1923 and the influential teachings of its former members, Michael Chekhov and Richard Boleslavski, who were now emigrés living in the United States.[1] Between them they imparted something of the dramatic technique of Stanislavsky, whose attraction to Americans in the theatre became linked in the thirties with an affirmative political attitude towards the Soviet Union. The subsequent emergence of the Group Theatre under Lee Strasberg, Harold Clurman, Cheryl Crawford and Elia Kazan was an important step forward in the promotion of American political theatre. But although Stanislavskian techniques were used by the theatre, it soon became clear that they worked more effectively in drama about contemporary American life than in productions of Chekhov or Ibsen. The failure to produce great European drama was offset by the success of the attempt to produce a theatre relevant to the crises of contemporary America. Integral to this development was the work of Clifford Odets, the outstanding American playwright of the early thirties.

Odets' work probably saved the Group theatre from disintegration in the period between 1932 and 1934 when they vulgarised Stanislavsky in their ill-fated production of Chekhov's *Three Sisters* and proved themselves incapable of coping with the figural aspects of European drama. When Odets betrayed his own talent by moving to Hollywood it soon became clear the theatre had no-one to replace him, and in 1941 it finally collapsed. Odets, however, was not a tragedian and his work differs significantly in its impact from that of O'Neill. It was more ostensibly political in its relation to the Great Depression than O'Neill's depiction of an earlier period in urban American life and it is more directly related to the fate of a particular ethnic group of

Americans that in O'Neill are conspicuous by their absence—the Jews. *Awake and Sing*, successfully produced by Harold Clurman for the Group theatre remains one of the most vivid and enduring portraits of any ethnic American family ever written for the stage. But there are few, if any, Jewish tragedians in American literature and Odets was no exception to the rule. The desire to survive and prosper, both as individuals and as members of an ethnic grouping, was probably stronger among the Jews than among any of the lower-class immigrant groups. The New World meant an escape from the ghetto, the pogroms and the persecution which were fundamental to the experience of large sections of European Jewry. There was perhaps a greater cultural and psychic investment in the promise of America than among other groups even though, at the same time, there may have been greater scepticism. For many hard-working Jews who believed in that promise, the Great Depression was a trauma of the first order.

Odets's drama portrays the subsequent revolt among Jewish intellectuals and trade unionists against the American way of life. By making the reference specific and incorporating the particular situation of an ethnic group, he effectively portrays the universal forms of discontent in the period. But the tone of the work is of a defiant endurance, a reaffirmation of the right to life in the midst of deprivation. The main beneficiary of the attraction to socialism amongst Jews and intellectuals was the American Communist Party whose impact was probably at its greatest during the period of Popular Front politics. This in many ways explains the complete volte-face which took place after the war when the House Unamerican Activities Committee started its hearings in earnest. Just as prior to the war, the Communist Party had sought to make socialism identical with its own organisation, so disillusionment with the Communist Party after the war came in many cases to entail disillusionment with socialism. What complicated the issue in the period of the Cold War was of course that Macarthyism and the forms of anti-communist witch-hunt it propagated, encouraged that identification. The pressure applied by Macarthyism on turncoat intellectuals was successful only if it is understood as tapping a genuine disenchantment with the Communist Party. The end of the war had meant the re-introduction of labour camps and massive repression by Stalin in the Soviet Union and the collusion of the Russian secret police in organising communist takeovers in Eastern Europe. A disillusionment with a genuine rationale was then distorted under pressure from the HUAC into a baiting of fellow communists or ex-communists and the playing of a ruthless kind of game entitled the 'naming of names' in public testimony, a game designed at ostracising all ex-communists from American cultural life. As the testimonies of Odets and Kazan before the HUAC in 1952 demonstrate, their willingness to become turncoats was due in no small part to the bitter feeling that the Party cheated them in the previous decade.[1]

The Cold War then inaugurated an era of introversion among many American intellectuals, particularly East Coast Jews. The radical intellectual fashion became psychoanalysis, Marx had by now been replaced in the Pantheon of the Greats by Freud, and there was a significant political shift from socialism to liberalism. The effect on drama was to stifle the development of a political theatre. Nonetheless the new drama of the period from Tennessee Williams, Arthur Miller and William Inge among others, was a profound response to changes in American society, and was linked to the new intellectual mood which immersed itself in the understanding of the individual personality.

The predominant figural stress of the new drama was psychosexual, and it portrays the conflict between the individual personality and society, where the sexual basis of personal disaffection now received an unprecedented recognition. What O'Neill had presented more formally and distantly in *Desire under the Elms* and *Mourning Becomes Electra*, became more vital and more immediate in plays such as *Come Back Little Sheba*, *Cat on a Hot Tin Roof* and *View from the Bridge*. The emphasis on psychosexuality complemented the economic and cultural changes in American life, the movement towards a mass consumer society based on massive expenditure and credit, bringing material prosperity to large sections of its middle-class and working-class population. This economic change weakened the hold of the Protestant ethic upon the moral code of most Americans quite substantially during the post-war years. While politics was diminished by the Cold War, the growing pursuit of hedonism was encouraged by market forces. The cult of the individual condoned by the American way of life was maintained, but it became increasingly the cult of the individual as mass consumer rather than the cult of the individual as producer. The emphasis changed from stressing individual capacities to stressing mass needs, and this took place within the context of a rather stifling political conformity which saw minority radical dissent temporarily disappear from the political system altogether.

This then constituted one of the major cultural contradictions of advanced capitalism in the United States.[2] The response of the major drama of the period was to show discontent in a personal light, and to place it in terms of the frustrations of individual human need. At the same time the legacy of O'Neill was, thematically speaking, formidable. The work of Williams and Miller was built centrally, and sometimes derivatively, on the thematic achievements of the Irish-American dramatist. Ethnic particularity, female victimisation, working-class life and personal insanity were all taken over and transposed into new settings. Moreover Williams and Miller both saw themselves consciously as being for the most part, tragedians, with Miller himself doing some special pleading for a 'tragedy of the common man'.[3] But the extent of their tragic vision was vitally limited by the degree to which psychosexuality could be portrayed as the basis of tragic alienation and lead organically to an authentic tragic strife.

The position of tragedy here is complicated by the legacy that the new American theatre bequeathed to Hollywood and to popular culture. With its extreme vulgarisations of Freud and Stanislavsky, the Actors Studio in New York produced a number of talented actors such as Lee J. Cobb, Marlon Brando, Paul Newman, Rod Steiger, Patricia Neal, Anne Bancroft, Montgomery Clift and others who were both vital to the stage performances of the new social drama, yet also Hollywood stars who popularised not only the acting style of the new theatre on the screen but also a film version of the heroic disaffection Williams and Miller had created. This was particularly true of the angry young rebel personified by Brando, Newman and James Dean. The tension between rebel and society was there, and a new kind of popular heroism emerged. But in Nicholas Ray's *Rebel Without a Cause* or Kazan's *On the Waterfront*, the rebellion of the hero is 'understood', exonerated and subject to processes of acceptable social incorporation. The disaffection, portrayed and acted brilliantly by Dean and Brando, was nonetheless recuperable and set in motion a general pattern. Moreover the actual film versions of the new drama were totally vulgarised. *A Streetcar Named Desire* was changed to mar its tragic ending, *Suddenly Last Summer* was glossy, sensational and superficial, while *View from the Bridge* was peculiarly wooden and without resonance. The difficulties went beyond the complex nature of changing from drama to film. There was an effective negation of tragedy in the more popular medium which highlights the rare achievement of Williams and Miller in the original dramatic form.

The rarity of nature and fully conceived tragic drama in their work is the main characteristic of both writers. Each has a particular stereotype vitiating the power of tragic writing in its psychosexual context. In Miller it is the paralysis of guilt and in Williams the paralysis of libidinal discontent. Their respective tragedies are achievements precisely because dramatically speaking, these limits are transcended. The three major tragedies of the period are *A Streetcar Named Desire*, *A View from the Bridge* and *Suddenly Last Summer*. Amongst their other works each dramatist has an outstanding play which is unable ultimately to emerge as the tragic drama its writer wished it to be. In Williams the failure is *Cat on a Hot Tin Roof*. For Miller it is *The Crucible*. Then come the lesser works conceived in the tragic mould—*The Glass Menagerie* and *Death of a Salesman*—and finally other works which capitulate rather more readily to the process of thematic stereotyping. What remains to be seen is how the exceptional themes of the three major tragedies demarcate themselves from lesser works. Here the different regional and ethnic traditions of the two writers are of vital importance.

As a Southern dramatist Williams is linked to a triumvirate of modern tragic writers in that region whose work has been of major importance for American fiction over the last fifty years. These are the novelists William Faulkner, Richard Wright and William Styron, one a predecessor, the others roughly contemporaries. In all three writers there are a variety of dialectical themes but the major one is the dialectic of country and city. In Williams and Faulkner this is fused with the dialectic of the aristocratic and the proletarian. In Wright and Styron it is also fused, in key works, with the wider dialectic of North and South in modern America. While Williams has tended to avoid the latter, he has been instrumental in using the aristocratic heritage of the 'old South' as a modality for tragic drama, and using in it in a way denied to O'Neill and other Northern dramatists. Unlike Faulkner, however, he does not use it historically, but transplants it to the contemporary settings of his own lifetime, where the tradition is strong but the social supports for that tradition are constantly being eroded by the modernisation of the South itself.

This latter theme is apparent in his first major play, *The Glass Menagerie* and its famous successor *A Streetcar Named Desire*, where it matures into a constituent element of major tragedy. The difference between the two plays in this respect is a vital one. Both trace the fate of people who have come from the country to the city, but while one heroine, Laura Wingfield, is forlorn and sentimental, Blanche Dubois has a startling tragic grandeur. While Blanche is supremely alone, Laura is protected by her family and overprotected by her mother.

The fate of isolation is then shared and as an individual person the daughter is unable to emerge out of her mother's shadow.

Aesthetically, the play is interesting because Williams explicitly tried to impose upon it a set of theatrical techniques for breaking with the realist tradition. He called it a non-realistic memory play. But by using Tom Wingfield as the narrator who steps back into the past action he narrates, Williams was merely extending the range of figural enactment. The memories themselves are profoundly real, and the screen device Williams had included in the stage directions of the text was abandoned in actual production as clumsy and obtrusive. A real innovation, comparable to those of the early O'Neill, was in danger of being too stylistically cluttered. But when this paraphernalia is cast aside, the play actually works as a narrated memoir of family life and of the different choices the children in the family make.

The thematic strength of the play hinges on the illusory expectations of the mother. As a lower-middle-class family isolated in a city apartment, the values of the Old South she had learnt in her family house in Blue Mountain are obsolete in St Louis. Still she lives in the past and still she tries to impose those values on her shy and crippled daughter. She thus embroiders a world of make-believe with disastrous results:

> Amanda. . . . Stay fresh and pretty!—It's almost time for our gentlemen callers to start arriving. (*She flounces girlishly towards the kitchenette.*) How many do you suppose we are going to entertain this afternoon?
> (*Tom throws down the paper and jumps up with a groan.*)
> Laura (*alone in the dining-room*). I don't believe we are going to receive any, mother.[4]

The alienation of the fatherless family is defined very precisely in terms of the mother's illusions and the passive defiance of them by her children. But the dramatic space of the drama cannot render them tragic. The enclosed apartment in which Laura escapes into arranging and re-arranging the animals of her glass menagerie, does not possess the resonance of Ibsen's strange loft and Hedvig's wild duck. The animals of the Wingfield's apartment are glass miniatures, and the closure of the dramatic space is such that there can be no real intimation of a free untrammelled life beyond, even though the neighbouring alleyways and fire-escapes are part of the stage setting.

Thus the alienation portrayed can only lead to escape and not to strife. When the gentleman caller does arrive he is straight out of romantic soap-opera, and reveals, according to the stereotyped Scribean pattern, that he is already engaged to another girl whom he must meet at the station. The effect then becomes one of domestic tragedy reminiscent of Hauptmann, in which inwardness can never be externalised to the point of rupture or conflict with the external world. The only resolution to the play is the escape of the narrator who leaves St Louis and thus 'lives' to tell the tale and to feel perpetually haunted by the sorry fate of the imprisoned sister he has left behind him.

A Streetcar Named Desire is on a different plane altogether. The initial production by Elia Kazan, before his capitulation to Macarthyist pressures, was one of the greatest achievements of his career. In his notebooks for the production, his response was both perceptive and immediate. He saw at once the monumental importance and originality involved in the creation of Blanche Dubois: '*Her problem has to do with her tradition.* Her notion of what a woman should be. She is stuck with this "ideal". It is her. It is her ego. Unless she lives by it, she cannot live: in fact her whole life has been for nothing'.[5] He had put his finger on the pulse of the whole play by showing the decisive way in which Williams developed the female hero in modern tragedy. Blanche has internalised the genteel living and graciousness of her plantation home and tried to take it with her into an alien world which no longer recognises it. While Amanda Wingfield can retain illusions of gracious living for her pitiful daughter in the privacy of their lower-middle-class apartment, Blanche goes forth, alone and vulnerable into the heart of New Orleans.

Through Blanche, Williams explores the difficulty of individual freedom for the single woman in a hostile environment. But he goes further than a similar presentation of such themes in the work of Jean Rhys. He fuses important elements of class and tradition with the psychosexual predicament of his heroine, to create the basis of a genuinely tragic alienation. On the one hand, Blanche's sexual desires constitute a transgression of a middle-class moral code concerning single women. On the other, the materialistic world of the urban South transgresses her own traditional code of gracious living. She is both violater and violated, transgressor and transgressed. The tragic resolution of the drama cannot come however from direct confrontation with middle-class life. In the course of the play it is gradually revealed to us that Blanche has already failed to adapt as a teacher to the demands of a small-town community. But the exploration of this theme alone would not raise the play to a tragic dimension.

Dramatically speaking it has to be a step downward already taken before the action begins, just like the failure and horrifying ending to her marriage. This cumulative failure in bourgeois life is the prelude to her confrontation with working-class life in the city, and it is this confrontation alone which generates such immense tragic power.

The confrontation arises out of the previous failure. Stanley Kowalski, her brother-in-law, takes a sadistic delight in revealing the compromised past of his wife's dreamy and rather precious sister. But the crudity of his tactics in doing so are possible only in a proletarian context. Both Blanche and Stanley are culturally inadmissable as far as middle-class life is concerned, but whereas Stanley has a received and positive identity as the proud dominant head of a working-class household, Blanche has no acceptable cultural identity at all. Kowalski benefits from the sexual double standards affecting men and women where his sexual freedom is never questioned as long as he remains head of the household, but Blanche's as a single woman, is increasingly brought into disrepute. Although Blanche and Kowalski are both alienated from middle-class life, Kowalski has a positive and stable identity. He lives in a world where, adapting the words of Huey Long, he can claim that 'a man is a king'. He is psychologically immune to the constricting poverty of his apartment and neighbour-hood because there are other ready forms of compensation. Alienated from society as a whole by virtue of his class, he is anything but alienated from his immediate surroundings.

The working-class subculture of the city caters for Kowalski's sexuality, and this is an important compensatory mechanism, allowing him an aggressive contentment with life in general. Blanche, by comparison, has an absolute sense of loss in which the denial of her sexuality is fused with the abandonment of Belle Reve. The extreme isolation of her position, which makes her so dependent on 'the kindness of strangers' is social rather than personal. The alternative fates of Blanche and Stella highlight this. Stella has sacrificed personal freedom and gracious living for marital security, while Blanche has remained alone under the illusion of fighting single-handed for their ancestral home: 'You are the one who abandoned Belle Reve, not I. I stayed and fought for it, bled for it, almost died for it.' In truth Blanche is too impractical to survive in a materialistic world. She squanders the money which should have maintained the hope and is forced to abandon it through bankruptcy. She is not ruthless enough to defend the tradition by pragmatic means, so the attachment instead is one of nostalgia and myth in which she accepts that her way of life is doomed.

She thus personified in her own mind the aura of the noble, having failed to make the plantation home financially viable.

That aura, which she attempts instinctively to cultivate in her everyday life, has an evanescent quality which makes her socially vulnerable. She confesses the vulnerability to Stella using the mode of poetic euphemism which is central, figurally speaking, to her persona:

> Blanche. You haven't heard any—unkind—gossip about me?
> Stella. Why, no, Blanche, of course not!
> Blanche. There was—a good deal of talk in Laurel.
> Stella. About *you*, Blanche?
> Blanche. I wasn't so good the last two years or so, after Belle Reve had started to slip through my fingers.
> Stella. All of us do things we—
> Blanche. I was never hard or self-sufficient enough. When people are soft—soft people have to court the favour of hard ones, Stella. Have got to be seductive—put on soft colours, the colours of butterfly wings, and glow—make a little temporary magic just in order to pay for one night's shelter! That's why I've been—not so awfully good lately. I've run for protection, Stella from under one leaky roof to another leaky roof—because it was storm—all storm, I was—caught in the centre . . . People don't see you— *men* don't—don't even admit your existence unless they're making love to you. And you've got to have your existence admitted by someone, if you're going to have someone's protection. And so the soft people have got to shimmer and glow and put a paper lantern over the light . . . [6]

The poetic euphemism employed here, and a characteristic of Blanche's speech throughout the play, is not an artificial front, a fanciful form of concealment which, as Kowalski imagines, can be annihilated by crude animal hostility. It exists, and prevails, because no other language exists which is socially apt to capture the real nature of Blanche's experience. She embroiders her own, because the social morality of the time offers up none which is remotely relevant to the passage of her life. At best, in terms of conventional morality, she is unstable and promiscuous. At worst, she is a whore. But these perjorative epithets omit the vulnerability which is at the foundation of her life. Moreover they shun any attempt at recognition of it.

The encounter with Stanley Kowalski recalls that of Yank and Mildred Douglas in *The Hairy Ape*. There is the same sense of female vulnerability before the crudely animal male, yet here the social roles are reversed. Blanche is no longer protected like Mildred Douglas by class and status, and the working-class male who confronts her is in no way subordinate to her. Rather, as the play progresses, she becomes increasingly subordinate to him. Despite her attempts to be dismissive by calling him a 'Polack', Kowalski can, within his own subculture, rule his dingy household like a feudal baron. She is privileged but alienated, while he is disprivileged but socially incorporated into the American way of life. The moral issue is not a clear-cut one of black and white with Blanche as a sensitive victim and Kowalski as a brutal villain. Blanche *is* insensitive to the hardships of the Kowalskis and to the genuine affection between husband and wife which does much to alleviate the harshness of their life. She is a social snob because of her class background and Kowalski's resentment of her is genuinely based on class differences. But by reducing the class dimension to a purely sexual one, he can also exorcise the sense of social inferiority with which she threatens him. His ruthless attempt to drive Blanche out of the household is not then a blow struck against class privilege, so much as confirmation of his incorporation within the existing social order. But without class hatred that confirmation, paradoxically, would have been impossible. Thus at times Kowalski acts in authentically proletarian terms but in the wrong way towards the wrong person and with the wrong moral justification.

The antagonism between the two leading personae, which overrides the mutual affection of husband and wife, and Blanche's fleeting attachment to the pathetic Mitch, is expressed theatrically in terms of a remarkable use of dramatic space. Williams suggests the integration of household and environment by using a skeletal set in which street exteriors and household interiors are combined, with the possibility of action taking place at the same time internally and externally. Moreover the apartment is divided internally into kitchen, bedroom and bathroom, so that Kowalski can explain in the kitchen to Stella his investigations into Blanche's shady past while Blanche is happily and obliviously taking a bath. But the central use of the divided interior is in the drapes dividing kitchen and bedroom. At night the kitchen becomes Blanche's temporary bedroom. During waking hours, she changes, applies make-up and talks to Stella in the bedroom while the kitchen becomes the preserve of Stanley and his poker-playing friends. The territorial switches highlight spatially the vulnerable situation in which Blanche finds herself, where her personal privacy in the apartment is flimsy and minimal. Stanley then is a constant threat territorially as well as physically and psychologically. There is nowhere she can really shut herself off from him whenever he is in the house. This then is the dramatic space which leads from the tragic alienation of life in the Elysian Fields to the tragic strife of being humiliated and finally driven insane by sudden and brutal rape.

The rape is more than an isolated act of brutality. It is the dramatic figural consequence of her summer residence in the apartment which becomes a growing trap for her. Drunk, demoralised, aware that she has been discovered, and entertaining illusions that she will be spirited away by a former beau who is now a millionaire, there is no escape even before Kowalski lays a finger on her. What Williams captures so well is the total breakdown in understanding between them which arises out of social and cultural strangeness. It is conveyed dramatically by the difference in speech which reinforces the difference in perception. Thus Blanche's drunken vision of her refined qualities contrasts completely with Kowalski's sardonic presentation of her as a sexual freak:

> A cultivated woman, a woman of intelligence and breeding can enrich a man's life—immeasurably! I have those things to offer, and this doesn't take them away. Physical beauty is passing. A transitory possession. But beauty of the mind and richness of the spirit and tenderness of the heart—and I have all of these things—aren't taken away but grow! Increase with the years! How strange that I should be called a destitute woman! When I have all of those treasures locked in my heart![7]

This, by contrast, is Kowalski:

> And look at yourself! Take a look at yourself in that worn-out Mardi Gras outfit, rented for fifty cents from some rag-picker! And with the crazy crown on! What queen do you think you are . . . I've been on to you from the start! Not once did you pull the wool over this boy's eyes! You come in here and sprinkle the place with powder and spray perfume and cover the light bulb with a paper lantern, and lo and behold the place has turned into Egypt and you are the Queen of the Nile! Sitting on the throne and swilling down my liquor! I say—*Ha! Ha!* Do you hear me? *Ha-Ha—Ha!* [8]

Kowalski's tirade accentuates the assault on Blanche's identity which the experience of moving to the city has had on her. But it takes the physical act of rape to destroy her sense of identity altogether.

Williams thereafter lacks the necessary Shakespearean intensity to convey the madness of his heroine. Madness, is not, as it is with Nora Clitheroe, an actual way of experiencing but rather a simple loss of faculties and of common sense. It is seen to be the outcome of the rape yet in her case the relationship between rape and madness is not clearly expressed. Its effect upon Stanley is seen more clearly, for it affirms his self-image as a sexual conquistador yet allows him, by destroying Blanche, to leave his home free for the return of wife and newly born child. Blanche meanwhile is ironically left to the kindness of strangers once more, the strangers in this case being officials from the state mental hospital who come to take her away. As she leaves her romantic vision of her own end has a freedom which her impending imprisonment will deny to her. The image of the sea is similar to that evoked by Edmund Tyrone but the sensibility is closer to that of his mother, Mary:

> I can smell the sea air. The rest of my time I'm going to spend on the sea. And when I die, I'm going to die on the sea. You know what I shall die of? (*She plucks a grape.*) I shall die of eating an unwashed grape one day out on the ocean. I will die— with my hand in the hand of some nice-looking ship's doctor, a very young one with a small blonde moustache and a big silver watch. 'Poor lady', they'll say, 'the quinine did her no good. That unwashed grape has transported her soul to heaven!' (*The cathedral chimes are heard.*) And I'll be buried at sea sewn up in a clean white sack and dropped overboard—at noon—in the blaze of summer—and into an ocean as blue as (*chimes again*) my first lover's eyes![9]

As a motif of limitless freedom, the sea is here transformed into a romantic image. In Blanche's deranged vision, ocean and passion are fused in the colour of the sea, in 'the ocean as blue as my first lover's eyes'. The passion here, like that of Emma Bovary's, is the love of love. In the case of Blanche however, it is the sensibility of the single and not the married woman. It is not a response to marriage and does not involve infidelity. It has both a greater freedom and correspondingly, a greater anguish. The social transgression is, if anything, greater and more elusive in nature. For while secret adultery sets up its own structured rituals of meeting and deceiving and loving, and becomes a popular formula in romantic fiction, Blanche's passion cannot be vulgarised in the same way at all, for it is without structure. The passion for the transient encounter in which mutual affection is shown is neither promiscuity rationalised as romance nor exonerated as sudden impulse. The impulse which makes Blanche embrace the newspaper boy as he stands momentarily at the entrance to the apartment is almost indefinable. In Blanche's case it remains passion because it contains hope and longing within an alienated life, a hope and longing which cannot be fully sublimated into romance, nor, at the same time, be reduced to the elemental desire of which she accuses Stanley Kowalski.

The tragic sexuality of Blanche contrasts with the psychosexual predicament of Brick Politt in *Cat on a Hot Tin Roof*, where discontent and the inability to find fulfilment are central themes, but not inherently tragic in their attempted resolution. The contrast is emphasised by Williams's own insistence on writing a tragedy according to Aristotelian convention. The play does observe the unities of time, place and action but it is a serious and not a tragic drama, an indisputable artistic success but not the kind of play which Williams had intended to write. There are two important losses here which constrain the tragic vision. The fixed setting of the plantation house loses the vital dialectic of country and city, and the transformation from heterosexual to homosexual discontent, closer biographically speaking to Williams' own sexual nature, actually mars the possibility of tragic strife. The dividing line is very fine indeed, but Williams' hero by stoically and passively accepting his marital and family role can never rise to tragic proportions.

The key to the affirmative nature of the work lies in the extent to which Big Daddy Pollitt, like Maggie the Cat, entices Brick back into the family fold in spite of the latter's infatuation with the dead Skipper. Familiar integration here works in spite of personal transgression, and in spite of the fact that for Brick, Skipper's loss is irreparable. Brick's homosexuality cannot be altered, but with Maggie's tenacious devotion he can be persuaded to accept inheritance of the plantation and his obligation to father the child. The latter, as the final scene shows, is a purely passive assent in which he does not resist as Maggie locks away his liquor and prepares to seduce him:

> Margaret. Oh, you weak people, you weak, beautiful people!—who give up—what you want is someone to—(*She turns out the rose-silk lamp*)—take hold of you. Gently, gently, with love! And—(*The curtain begins to fall slowly*.) I *do* love you, Brick, I *do*!
> Brick (*smiling with charming sadness*.). Wouldn't it be funny if that was true?[10]

Like Chekhov, Williams opts for the landed country house, but its owners do not exemplify the aristocratic spirit of the Old South. Pollitt is brash, ruthless and *nouveau riche*, a rural capitalist of the new age. The plantation is not therefore comparable with the lost reality of Belle Reve which is never shown in the earlier play. The embourgeoisement of the plantation home is a precondition for the cultural containment of the prodigal son. Through his own lack of pretension to cultural refinement or middle-class respectability, Big Daddy can prefer his alcoholic homosexual of a son to Mae, Gooper and their hordes of children. And Brick's prodigality, though based on his sensitive sexual nature, is itself without cultural refinement. Blanche Dubois tries to uphold the privileged status derived from a refined culture only to find that status is no longer recognised, but Brick's material privileges are so assured that status is irrelevant. Indeed as acted by Paul Newman in the Hollywood movie, it was possible to give Brick the cultural attributes of a rebellious working-class hero, to turn him into a sympathetic version of Stanley Kowalski. But this was merely an impression created by the Method style of acting which Brando and Newman had imported into Hollywood, and Brick's circumstances are always more privileged than those of Kowalski's.

The failure to transform the confrontation between Big Daddy and Brick into the play's tragic climax, resulted in an important difference of opinion between Williams and Kazan during the original Broadway production. Kazan felt that the disappearance of the patriarch from the third act, where instead he becomes the absent subject of the doctor's gloomy diagnosis, meant a disastrous weakening of the play's dramatic impact. But Williams, who reluctantly rewrote the third act to include him again, was instinctively right in realising that such an interpolation spoilt the dramatic balance of the play. Big Daddy exhausts his figural role in extorting from Brick a confession of his relationship with Skipper, and yet the revelation alters nothing since the father's sympathy for his son is fixed and unassailable. In the third act there can be no real dramatic development because the catharsis at the end of the second is necessarily premature and non-tragic. In the Broadway version of Kazan, Big Daddy could only reappear in the Third Act as a diminished man.

After *Cat on a Hot Tin Roof* Williams tended to vulgarise psycho-sexual discontent into a literary formula which often read like a parody of his more serious work. In Hollywood screen plays such as *Baby Doll* and *The Roman Spring of Mrs Stone* discontent is given a stereotyped glamour, and there follows in much of his stage drama the typical theme of an abortive affair between a wealthy middle-aged woman and a young gigolo. The most serious of these was *Sweet Bird of Youth* in which Williams did try to integrate authentic political themes. But the attempt to write political drama was a failure. The all-American stud, Chance Wayne, whose name captures exactly his stereotyped qualities, is having an affair with a spoilt ageing Hollywood star and at the same time, with Heavenly, the daughter of a Southern racist politician, Boss Finlay, whom he scandalously impregnates. The attempt to link torrid political drama with sexual transgression here has a rather camp quality in which the power of figural composition is lost. Studs, violated women and politicians have a phantom and freakish quality unrooted in any recognisable social reality. The exotic setting, as in much of Williams' later work, is coated with a thick layer of conspicuous opulence which says less about American life as such than about Williams' own predicament as a wealthy and successful writer.

His second major tragic work should be seen in the context of the more general decline in his writing, as a renewal of genius which stands out very distinctly yet has never been given the critical recognition it deserves. The work is *Suddenly Last Summer*, produced in 1958 along with *Something Unspoken*, one of the best short plays of the post-war period. In *Suddenly Last Summer* Williams rediscovered the vein of tragic writing in which he started his career, and it was a curse on his own reputation that the play should be made into a travesty of a film which obscured the importance of the original stage work. In this play Williams takes one stage further the theme of the incipient madness of his earlier female heroes, Laura Wingfield and Blanche Dubois. It also reveals a lineage of European influence very different from that of O'Neill. Whereas the Irish-American had been strongly influenced by Ibsen, Strindberg and the Irish realists, the flavour of Williams's work is more distinctly Chekhovian. *Cat on a Hot Tin Roof* possesses more than an echo of *Three Sisters* while *Suddenly Last Summer* shows remarkable thematic similarities with *The Seagull*. In both these plays, Williams reproduces the Chekhovian device of the ensemble as discordant community, arguing amongst themselves, continuously interrupting each other and clamouring for attention. Often the effect is ugly and strident, unlike Chekhov, where it is lyrical and invigorating. But in *Suddenly Last Summer* tragedy hinges, as in *The Seagull*, on the nature and betrayal of art.

In the two tragedies, the compromise of the writer hinges on contrasting strategies. Whereas Trigorin largely exploits life for the sake of his literary art, Sebastian Venable has exploited his rather limited art for the sake of his prevented life. The exploitation of writing is linked to the exploitation of other people. Trigorin uses Nina while Venable uses first his mother and then Catherine Holly as a means of procuring young men. But the difference in priorities is paramount. Trigorin subordinates everything to writing while Venable has let his sparsely produced poetry take second place to sexual desire. Another difference is crucial. We see and hear Trigorin extemporising on the work of the writer but Venable is already dead, like Beata in *Rosmersholm*, and his absence dominates the whole play. The play is essentially about how his life and its horrific ending are recalled in contrasting ways by his mother and by Catherine Holly. Like Nina, Catherine is the victim of a gradual process of exploitation over time, but in reverting to a unity of time and place, Williams portrays that victimisation in the compressed manner of Ibsen. Catherine first appears already in shock, the inmate of the state hospital, still horribly obsessed by the manner of Venable's death. Her entrance then follows on from where Blanche made her exit in *A Streetcar Named Desire*. Whereas Nina's abortive affair with Trigorin takes its toll over many years, gradually wearing her down into resignation, Catherine's trauma has been instantaneous, or as the title has it, 'suddenly last summer'.

The use of dramatic space similarly invites comparison with Ibsen. In *The Wild Duck*, the attic with its rabbits and wounded pet was a residual reminder of rural wilderness. Here the miniature of a tropical jungle is reproduced in the interior of a Victorian Gothic mansion in the Garden district of New Orleans. Though they reveal contrasting aspects of nature, the attic and the jungle-garden theatricalise in much the same way the incorporation of wilderness within civilisation. A similar comparison can be made between the seagull or the wild duck, and the Venus Fly-Trap, the rare plant which feeds on insects and which Sebastian made a point of supplying with fruit flies from a Florida laboratory. But there is equally a subtle transformation. The Fly-Trap is the predator and not the victim, and the tropical garden is at the centre of attention and the centre of the stage.

Homosexuality in this play is a more effective basis for tragedy than in *Cat on a Hot Tin Roof*. The subterranean strategies of Sebastian are tragic in their consequences whereas Brick, alcoholic and unloving, remains discontentedly within the family fold. The tragic experience of Sebastian's death fuses two elements—the actual murder and Catherine's witnessing of it—so that it not only lies in the brutality of the act and the ensuing cannibalism but also in the witnessing of it as a nightmare which can never be forgotten. Only when Catherine relives it, on the verge of madness, her own sexual identity destroyed, does it become genuinely tragic. Mediated by her own sensibility the brutal incident is transformed into tragic experience.

The main strife in the play concerns the struggle of the two women who knew Sebastian best over the recognition of that experience. Mrs Venable wishes to deny and suppress it for good, Catherine to make it public for the first time. Mrs Venable's memories are thus riddled with euphemism, a euphemism which makes Catherine all the more desperate to tell what has really happened. Here is the mother's extravagant aesthetic metaphor of their cosmopolitan travels together:

> My son, Sebastian, and I constructed our days, each day, we would carve out each day of our lives like a piece of sculpture—yes we would leave behind us a trial of days like a gallery of sculpture! But last summer— . . .[11]

Here by contrast is the accusation of the girl she accuses of being a 'vandal' with a 'tongue for a hatchet'. Later that afternoon Catherine is explaining to the doctor why Sebastian has made her wear a transparent swimsuit on the beach:

> Don't you understand? I was PROCURING for him!
> (*Mrs. Venable's gasp is like the sound that a great hooked fish might make.*)
> She used to do it, *too*.
> (*Mrs. Venable cries out.*)
> *Not consciously*! She didn't know that she was procuring for him in the smart fashionable places they used to go before last summer. Sebastian was shy with people. She wasn't. Neither was I. We both did the same thing for him, but she did it in nice places and in decent ways and I had to do it in the way that I just told you![12]

Much of the onus for creating the power of tragedy lies in Catherine's final speech. Unlike *Long Day's Journey* where there is a continuous and lyrical movement towards dramatic climax, the scene of the family visit slackens the dramatic pace, and the power does not seem recuperable. Yet Catherine's speech is comparable in its breadth of vision and depth of horror to the final speech of Mary Tyrone. It shows the evil of personal manipulation moreover in an unexpectedly wide and far-reaching dimension, a dimension which is new not only to the action which has preceded it but to Williams' work as a whole. The evil embraces a whole class of underprivileged beings, the young boys of Cabezo de Lobo who exist for Sebastian only as possible objects of pleasure, and who claim their unexpected revenge. The symbol of the Venus Fly-Trap comes full circle as the potential victims transform themselves into vengeful predators.

The nature of the retribution takes the play into a new dimension. Venable, who had thought all retribution came from God, becomes instead the victim of 'the damned of the earth'. His fate is the outcome of social and sexual degeneration, not of divine retribution. Here is the climax of Catherine's account:

> . . . White hot, a blazing white hot, hot blazing white, at five o'clock in the afternoon in the city of—Cabezo de Lobo. It looked as if . . . as if a huge white bone had caught on fire in the sky and blazed so bright it was white and turned the sky and everything under the sky white with it ! . . .
> The band of naked children pursued us up the steep white street in the sun that was like the great white bone of a giant beast that had caught on fire in the sky!—Sebastian started to run and they all screamed at once and seemed to fly in the air, they outran him so quickly. I screamed. I heard Sebastian scream, he screamed just once before this flock of black plucked little birds that pursued him and overtook him halfway up the white hill . . .
> Waiters, police and others—ran out of the building and rushed back up the hill with me. When we got back to where my cousin Sebastian had disappeared in the flock of featherless little black sparrows, he—he was lying naked as they had been naked against a white wall, and this you won't believe, nobody *has* believed it, nobody *could* believe it, nobody on earth could possibly believe it, and I don't *blame* them!—They had devoured parts of him.
> (*Mrs. Venable cries out softly.*)
> Torn or cut parts of him away with their hands or knives or maybe those jagged tin cans they made music with, they had torn bits of him away and stuffed them into those gobbling fierce little empty black mouths of theirs. There wasn't a sound anymore, there was nothing to see but Sebastian, what was left of him, that looked like a big white-paper-wrapped bunch of red roses had been torn *thrown, crushed!*—against that blazing white wall . . .[13]

Up to this point in his writing, Williams' portrayal of lower-class life had been largely urban in context, and in his later work he had increasingly deserted it for the snares of upper-middle-class opulence. The rural South of Faulkner, Caldwell and McCullers, its quasi-feudal poverty, is missing from his work. The final scene in this play adds a different dimension which partially atones for that gap. The naked young beggars of Cazebo de Lobo are hungrier, more primitive and more desperate than their Southern counterparts and their cannibalism is an ultimate transgression against any moral code. In the context of the absolute gap in wealth between rich American and poor Latin it possesses a social dimension which saves the horror from being gratuitous. Having ignored, for the most part, the damned of his own, Williams discovers suddenly and without dramatic precedent the damned of the earth. He thus preserved and extended the link cemented in O'Neill between lower-class life and tragedy by giving it a global basis.

In Arthur Miller's play *A View from the Bridge*, the link is also preserved, this time internally within the life of the northern city. The power of this tragedy is in direct contrast to the rest of Miller's drama where he failed to attain the 'tragedy of the common man' he wished to create.[14] As a contemporary of Williams, there are some remarkable similarities in stage setting and in the motif of the city. But Miller was essentially a Northern writer and his life as a whole had a much more political dimension to it. Like Odets and Kazan, he too was forced to testify before the HUAC. But unlike them, he did not publicly regret his past or incriminate others.[14] Ironically too, his most celebrated drama of witch-hunting, *The Crucible*, was written before he was subpoenaed. Yet despite greater political resilience than most left-wing intellectuals of the period, his drama tends to reflect a set of social dilemmas which have a more direct reference to liberal guilt. In some respects his work seems in direct line with the early social drama of Ibsen. He retains the same concern with the all-pervasive and ambiguous guilt of the respectable man who betrays the moral code of his society, and this concern makes him ultimately one of major writers of bourgeois drama during the post-war period.

His drama usually works at two levels, that of the private, mostly loyal family and that of the public, mostly hostile world. The link between them is made by the guilty behaviour of the imperfect and often victimised hero, a guilt stemming from his personal failure to live up to a public ideal. This conflict, however, does not provide the basis for tragic strife. True, it comprises personal failing and reversal of fortune, but class and family associations pre-empt the establishment of tragic alienation. The reason lies not only in middle-class or lower-middle-class background, but in the ethnic affiliation which Miller suppresses. Robert Warshow and Morris Friedman have both pointed out that Miller systematically conceals the Jewish background of his characters in many of his plays, and instead tries to present them, awkwardly and unconvincingly, as 'typical Americans'.[15] Deprived of that concrete background, of an ethnic group in American society which has had its own special history of suffering and endurance, the nature of the individual guilt becomes mystified. Heroes such as Joe Kellner and Willy Loman, one senses, have more to answer for than their occupational and familial transgression, but what that is, one never knows. The failure of Miller's heroic victims to fulfil the promise of the American Dream in their own lives is artistically flawed by Miller's unwillingness to give them a concrete ethnic identity, and to comply instead with the myth of the 'melting-pot'.

Death of a Salesman is similar in spirit, perhaps, to a sociological classic of the period, C. Wright Mills' White Collar. There is critical disaffection and inflated pathos running through both. The gap between the promise of the American Dream and the predicament of the anguished salesman who can only act out his occupational role by destroying his personality is a common feature. Miller's hero is very much the little man, dwarfed by the very processes to which he defers and allows to control his life. The figural dimensions of the potentially tragic hero are shrunk by the class context of the action. The tenacity with which Loman clings to the punitive values of the system, his capacity for constantly obeying, reduce the dramatic space within which defiance can be expressed. There is little basis for alienation here at all, and Loman's discontent is diverted into personal channels of transgression. Failing to defy the company in any substantial way, his real violation is adultery. This explains the abundance of guilt in the person who is really the victim in the play. Moreover, it is not repressed guilt. Like nearly all of Miller's heroes, it is expressed openly, and Loman tries to incriminate his own family, to taint them with the odour of corruption he feels within his own soul, and which stems paradoxically from his betrayal of their trust.

Only in The Crucible and A View from the Bridge where Miller specifically and openly departs from his own ethnic background, does he begin to write tragic drama. He also moves away, at the same time, from contemporary middle-class and lower-middle-class life. The Crucible was the most ambitious historical drama in the American theatre since Mourning Becomes Electra. At the same time it had a more direct concern with ongoing political events in America. The witch-hunts of Salem were directly comparable, in some respects, to the witch-hunts of Macarthy and the HUAC. It is wrong, though, to fault Miller for not producing a rigorous ideological parallel. By its very nature, seventeenth-century Puritanism in New England is part of a different universe of thought from the political anti-communism of the Cold War. The threat to Salem was an elusive and irrational phenomenon, distorted by manipulating a zealously held and very rigid code of theological belief. The Puritans knew on the whole what they were for, whereas the common focus of the Macarthyites was what they were against. In this respect, the Moscow show trials of the thirties have more in common with the Salem trials than the American hearings of the forties and fifties.

Despite this, the play does have the power to illustrate the objective social workings of history within which the individual is hopelessly implicated and powerless, despite personal commitment to alter it. Outside of Germany, this is one of the most important historical dramas to be set at the beginning of the bourgeois epoch. It certainly makes no attempt to explain the hysteria about witchcraft which dominates it, but this lack of explanation is dramatically legitimate. Miller is concerned with the institutional consequences of the hysteria—the accusations, the witch-hunt, the casuistry of legal argument, the severity of punishment and finally the question of defiance or false confession. As a dramatic extrapolation of that process the play is gripping and to the point. John Proctor is one of the most positive heroes of all Miller's work, rational and eloquent in the defence of human justice. His resistance to the witch-hunt is not merely that of the rational man against irrational hysteria. It is his consistent opposition to the *rational* manipulation of irrational hysteria which gives the play its strength, the contrast between his own fortitude and the weakness of those who allow themselves to be manipulated and intimidated despite their disbelief in the whole process of judicial persecution.

But the strength of the play is compromised at a personal level. One significant change that Miller made from the court records at Salem was to transform Abigail Proctor from a child of eleven into a girl of seventeen and make her Proctor's former mistress. This liberty with history makes the exemption of Proctor from her general accusations seem more credible. But it also smuggles in by the back door the familiar and decisive private guilt of the Millerian hero, a guilt which destroys the tragic quality of his defiance of the unjust. At a crucial moment in the trial, Proctor humiliatingly admits his adultery with Abigail to the court. His wife is brought in to verify it, unaware of the confession. Hoping to save her husband's reputation, she denies it. The moment is dramatically convincing, but intellectually dubious. Why should the fate of Proctor hinge on the verification of adultery? Largely because it turns Proctor's guilt into the open wound familiar from the lesser plays, publicly displayed and then instrumental in compounding his unjust fate. 'I have made a bell of my honour', Proctor confesses, 'I have rung the doom of my good name—'. When his wife denies the adultery, he protests 'she only thought to save my name'. That very instinct condemns him to prison.

But this 'saving of Proctor's name' is only the prelude to a much greater compromise in the final act when the stain of guilt irreversibly mars the tragic vision. Proctor decides to confess to save his life, but is not prepared to implicate others in the confession. The crucial passage in which the conflict between Proctor and his prosecutors occurs is after the initial confession of guilt, when it is made clear to the defendant that he must publicly condemn others. But whereas Proctor is prepared to betray himself, to dishonour his own soul, he is not prepared to make public denunciations of other members of the community. The distinction between the public and private dimensions of dishonour are therefore paramount. Capitulation is a lesser evil than betrayal:

> Proctor . . . What others say and what I sign is not the same!
> Denforth. Why? Do you mean to deny this confession when you are free?
> Proctor. I mean to deny nothing!
> Danforth. Then explain to me, Mr. Proctor, why you will not let—
> Proctor (*with a cry of his whole soul*). Because it is my name! Because I cannot have another in my life! Because I lie and sign myself to lies! Because I am not worth the dust on the feet of them that hand! How may I live without my name? I have given you my soul; leave me my name![16]

Proctor's resistance here, the triumph of public conscience over private capitulation, is a victory. What matters to him is not the nature of the evil which persecutes him but the special defiance by which he refuses to share in that evil. He can be its victim, but not its accomplice. The compromise vitiates the tragic sense of loss. Something can be salvaged and saved, so the complete horror of facing the abyss is never reached.

Elizabeth's final cry after Proctor is led away, 'He has his goodness now', is a false note of affirmation. Her subsequent and concluding remark is more revealing. 'God forbid', she gasps anxiously, 'that I should take it away from him'. She is already beginning to believe the blame that is his, could eventually be her own, the guilt transferred from husband to wife.

In his own life, Miller was to show a firmer and more unwavering attitude towards the HUAC than his hero did to the judges of Salem. But in terms of the pressure exerted, and the possible punishment, there was no comparison. In one respect, life had imitated art, but in another, it had not. Indeed a grave weakness in the structure of the play results from the disparity between the attitudes of Proctor and those of his persecutors. His is the sensibility of a modern twentieth-century American liberal, with which Miller's audience could readily identify. His judges, on the other hand, are more accurate historical transcriptions of the religious fanaticism of seventeenth-century Salem, culturally alien to modern liberalism but also to its persecutors. This disparity between anachronism and authenticity illustrates the central dilemma of the kind of historical play which Miller is trying to write, and it is a dilemma which he never genuinely resolves. The indecisive and very contemporary hero is the victim of a strikingly archaic world.

The whole question of betrayal, especially betrayal of community, which is posed here, finds a clearer and more decisive answer in Miller's subsequent drama of contemporary Brooklyn, *A View from the Bridge*. This is the one unconditionally tragic work which Miller ever wrote, free from the spectres of repressed Jewishness and liberal guilt. It was based on a real-life incident told to Miller by a Brooklyn longshoreman, and is set in an Italian-American working-class community near the waterfront. The similarities with *A Streetcar Named Desire* are very strong. There is a working-class neighbourhood and a skeletal set, showing both the inside of the Carbone's apartment and the street outside. In Peter Brook's English production of the play, the sense of community was emphasised by showing people in the street going about their everyday lives while action took place inside the apartment. The lineage with O'Neill and Williams is therefore clear, but the sense in which this play represented Miller's only genuine mastery of modern tragedy has to be seen in a rather different light.

Miller first conceived the play as a poetic tragedy based clearly on the Greek form. The first version, then, recalled in its nature and purpose O'Neill's *Mourning Becomes Electra*. Yet it was clearly inferior.

Unlike O'Neill, Miller was trying here to write about contemporary life and produced a rather distant austere drama anomalous with its setting, and pretentious in its use of verse. Eddie Carbone, the hero-villain of the piece, appeared as a rather freakish and dehumanised monster. The choral effect which Miller attempted to create through a lawyer-narrator speaking in verse form was a disaster. In the second prose version the language of the social context is discovered with resounding effect. Carbone becomes demotic and human, Alfieri, the lawyer, still has a choral function, but this time it contains a terse and measured social comment on the life of the hero. Moreover, it has that distant and balanced judgment of the middle-class professional whose own life is partially detached from the community processes which finally drive Eddie to his doom. Alfieri is a mediator between hero and audience, more articulate and more knowing, but by that very token, removed from the social action which becomes inescapably tragic. He articulates the moral dilemma which Carbone is unable to articulate for himself.

There are strong similarities between Carbone and Stanley Kowalski. Both exhibit a qualified acceptance of the American way of life, in which they compensate in different ways for that lack of social power and privilege which is the fate of the working-class male. They compensate for these deficiences through control over women, control over the household, and the cultivation of an image of uncompromised virility. Stanley dominates Stella and brutally humiliates Blanche. Carbone exercised a tyrannical protectiveness over the lives of his wife and stepdaughter. It is the price of social integration and in each case has tragic consequences. There is, however, a significant switch of direction in Miller's play. Rather than the confrontation of social differences which Williams pursues, he is interested in the confrontation between individual desire and communal code. In Carbone's ethnic community there is a more strongly defined sense of loyalty and honour. It is something which Carbone himself cannot shed even as he violates it irreparably and pays with his life. This contradiction makes Carbone a tragic figure, where, without the presence of that code, he would merely be a monster. Miller did not therefore create a pure villain since the tyrant is also a victim; neither did he create a pure victim, like John Proctor or Willy Loman, because the victim here also victimises; and in his dual role, the one is inseparable from the other.

The proximity of Miller and Williams in these two plays is not merely confined to the working-class hero. It also lies in the dominance of a psychosexual motif which for Miller is unique. Admittedly there are sexual themes in his other work such as adultery, but here the personal and the social possess an organic relationship through the psychosexual displacement of the hero. This is not to posit a Freudian pathology, but rather to point out that the displacement derives from Carbone's social dilemma. The compensatory device of control over the women of the household in modern culture necessarily has an important sexual component. In this case, Carbone has displaced his affections from his wife to his niece, Catherine and when she falls in love with the younger of the illegal immigrants they are harbouring, Eddie regards him as a sexual rival. His jealousy transforms itself into authoritarian rage and insinuations of Rodolpho's homosexuality. The point is that he conceals and rationalises his desire within the code of the community until its credibility is totally strained. But his resentment and envy do have a social origin, which becomes clear when he explains himself to the lawyer Alfieri:

> Eddie (*with a helpless but ironic gesture*). What can I do? I'm a patsy, what can a patsy do? I worked like a dog twenty years so a punk could have her, so that's what I done. I mean in the worst times, in the worst, when there wasn't ship comin' in the harbour, I didn't stand around lookin' for relief—I hustled. When there was empty piers in Brooklyn I went to Hoboken, Staten Island, The West Side, Jersey, all over—because I made a promise. I took out of my own mouth to give to her. I took out of my wife's mouth. I walked hungry plenty days in this city! (*It begins to break through.*) And now I gotta sit in my own house and look at a son-of-a-bitch like that—which he came out of nowhere! I give him my house to sleep! I take the blankets off my bed for him, and he takes and puts his dirty filthy hands on her like a goddam thief![17]

Though Carbone exaggerates social rationale to conceal personal jealousy, the two are inextricable. Rodolpho challenges his sense of household possession and without the confidence of that possession, the feeling of purpose is lost to him. Even then, however, the basis of that possession has already been undermined. His repressed desire for Catherine compels him to neglect his wife and no longer sleep with her. When Rodolfo arrives, his authority is already on the wane and the immigrant's presence is a catalyst to an inevitable process. Here is the poignant scene in which Eddie, after failing to prevent his niece taking up a secretarial job on the other side of Brooklyn, acknowledges the inevitable:

Eddie (*smilin' sadly yet somehow proud of her*). Well . . . I hope you
have good luck. I wish you the best. You know that, kid.

Catherine (*rising, trying to laugh*). You sound like I'm goin' a million
miles!

Eddie. I know. I guess I just never figured on one thing.

Catherine (*smiling*). What?

Eddie. That you would ever grow up.[18]

The theme of lost innocence is common in American literature and
there is an echo of Ella Downey in *All God's Chillun'*. Both Eddie and
Catherine feel a sense of loss. But whereas Catherine, prompted by
Beatrice, begins to realise she can no longer behave like a child in front
of Eddie, the part of her which Eddie is also losing is her growing sexual
maturity which has captivated him. The reference to her growing up is
ambiguous, since he wants her most for the very reason that he has to
lose her. But the loss of a loved one is tied up with the more sensuous
dilemma—the imagined loss of virility. Virility, or machismo, is the
saving grace. It is why Stanley Kowalski is a born survivor, because he
has cultivated it on the basis of his physical capacities. Carbone, on the
other hand, an older man, strives desperately not to see himself as a
sexual failure. He can no longer satisfy his wife. He knows his desire for
Catherine is illicit yet he is too homely to try and find a substitute for
his niece. He has no institutional power to prevent Rodolpho working
because dock work is controlled by the syndicate. Therefore his virile
posturing becomes overt and embarrassing, ultimately counter-
productive. He tells Beatrice, referring to Rodolpho, 'I can't cook,
I can't sing, I can't make dresses, so I'm on the waterfront'. But
Beatrice also knows that he cannot bring himself to make love to her.
When he hits Rodolpho hard in a playful boxing match, he does not
establish his superiority. For Marco immediately challenges him to a
trial of strength—lifting a chair by its leg which Eddie fails humiliatingly to do. The last chance for him to recapture his virility, and
disprove Rodolpho's, is an act of desperation. Brilliantly conceived,
dramatically speaking, it is the famous scene in which Eddie, drunk on
Christmas Eve, catches the lovers together in her bedroom. It is the
climax of the whole process of rationalisation by which Eddie,
claiming to defend a moral code, violates it more severely than those he
accuses. He passionately kisses Catherine out of desire and Rodolpho
out of contempt, one after the other. The action meant to reflect on
them, only succeeds in reflecting on himself.

It is only when the myth of his virility is broken that he tips off the two Italians anonymously to the authorities. The code and his own desire are finally incompatible. Even then, he tries to rationalise his own actions in terms of the code, denying his guilt and claiming his name. As Marco comes to fight him for the betrayal, Eddie facing death demands a respect which can never be given to him in terms of the code he has broken. As he addresses the assembled neighbourhood his demand has a genuine tragic pathos, which eludes Miller in *The Crucible* where he is more concerned to justify Proctor, despite the latter's guilt and indecision.

> He knows that ain't right. To do like that? To a man? Which I put my roof over their head and my food in their mouth? Like in the Bible? Strangers I have never seen in my whole life? To come out of the water and grab a girl for a passport? To go and take from your own family like from that stable—and never a word to me? And now accusations in the bargain! (*Directly to Marco.*) Wipin' the neighbourhood with my name like a dirty rag! I want my name, Marco.[19]

The naming of names finally assumes a tragic context, because the violation is irreparable. Although this play is not a direct comment on Macarthyism it contains a more universal theme out of which that specific evil comes, and it is directly about the contemporary America in which Macarthyism had thrived. The sense of tragic fate springs directly here from the code, the proletarian code, of community retribution. Thus in discussing Eddie's fate, Alfieri tells the audience he feels powerless to stop it. There is no place here, as in *The Crucible*, for a potentially rational court of law and the lawyer-narrator is relating a tale which exists beyond his own domain. Like Horace Benbow, another middle-class lawyer in Faulkner's *Sanctuary*, he has no real brief to prevent retribution or the miscarriage of justice. 'I mourn him—I admit it—with a certain . . . alarm', he concludes. In that confession, lies a significant social role-reversal. The working-class docker is the tragic protagonist and the middle-class lawyer the narrator of his fate. Miller thus takes his rightful place in the literary transformation of Western drama. Equally the device is a reminder that the audience of Miller's play will be like those of other working-class dramas, predominantly middle class. Alfieri talks to them in a language they can understand. But that power of mediation, it is soon apparent, can take place only because the action cannot be altered. Liberal guilt, as it were, is externalised into the role of the narrator where it has a detached rather than a frantic quality. Fate is thus purified of the reflective understanding which eludes its heroic victim, and is portrayed with an immediacy and an intensity which Miller was never again to recapture.

In the work of most dramatists, tragic writing is usually indicative of a creative maturity, an achievement reached after intense creative struggle. But because tragic drama has a very rooted social context, it cannot be explained solely in terms of that individual struggle. The point is aptly made by the example of Edward Albee. Albee wrote at the end of this phase of tragic drama in American life and thus, paradoxically, his first work attained it with a purity and a strength which he never repeated. *The Zoo Story*, written in 1958 and first produced in Berlin the following year, is arguably his best single work. The immediate response to it was to claim it for a modern experimental theatre, or the theatre of the absurd in which naturalist techniques had been rejected or superceded. Albee's play seemed at first sight to have much in common with the work of Beckett, Ionesco and Pinter. It made little attempt to identify its characters. Their social background seemed of minimal importance; the references to their past life were often veiled and oblique. The encounter of the two main protagonists in Central Park in fact appeared to have little relationship to any other kind of social event at all. It seemed existential and self-contained. Yet the most significant fact about the play—often overlooked—is the link it has with past American tragedy. Just as *Suddenly Last Summer* echoes *The Emperor Jones* in the emphasis on primitive horror, so Albee's play echoes O'Neill's concern in *The Hairy Ape* with animality and social exclusion. The short plays inaugurating American tragic drama are echoed in the short plays which end it forty years later.

The obvious similarity between Yank and Jerry is their desire to communicate with animals where they have failed with fellow humans. It seems fitting that Jerry may have visited the same zoo in which Yank had been crushed to death by a gorilla. But there is a significant difference of time and of identity. Unlike Yank, Jerry is a flabby overgrown beatnik of fifties vintage. His protagonist is a respectable office worker. In a way, the play is prophetic of the counter-culture of the late sixties and early seventies, because it reveals the enormous gulf between the two characters. Yet, despite the opinion of most critics, it does this realistically. Many have confused the lack of a strong social identity with the transient nature of the encounter, which is itself highly realistic. Jerry indeed calls himself at one point, '*a permanent transient*' and the play dispenses with the normal forms of social signposting. We only know about them what they can convey naturalistically in conversation to one another. The sense of the unknown is not a quality of the writing but a feature of the social situation where each confronts a stranger about whom he has no previous knowledge. In that engrossing but limiting case, the drama possesses that same relationship to Erving Goffman's sociology of interaction rituals as Miller's early work does to *White Collar* and theories of mass society. It is the dramatic working-out of a first encounter, which as Goffman claims, is itself a dramatic event.

The question of animality operates through interaction, and dramatically works on two levels. The 'zoo story' Jerry recounts is his attempt to communicate with animals, in this case his landlady's ill-nourished dog, where communication with humans is impossible. Subsequently he tries to direct his abortive relationship with Peter in the direction of an animalistic struggle for territory. But this territoriality, though an animal phenomenon, involves symbolic rituals which are distinctly human and social. Like *The Hairy Ape* it involves a descent to the level of animality. But the meaning of that descent similarly entails a stripping away of civilised artefact, an unmasking of the civilised forms of human ritual as superficial and dispensable. Jerry's taunting of Peter is not merely a knowing and deliberate ritual. Underlying it emotionally, is a combination of anguished desire and nihilistic despair. The encounter has strong homosexual overtones. Jerry's confession of his adolescent homosexuality and the transience of his sexual encounters with women tend to this direction, as does Peter's willingness to stay and absorb the ritual punishment handed out to him. There is then the veiled promise of mutual need which the direction of the actual encounter systematically erodes.

Although the metaphor is animality, the erosion is social. The social difference of the protagonists has the strength of the difference of odour among animals, and the play prophetically acts out a major social division of American life in the late sixties—the revolt of a radical middle-class youth against its respectable parentage, the resistance of a counter-culture to the predominant mores of middle-class life. For despite the social hiatus, the play hinges upon a distinctive kind of knowingness. Jerry can almost always tell in advance what the response of his respectable protagonist will be. Whereas he is outside that culture and therefore unpredictable to Peter at every turn, the opposite is true of the man in publishing. Jerry knows him from the inside, almost as if their confrontation was an affair *en famille*. Albee captures the quintessential nature of the American counter-culture with remarkable perspicacity. It knows its enemy but camouflages itself in order not to be known for what it is. The counter-culture's estrangement is Jerry's ritual of 'making strange', of deliberately disfiguring conventional forms of accessibility and engagement. The ritual throws Peter into confusion. His strange reluctance to leave appears as an ambiguous form of bourgeois masochism, as if almost inviting the humiliation he suffers. Despite this, it is not he but his tormentor who ends up as the real victim.

Though a ritual of humiliation in some respects, the taunting is never a means to conquest. It is rather a means of goading the publisher into a violent defensive act, mirroring the rationale of that kind of political violence which a few years later was seen to be the necessary means of revealing the true repressiveness of a state apparatus conventionally concealed under the veneer of liberalism. But as a political tactic, the manoeuvre is self-defeating, and at a personal level, it is suicidal, the explicit crystallisation of a very specific kind of death-wish in which the victim dictates the terms of his own destruction. The vital aspect of that 'revolutionary' suicide is captured in Jerry's death. It is not amenable, in its execution, to any process of recuperation. Jerry's murder is genuinely tragic, born out of tragic strife. He can only control his destiny by destroying himself while Peter, by unwillingly killing his protagonist, is drawn into a living nightmare he neither wishes nor believes could possibly happen.

The denouement starts with a territorial fight for possession of the bench on which Peter is originally sitting by himself. There are two stages to the provocation. Jerry goads Peter into possessively defending the bench as if it were his own property, then he prompts him in desperation to call for the police:

Jerry. I said I want this bench, and I'm going to have it. Now get over there.
Peter. People can't have everything they want. You should know that; it's a rule: people can have some of the things they want, but they can't have everything.
Jerry (*laughs*). Imbecile. You're slow-witted!
Peter. Stop that!
Jerry. You're a vegetable. Go lie down on the ground.
Peter (*intense*). Now you listen to me. I've put up with you all afternoon.
Jerry. Not really.

Peter. LONG ENOUGH. I've put up with you long enough. I've listened to you because you seemed . . . well, because I thought you wanted to talk to somebody.

Jerry. You put things well; economically, and, yet, . . . oh, what is the word I want to put justice to your . . . Jesus, you make me sick . . . get off here and give me my bench.

Peter. MY BENCH!

Jerry (*pushes Peter almost but not quite off the bench*). Get out of my sight.

Peter (*regaining his position*). God da . . mn you. That's enough! I've had enough of you. I will not give up this bench; you can't have it, and that's that. Now go away.

(*Jerry snorts but does not move.*)

Go away, I said.

(*Jerry does not move.*)

    Get away from here. If you don't move on, you're a bum . . . that's what you are . . . If you don't move on, I'll get a policeman and make you go.

(*Jerry laughs, stays.*)

I warn you, I'll call a policeman.

Jerry (*softly*). You won't find a policeman here; they're all over the west side of the park chasing fairies down from trees or out of the bushes. That's all they do. So scream your head off; it won't do you any good.

Peter. POLICE! I warn you, I'll have you arrested. POLICE! (*Pause.*) I feel ridiculous.[20]

The immense theatricality of the territorial combat relies on very simple props, on a 'poor' theatre in which nonetheless the whole issue of a possessive individualism is brought to light. While Peter is goaded into aggression, that aggression is explicitly rationalised as a defence of law and personal property in the interest of self-possession. That Jerry manages to elicit it, and annihilate the assumptions on which in everyday middle-class life it is taken for granted, is a pyrrhic victory. He offers himself as a sacrifical victim to that process of annihilation, and his own death, where he impales himself on the blade of the knife in Peter's hand, is the culmination of that process. His strategy is only complete when Peter has been transformed into a murderer and must go home to see the picture of his victim on television later that night. But in order for the publisher to become a murderer his protagonist must be his victim. The tragedy lies in the destruction of the relationship and the death which is both murder and suicide. The coaxing toward destruction is inseparable from the coaxing toward understanding, toward the promise which is then wilfully destroyed.

The power and intensity of Albee's vision is in part a function of its shortened and concentrated form. This is the link with *Suddenly Last Summer*, and it becomes clearer when Albee opts for a more extended form and a more conventional setting in *Who's Afraid of Virginia Woolf*. Savagely funny in parts, Albee's attempt to go beyond comic situation to the creation of a tragic denouement is an outright failure. The play is the first major American work since *Strange Interlude* to use an academic setting. But the enclosed universe of the academic world becomes a decisive limitation. The strategies of the transient encounter which in *The Zoo Story* have a genuinely tragic pathos are transformed here into stereotyped ploys of domestic humiliation, the institutionalised baiting of a sophisticated intelligentsia. Albee is to be commended for dispensing with the aura of academic gentility. But the ugliness which replaces it reveals the limitation of his dramatic vision. 'Humping the hostess', 'Getting the guests', Inventing the child' are ingenious games behind which lies a permanent emptiness. Like Goffman, Albee has a very vacuous conception of human nature because he can present nothing beyond the playing out of roles. True the dramatic effect lies in the impact of the game—how it can hurt or wound, the emotional response it draws when it breaks down. But emotional response can never break free from the tyranny of the game, which reigns supreme.

This play in many ways marks a point of transition not only in American, but western theatre as a whole, between a drama of experience and a drama of sensation. The dramatic impact of Albee's work, its *immediate* impact, is undeniable. To that extent it is aligned with the new work of the sixties by Jack Gelber, Arthur Kopit, Leroi Jones, Rochelle Owens, Sam Shepard and Jean Claude van Italie. But this transition with its concern to shock and its devotion to immediacy, also loses the dimension of experience which is offered in different ways by the realist and the epic theatre. The hollow quality of *Virginia Woolf*, despite its comic brilliance and theatricality, places it at the crossroads. Albee subsequently abandoned social experience and naturalist technique, much to the detriment of his own work. In *Virginia Woolf* the transition can be seen and the subsequent loss felt. The attempt to retain with a theatre of sensation some serious figural dimension—on which all tragedy is based—results in an almost unparalleled ugliness in the portrayal of human nature. The dramatic portrayal of shock and horror has to remove itself from social experience in order not to disfigure human nature as such. But the price of that removal has usually been the death of tragedy.

'In my beginning is my end.' Eliot's statement in *The Four Quartets* would seem highly appropriate to the development of tragedy in the American theatre. *The Zoo Story* and *Suddenly Last Summer* extend and consummate *The Hairy Ape* and *The Emperor Jones*. The point of cessation is relatively clear, and can be shown by looking at three of the most important American plays of the sixties—Albee's *The Death of Bessie Smith*, James Baldwin's *Blues for Mr Charlie* and Leroi Jones' *Dutchman*. All three are explosive dramas of racial conflict which bear immediate comparison with *All God's Chillun*, the first of O'Neill's social tragedies. But they fail, in a variety of ways to extend it, and its social and artistic strength actually becomes clearer when the later works are seen side by side with it. The common denominator in all the plays is the vital relationship between black and white. But each of the modern plays represents, in one aspect at least, a falling short of O'Neill's achievement. Of the three, Albee comes nearest to capturing dramatically speaking the vicious and corrosive quality of white racism. But the achievement is ambiguous. It derives from the more general flair he has for uncovering human ugliness and is confined to the circumstance of a rather shiftless role-playing at the admissions desk of the hospital. Moreover the racial imbalance is a vital flaw. Albee makes no real attempt to portray blacks as more than dramatic ciphers and Bessie Smith is the absent heroine who never appears on stage. In the case of Baldwin's play, the flaw is perhaps the opposite. The play suffers from a surfeit of human sympathy. Of the white murderer of the black youth (based on Emmett Till who was murdered in Mississippi in 1955), Baldwin wrote in his introduction: 'It is we who have persuaded him that Negroes are worthless human beings'. But in his desire to present a social understanding of the poor white, Baldwin misses the quality of evil which needs to be there in spite of human sympathy. Although he remains nearest to O'Neill in spirit, he again succumbs to an imbalance in which the portrait of the whites in the play is nowhere near as dramatically convincing as that of the blacks. A severe judgment would be that it verges at times on apologetics. Of Leroi Jones, that could never be said. Jones captures the vital element in O'Neill which is missing from Albee and Baldwin—the immediate impact of racial humiliation. The chance encounter of Lula and Clay is similar to Jerry and Peter in *The Zoo Story*. But the white girl's humiliation of the black man recalls Ella and Jim in *All God's Chillun*, to which it is close in spirit, and which it finally ends, artistically and historically, by Clay's violent repudiation of Uncle Tomism. But Lula is a fragmentary and incomplete persona, at times a fear-haunted sexual fantasy, at other times the crystallisation of Clay's inner conscience condemning his docile conformity. She does not stand out like Ella Downey as a tragic figure, rather as a dramatic device for Clay's transformation. At times she is little more than a figment of Clay's imagination. The tragic alienation of Jones's hero is marred by the failure of the dramatist to make the denouement truly convincing. While Clay has a more intensely wounded alienation than the arrogant and militant young hero of Baldwin's play, Jones resorts to a sexual reductionism which loses the wider historical and cultural dimensions of racism Baldwin manages to create. The dilemma is a real one. By comparison with the resounding impact of *Dutchman*, Baldwin's play is theatrically fuzzy and at times too literary. But it does not succumb to the process of figural decomposition which distorts, in Jones's case, the nature of what is a potentially tragic work. The hiatus between the conventional forms of realism and the new theatre of sensation has illuminated a more general divergence of tragedy and realism in the theatre by which both have been substantially diminished.

The division was mirrored in the American theatre world by the development of the national theatre at the Lincoln Centre which opened in 1964. It has largely been the preserve of the old guard and has had little use for the new forms of theatrical experimentation which have revitalised the off-Broadway theatre in the last ten years. It is perhaps significant too that Baldwin, Jones and Albee were all absent from the opening programme. Despite the euphemistic tone of Elia Kazan in his speech to the first meeting of the acting company, the choice of opening productions was indicative of the malaise of the American theatre as a whole.[21] From O'Neill's work, the company performed *Marco Millions* and *Strange Interlude* and from Miller's work, *Incident at Vichy* and *After the Fall*. Two of America's major playwrights were thus celebrated with indifferent productions of their inferior work. No tragic drama was attempted. The Lincoln Theatre became the high temple of a stale bougeois drama while the vital developments in drama took place more and more within the context of a counter-culture where shock and immediacy were regarded as the legitimate and effective weapons of a struggle against the cultural establishment. As a result there was no genuinely national theatre. The cult of

American egoism, which first reflected itself in the drama of liberal guilt and the Method adulteration of psychoanalysis, now gave way to highly individualised expressions of outrage, many of them original and harrowing but most of them faddish and transient. As the most substantial source of tragic drama in the twentieth century, the United States still had no enduring theatre to do that achievement justice.

Postscript:
The Absence of Tragedy
in the English Theatre

The modern period of English drama, starting with the first productions of Ibsen, the comedies of Oscar Wilde and the emergence of George Bernard Shaw, is notable for two things—an insular neglect of theatrical innovation and the absence of tragedy. From 1890 to 1956, the English theatre was one of the most conservative and unadventurous in Europe. From 1918 to 1956, its stylistic torpor and its neglect of the social content of English life made its complacency unparalleled in the Western World. Impervious to the transformations of its own art, it was equally impervious to the transformations of the society around it. In the twenties it was dominated by farce and musical comedy and came to be regarded as a place for social escapism. The Great War, the general strike and later the Great Depression might, it seemed, never have happened. Though some changes occurred after 1945, this large-scale neglect of social life does much to explain the spontaneous and explosive acclamation of *Look Back in Anger* in 1956. John Osborne's play was not only looking back in anger at post-war Britain's colonial past but also at the English theatre which had developed as if the threat to Empire never even existed. The play appeared to many people to mark the end of a lengthy and unnerving silence, during which complacent drama over several decades had never really questioned the basic institutions of British life.

There were strong institutional reasons for this complacency. With the decline of the actor-manager at the turn of the century and the advent of the commercial West End theatre, there was a heavy bias towards London and respectable theatre-going became a convention by which the *nouveau riche* bourgeoisie could imitate the social manners of the upper classes.[1] The archaic but effective censorship of the Lord Chamberlain set drastic limits upon the development of serious drama, and lack of state patronage handicapped those theatre companies

241

committed to producing it. Moreover 'seriousness' in the English theatre had now become strongly linked with tradition, above all with the godlike figure of Shakespeare. Shakespearean drama of course had benefited enormously from developments in the Victorian theatre, but the Bard inspired no tradition of theatrical writing in the way that he had inspired new directions in acting and producing.

The major failure, however, taken in conjunction with all these factors, was the artistic inability to respond to dramatists and theatres of other countries. Despite the efforts of his most fervent supporters, Shaw amongst them, Ibsen was never given a true theatrical voice in the English theatre. As a serious dramatist, Shaw proved unable to fill the vacuum. The Edwardian age thus saw the English stage divided in tripartite fashion between a truncated Ibsen, a satirical Shaw, and a rather stiff and old-fashioned Galsworthy. By the beginning of the war, this legacy was insufficient to create a new and vital body of dramatic work to act as a springboard for major innovation. As experimentation and change increased in Europe, English drama became more insular, not less, a rather bland and eccentric version of theatre in one country. Of course Chekhov and O'Casey, O'Neill and later Williams were successfully produced on the English stage. But until the 1950s their artistic impact was minimal. Certainly the work of Williams and Miller did have its effect on the Renaissance of 1956, but the wider issue was the reassertion of the social relevance of the theatre and the ending of England's cultural isolation. This could only come with the end of Empire and for that very reason seemed deceptively at the time as if it had come out of nowhere.

There are, however, continuities in English drama throughout the century which must not be overlooked, continuities possessing both stylistic and thematic durability. One enduring theme which links Shaw and Galsworthy to John Osborne and Peter Shaffer is the attitude towards authority. Galsworthy's work is particularly important here. Though dealing with social issues of its own time, it was a throwback to the early Victorian novel and the lower-class melodrama of the mid-century. In his most important plays *Strife* and *Justice*, Galsworthy's main emphasis is on the unnecessary hardship and ill-treatment of the lower classes. The didactic judgment about that hardship and ill-treatment is always from the viewpoint of an existing authority and the prevalent moral code of the day. The plays are an appeal to the moral conscience of that authority to be more enlightened and humane in its dealings with people of subservient social position, while remaining rational and loyal to its basic function of exercising power for the respectable and the privileged. The same appeal is made by Shaw in a more comic vein, where he attacks those who accept privilege as a fact of life needing no further moral justification and ignore the sufferings of those excluded from it. The appeal of the dramatist, however enlightened, is to the possessor of power and privilege. Edwardian drama thus reflected the wider ideological concern of reform from above which had profoundly affected English parliamentary and social life since 1848 and gathered momentum towards the turn of the century. Iconoclastically, Shaw and Galsworthy, like the major novelists before them, extended the acceptable boundaries of 'enlightened' action. But their ideological frame of reference is still one within which, though class differences are recognised, a spirit of social reconciliation based on existing authority prevails.

The consequence is that the dramatic space for tragic alienation is never available to them. Attempts to write tragedy are ultimately unsuccessful. *Justice*, in terms of its social theme a predecessor to *Death of a Salesman*, is an attempt to inject tragic pathos into the predicament of a poor clerk caught embezzling from his employer in order to give financial support to a battered wife desperately trying to escape the clutches of her husband. Falder, the clerk, then becomes the victim of a process of excessive judicial severity, imprisoned unfairly for his misdemeanour, and subsequently refused the opportunity to start afresh after his return to civilian life. But though he transgresses, Falder is never truly rebellious. He remains deferential to the bitter end, accepting the wrongful advice of his social betters which finally destroys him. Similar displays of social deference pervade the comedies of Shaw even when the satire is directed against the privileged. While it clearly did reflect something basic to the social manners of the period, it equally ignored the possibilities of a more fundamental challenge to the class-ridden values of British society.

In the most powerful of his dramas, *Strife*, the power of Galsworthy's writing actually lies in the abandonment of rational and humane attitudes by its two main protagonists. These are the two leaders of capital and labour respectively, who confront each other during a miner's strike—Anthony, chairman of the board, and Roberts, leader of the strike committee. The irony of the piece soon becomes apparent. Galsworthy is counselling reason and moderation, yet the dramatic strength of the work comes entirely from the two men who are intransigent in their attitudes, who tend to extremes and refuse all accommodation. It is the nearest thing in Edwardian drama to a realistic conception of the demonic, an achievement far beyond the grasp of Shaw. But since extremism on both sides is portrayed as a rearguard action causing widespread human suffering before the eventual triumph of reason, the 'strife' of the play's title does not eventuate in tragedy. Rather the opposite. The power and threat of implacable strife is there from the very beginning and only at the end is it finally contained. The eventual triumph of reason is an alternative to tragic strife, but the figural dimensions of the play are such that Galsworthy had the artistic potential to create it. The reason why he did not lies in the ideological vindication of 'humane authority'.

Having found a genuine language for rebellious miners and shown his figural power, Galsworthy's attempt at tragic drama overshadows that of Shaw, whereas his overall contribution to the theatre was substantially less. Shaw attempted to theatricalise intellectual controversy by comic means and the vitality of the work lies in the wit derived from personal self-contradiction and social hypocrisy. But the use of language is stereotyped. The predominant mode is that of the Edwardian drawing room, at times brittle, at times flaccid, but always flippant in tone. It lacked the epigrammatic purity of Wilde and did not create the dynamism of new speech patterns to put it in its place. The wit is that of an essayist adapted for the theatre, and the human voice becomes the comic mouthpiece of verbal interplay. The occasional intrusion of the lower classes into the world of the privileged provides the audience with a refreshing honesty and openness, but generally the lower classes are naive and parochial. While their plight is to be taken seriously, they themselves are not. Though Shaw had been effective in ridiculing the Establishment, the experience of the Great War prompted him to write more serious and ambitious drama than he had done previously.

Shaw's two most important plays of this period were *Heartbreak House* and *Saint Joan*. The former was his idiosyncratic attempt to present Chekhovian themes to the English theatre audience for the first time. Later during the twenties Chekhov's plays were produced in England, notably by the Russian emigré Theodore Komisarchevsky. But Shaw's Chekhovia, which he called a 'fantasia on Russian themes' was a distinct travesty of the work of the Russian dramatist. It modelled itself on the landed family and the Russian country estate, and was written with the hindsight of the war and the Russian revolution. The transposition from Russia to the English upper classes and to the setting of the North Sussex Downs was ingenious but insubstantial. Shaw overbalances into a fantasy of the destruction of the upper classes largely because their actual destruction, as happened in Russia, still seemed remote and unreal in England. The room in which the play is largely set 'has been built to resemble the after part of an old-fashioned high-pooped ship with a stern gallery'. The names of the characters—Chaptain Shotover, Lady Utterword, Mrs Hushabye—speak for themselves. The explosions, never explained, which shake the 'ship' at the end of play are obviously the air bombs of a new stage of modern warfare, but the reason as to why they should fall on Heartbreak House as opposed to homes and factories in large cities is never explained. Shaw was too literal and too sensational in bombing the upper classes out of existence, and too insubstantial in making the parasites of his eccentric 'ship' no better than caricatures. The problem was not merely thematic. He had failed to find a suitable form for serious drama, and any tragedy of contemporary life then became impossible.

As a historical drama, *Saint Joan* by comparison stands on more solid ground. His heroine is perhaps the most substantial of all his creations, and has many links with the female figures of modern tragedy. Moreover the choice of the historical subject seemed very apposite. The Suffragette movement had finally secured the vote for women after a long and ardous campaign. In Ireland, a Free State had been created with minimal help from the Catholic church which dominated its people, and the British withdrew from Southern Ireland after centuries of Imperial rule. The fight of Joan against the English and against the Church provides an echo of both the feminist and the nationalist struggles of Shaw's own time. As for Joan herself, Shaw regarded her as a tragic figure, and wanted to transform the dramatic conception of tragedy in his work. He reacted strongly against the earlier tradition of using absolute notions of good and evil in tragedy which he thought melodramatic and sought instead for a formula more appropriate to a sociological understanding of modern life. He thus claimed that Joan was burnt by 'normally innocent people' and that 'the tragedy of such murders is that they were not committed by murderers'. He portrays her execution not as criminal but as wrongheaded, the result of blind ignorance rather than evil intent. There is, implicit in this, a sociological challenge to traditional conventions of tragedy. If the social and political origins of wrongdoing are uncovered, then surely the ideas of good and evil are inappropriate to human action? For if those origins can be identified and eradicated, surely what previously was thought of as evil can now be seen as stupidity and error, faults which can be eradicated by practical reforms? The persuasive logic of Shaw's argument is not matched by his dramatic presentation. The main feature of modern tragedy, as we have seen, is that good and evil do prevail as human attributes within the context of social alienation. Shaw's moral relativism, intended as a declaration of enlightenment, erodes the figural dimension of his writing, and as far as tragedy is concerned undermines his ability to create irreparable loss.

This can be seen most clearly when Joan's prosecutors from the Church and the Inquisition are presented as judicious and convention-ally intelligent. In establishing their role in the play, Shaw uses a method similar to that of Brecht's 'complex seeing'. They make the play intelligible to their audience by commenting on the action in ways of which they would have been historically incapable before the limits of their own understanding are exposed. The functioning of Church and Inquisition is thus explained in the language of the twentieth century. This has the benefit of making heresy an under-standable phenomenon. But in the course of dramatic action, there is a dubious switch of emphasis. At first we see the play through the eyes of the heroine, but latterly through the eyes of her persecutors. The reversion to established authority is paramount. It is a myopic yet conscience-stricken authority, no doubt, but the change destroys the potentially tragic climax. Both Cauchon and the Inquisitor are such articulate practitioners of ecclesiastical authority, that Joan's predica-ment is stifled during the trial scene by the sheer weight of their unchallenged verbosity. The voice that is heard at the trial is not that of the rebel but that of the apologists, and the tone of that voice is authoritative, despite its failures of insight.

The role of the clergy is vital in fact. It restores to the French ruling class that tone of authority which the Dauphin and the nobles had discredited through weakness and incompetence. It is her ability to trample down public objections to her military strategy which makes Joan so formidable in the first act. But later, when confronted by the stern and unrelenting accusers of the Church, her rustic wisdom is gradually exposed as the naive and lower-class superstition so familiar from Shaw's more contemporary plays. The displacement involved here is a fascinating one. Shaw transposes the dilemma of the British ruling class of his own time into late Medieval France (though the nationalist cause of Joan herself is much closer to that of Britain's Irish protagonists). It makes sense of Shaw's view that the political stature of British leadership was flimsy and laughable while its legitimacy, on the other hand, was quite formidable. The division between nobility and church encapsulates this very succinctly. But the nobility are in fact too weak and insipid to be anything other than figures of fun. Their language remains that of the Edwardian drawing-room, and they lack any formal dignity, eloquence or power of expression. The cosy upper-class vernacular makes nonsense of the historical form. While Shaw wanted to deflate the pretensions of historical melodrama he had no viable speech to put in its place, and his nobles simply became straw men.

Joan's real struggle, consequently, is with her religious masters, not her political ones, and she is too weak to confront her enemies on her own terms. The weight of ecclesiastical authority is too great for her to consistently defy. The crucial exchange is in scene six where Joan signs a written confession of heresy only to find that while it lifts the threat of execution from her head, she is still faced with life imprisonment. Her resistance collapses, and her plea for mercy is one of sentimental pity, not tragic defiance. She pleads against being shut out 'from the light of the sky and the sight of the fields and the flowers' and her will is broken. Like Brecht's Galileo there is a willingness to compromise under pressure. But as in the case of John Proctor, there is a retreat from absolute co-operation back into defiance. Yet the return to defiance is sentimental and lacking in credibility. She remains the inspired courageous simpleton suddenly shown to be weak and vulnerable. As if to wilfully deny the tragic character of her ending, Shaw produces the damaging epilogue where his heroine returns from the dead to see how everyone is living without her. The intellectual intention here is to show how suddenly historical fortunes can change, but the effect is simply to detract from the seriousness of the heroine's fate.

To be fair, Shaw's work cannot be labelled simply as drama of social reform. He recognised the growing challenge to the established order in the twentieth century and the intransigence of much lower-class discontent. But his dramatic focus remained to the end the blindness and stupidity of the upper classes in failing to understand that discontent. The fact that in the one play where he really confronted the issues head on, he resorted to historical drama, meant that his dramatic work lost much in the process. Joan was a fascinating historical figure in her own right—which explains the attractiveness of the play for modern audiences—but direct references to Shaw's own life and times which the play might evoke invariably take second place. When a drama critical of English institutions re-asserted itself, Shaw's influence was small, and the tone of the new work clearly had a new dimension which could not traced back to his own.

What brings the drawing-room drama to an end, is not primarily the internal changes in English society—the decline of the landed aristocracy, the rise of the Labour party, and the introduction of the welfare state—so much as a related external factor—the disintegration of Empire. The first production of *Look Back in Anger* sparking off a minor English revival came in the same year as the last great Imperial adventure—the fiasco of Suez. It then became clear that the cushioning effect of tolerance in the British parliamentary state was to be sought and found in the overarching security of Empire. Even the war against Hitler took place within this context. Although it temporarily enhanced the sense of national consciousness, the gradual and irreversible loss of the colonies both revealed and then destroyed the dependence on Imperial legitimacy. *Look Back in Anger* did two things. It inveighed against a society which had seemingly not changed in value since Edwardian times, and simultaneously condemned by implication a stasis in form which had atrophied the English theatre since then. Jimmy Porter's anger is directed against the stereotypes of upper-class England, and reflexively against their unjustified monopolisation of the English stage.

The impact of the diffuse and often inchoate anger of John Osborne's hero works because it combines these two things. It appeals both to the social experience of its audience but also to their experience of the theatre, to their collective memory of the English plays they had seen in their own lifetime. The link becomes most explicit during one of Jimmy's more devastating speeches in the play, the character-assassination of Alison's brother Nigel:

He's a big chap. Well, you've never heard so many well-bred commonplaces come from beneath the same bowler hat. The Platitude from Outer Space—that's brother Nigel. He'll end up in the Cabinet one day, make no mistake. But somewhere at the back of that mind is the vague knowledge that he and his pals have been plundering and fooling everybody for generations (*Going upstage and turning*). Now Nigel is just about as vague as you can get without actually being invisible. And invisible politicians aren't much use to anyone—not even to *his* supporters! And nothing is more vague above Nigel than his knowledge. His knowledge of life and ordinary human beings is so hazy, he really deserves some sort of decoration for it—a medal inscribed 'For Vaguery in the Field'. But it wouldn't do for him to be troubled by any stabs of conscience, however vague. (*Moving down again.*) Besides, he's a patriot and an Englishman, and he doesn't like the idea that he may have been selling out his countryman all these years, so what does he do. The only thing he can do—seek sanctuary in his own stupidity. The only way to keep things as much like they have been as possible, is to make any alternative too much for your poor tiny brain to grasp.[2]

The real fire in Jimmy's anger derives not from the directly odious nature of his enemies—at times his contempt for them verges on pity. It comes instead from the fact that they have got away with so much for so long. Thus Nigel and Colonel Redfearn, the 'Edwardian brigade', are hated because they have been exemplary models of Englishness for so long, their hegemony unchallenged over generations. And once that challenge has been made, nothing can atone for the years of compliant silence. It is the anger at what had not previously been done which consumes Osborne's hero, and also in a way destroys him. For his Sunday afternoon bed-sitter eloquence is a verbal display of impotent fretting, lacking aim or direction and only hitting its target when it becomes personalised. His hatred of society is reduced quite knowingly by its perpetrator to venom against his wife and her family. And here the play hopelessly betrays itself. Jimmy is never seen to confront the 'Edwardian brigade' in the flesh and his maligned spouse is never endowed by the playwright with the power to answer. She needs to be masochistic and inert since resistance of any sort on her part would stem the flow of Porter's eloquence and disrupt the theatrical effect Osborne is striving for. It is in the nature of the play itself that she is doomed to be the victim of sustained misogyny. Far from maintaining equilibrium between the social and the personal, the play is an expression of a classic form of scapegoating. The absence of any coherent means of social expression of discontent leads to personal victimisation. Here the victimisation is that of man against woman, and more specifically, husband against wife.

A question-mark must hang, therefore, over Jimmy Porter's rebelliousness from the very beginning. And that questioning points itself also at the form in which the play has been written. Osborne transforms the naturalist conventions of the English bourgeois drama from the drawing room to the bed-sitting room, but the oppressive identity of the three-walled room is as strong as ever. It incorporates the whole of the Porter's domestic existence, and implies among other things, no physical escape from one another. The overall effect is that of a prison-house of naturalism, in which the absence of escape signifies the ineffectiveness of revolt. Moreover, having made the break iconoclastically with the English dramatic tradition, Osborne has to resort to that tradition in order to guarantee the play's structure. It is, as he himself has admitted, a variant of the well-made play, in which the replacement of Alison by Helena in the flat and in Porter's affections has a contrived symmetry posing as dramatic development. Moreover Jimmy's dual lament for his father—a Spanish Civil War veteran—and Hugh's dead mother, are mechanical contrivances designed to 'show' the hero's 'real' compassion and exonerate his behaviour onstage which displays no compassion at all.

As the ending of the play makes clear, the room is a prison to which husband and wife eventually accommodate themselves, largely through a private world of make-believe where they seek mutual solace in their famous game of 'bears and squirrels'. But this acceptance cushions the tentative estrangement of the play's hero. His alienation from the social world is provisional, and instead of testing its resilience by pitting him against it, Osborne undercuts it with the easy refuge of domestic fantasy. In terms of dramatic writing like this, alienation can never become tragic, because it offers an evasion of strife. And the social context of that alienation is itself suspect. Certainly, Jimmy is the university drop-out with working-class connections, living in some degree of material discomfort. But the almost gratuitous occupation which the dramatist gives him, that of a sweet-stall owner, is unintentionally to the point. The anger at the upper middle classes is coloured by a petit-bourgeois resentment, and its concomitant sense of powerlessness. It is reinforced by his attitude to his wife which can only be described as one of proprietory contempt.

While Osborne's play is regarded as a watershed in English drama, the real entry of the lower classes into English drama outwit the ethos of deference which Shaw and Galsworthy had created for them, comes in Arnold Wesker's *Chicken Soup with Barley*, the first play of his important trilogy first performed in sequence in 1960. Wesker's milieu is uncompromisingly working class and autobiographical. It is also urban and political. Set in the East End at the time of the anti-fascist protests of the thirties, it centres on a family which is working class, socialist and Jewish. One is immediately put in mind of Odets' *Awake and Sing*. The omnipresent quality of the Jewish family in both cases is to endure, to survive the tribulations which are forced upon it and which it forces upon itself. In both plays the role of the mother has an extraordinary theatrical power based partly on Jewish cultural tradition and partly on the resonance of a demotic language as compelling as anything in O'Casey or O'Neill. If Jimmy Porter's eloquence derives from the speech patterns of a very individualistic form of iconoclasm, those of Wesker are more socially rooted in a distinctive living community.

Because this play, and the trilogy in general, are about endurance and change over time one would not expect the components of tragedy to be relevant in a central way. Yet the trilogy taken as a whole, is about a painful kind of loss over the space of two generations, a loss about which Wesker attempts to make a specific kind of judgment. He calls the characters in the trilogy 'my people' and adds: 'The picture I have drawn is a harsh one, yet my tone is not one of disgust—nor should it be in the presentations of the plays. I am at one with these people. It is only that I am annoyed with them and myself.' The counter-current to the theme of endurance is that of collective failure. The failure is not a tragedy but an indictment. Wesker's personae all have a working conception of socialism which in some measure, they or others judge to be inadequate and unrealised. In the family recriminations which take place throughout the trilogy they personalise the blame for the general failure of principle. The families endure and survive, but they are severely judged, not least by each other.

In the plays, it is the women who have a startling power of eloquence and conviction, the men who ultimately waver and fail. In *Chicken Soup with Barley*, Sarah Kahn is not only the provider for the family where her husband has failed her. She is also the political conscience of the family, a communist party militant, contemptuous and scathing about Harry's failure to give his full support to the anti-Mosley demonstration. In *Roots* Beatie Bryant carries through the ideals of Ronnie Kahn even after Ronnie deserts her—and them. The gender distinction is not absolute for in the first part of the trilogy at least the fight against Mosley is predominantly the work of the men. But the dramatic context, where the setting is the Kahn's basement and not the barricaded street, and where Beatie is preaching to her own family in the front room of their tied cottage, not to the villagers in the market square, enlarges the figural dimensions of the female hero. The ambiguous attitude of Wesker towards the female dominance of his domestic dramatic setting is exemplified in the final part of the trilogy *I'm Talking about Jerusalem* when Libby Dobson, an old friend of Dave Simmons and a trenchant misogynist, attacks women as domesticated destroyers of male idealism. 'A woman dirties you up . . . She and the world, they change you, bruise you, dirty you up between them.'[3] If the persona of Beatie seems more than an answer to that accusation, her excessive dependence on Ronnie still leaves the question very much open.

Seen as a whole, the trilogy looks at questions of politics in terms of changes in modern England over a period of twenty years or more, and also the dialectic of the country and the city which Wesker explores more seriously and more originally than any other modern English playwright. The two are linked. The changes in post-war England prompt the younger Simmonds and Kahns to look to the country as a more promising and less oppressive environment to put into practice their socialist ideals. Ultimately they fail to do so. Ronnie's relationship with Beatie breaks up. Dave and Ada move to Norfolk, but his career as a furniture craftsman ends in disillusionment. The choice is a difficult one. The East End community had offered comradeship and mutual support but a poor and dreary existence. The move away from it offers greater opportunities of self-fulfilment but in the process something is lost. The old world, including the communist party, is too inflexible and unimaginative, but the new breaks down the sense of community built up through material hardship.

The idea of changing the rural community to which they move, or with which they have connections, is one in which, significantly, Wesker fails to pinpoint the potential strife between the rural community and the outsiders. In *Roots*, Ronnie Kahn, the moving force of Beatie's radiant creed is conspicuous by his absence. In *I'm Talking about Jerusalem*, by complete contrast, there are no locals on hand except for the colonel, Dave's initial employer, who is something of a caricature. In *Roots*, Ronnie's failure to arrive at the cottage and the self-pitying letter he sends instead to announce the end of his relationship with Beatie, illustrates the wider weakness. The locals and the Londoners never confront each other head on. We are never shown the basis of Ronnie and Beatie's relationship since they never appear on stage, or in the same play, together. In Beatie's vivid imagination Ronnie is a charismatic figure. In the flesh he is self-pitying and weak, constantly lamenting his failure to change the world. The title too comes to have an ambiguity which Wesker did not intend. Beatie accuses her family of having no roots, yet it is quite clear that they do. The 'roots' they do have are in a rural community which is deeply traditional and conservative, the opposite in fact of Ronnie's 'roots' in a socialist Jewish working-class family in the East End. The point is that the experience of the urban family does not easily transfer to the experience of the rural one. Even though Beatie is personally converted to Ronnie's cause, to the extent of quoting him word for word, her exhortations fall on stony ground. At the end, when Ronnie has written to explain his failure to come, she claims to have found her own voice: 'D'you hear that? Did you listen to me. I'm talking . . . not quoting anymore.' But the voice continues to talk into thin air. Her family do not understand and at the end, they do not listen. The roots of the rural community are embedded in a tradition of class deference with which the Kahns and the Simmonds as Jewish immigrants to the East End were never directly confronted. Beatie's growing eloquence, inundated with Ronnie's vague abstractions, is too remote to make it change, even though it, too, has grown from those very same roots.

Wesker's trilogy is the most powerful composite dramatic statement in the post-war English theatre. It gives a multitudinous voice to the lower-class English, urban and rural, and with a magnificent ear for the demotic. Moreover it threw away more decisively than Osborne the perspective of enlightened authority, with which Jimmy Porter has such an intense love–hate relationship. In Wesker such a perspective is alien to the experience of the socialist family and is of no emotional consequence. Yet tragedy is also outside the range of Wesker's dramatic expression and the success of the trilogy, which he never again repeated, highlights the divergence between tragedy and realism in recent English drama. Wesker was in fact writing the trilogy as the age of modern tragic drama was drawing to a close but where serious realist drama such as *Blues for Mister Charlie* or Miller's *The Price* have continued to make an impact. The feeling that tragedy was no longer possible within the framework of naturalist conventions led other dramatists of the English revival to decompose the figural dimensions of their work in order to create more theatrically compelling expressions of menace, fear and human loss. This movement, visible in the work of Harold Pinter and less destructively in David Rudkin's *Afore Night Come* was part of a general historical trend, but in an English context had a number of interesting peculiarities. Both Pinter and Rudkin retained a minimal sense of the tragic and continued the new tradition of the demotic established by Osborne, Wesker and some of the lesser realist dramatists. Their ear for ordinary speech is acutely perceptive, but the source of menace, which often culminates in capture or death, is opaque. It becomes threatening precisely because its social referents are blurred and cannot be identified. At its extreme in Pinter, the audience can only experience the menace as an eavesdropper might overhear a conversation between strangers which was not intended for it. The dramatic personae must remain strange and the growing familiarity the audience comes to have by seeing and hearing them over a period of time must be countered by the obliqueness of the references made. Sympathy or identification with the personae are not really possible.

The single phrase or expression can be moving but the persona uttering it remains inscrutable, yet only through a deliberate strategy of evasion on the part of the dramatist. The other interesting feature of this dilution of the tragic, very apparent in *The Caretaker*, is the harnessing of Beckettian sensibility to the naturalist setting of the three-walled room where its universality is constricted by the box-like usage of dramatic space. The effect is to see tragedy through a glass darkly aided by many of the familiar props of the traditional English drama, and to feel once one has seen it, that the real experience of tragedy is no longer accessible. At its most damaging, the realisation can bring with it the feeling that one has been the victim of an elaborate confidence trick.

There were, however, other more important developments where the retention of figural modes suggested the possibility of tragic expression, and this was particularly so of the two great historical dramas of the period, Osborne's *Luther*, and Peter Shaffer's *The Royal Hunt of the Sun*. These plays were only really possible in Britain's post-colonial era. Their concerns are global, and become possible, ironically, only when the global power of Britain is in absolute decline. In Imperial Britain, English drama had been incredibly parochial but once British power and status became uncertain then the relationship of the country to the world as a whole as called into question. Neither Osborne's nor Shaffer's play is set in Britain nor does it have British protagonists. Both dramatists are concerned, in rather different ways, with the origins of the modern bourgeois societies of the West as a whole. That wider perspective is only available for historical drama once Britain has been effectively reduced from an Empire to a multi-national bourgeois state. In both there is a concern with the voice of enlightened authority traceable to Shaw and Galsworthy, but operating in rather different ways. Luther is the rebel who defies authority before eventually succumbing to it. Pizarro, in Shaffer's play, is the semi-legal custodian of authority who in effect is able to make his own rules in the treatment of savages. Both are heroes of a new bourgeois world in the making, one challenging the medieval authority of the church, the other involved in imperial conquest for the precious metal, gold. Their boldness and desperation make neither of them typical heroes of the English stage. Each has a Promethean quest, which in a way makes him a candidate for tragic heroism, yet the dramatic outcome in each play is never tragedy. For each of the heroes survives to win a flawed, ambiguous victory.

Luther is an historical drama which succeeds where *Saint Joan* fails. It was only possible because Osborne had already made the break with the voice of enlightened authority. By historically transposing the voice of his defiant rebel from the present to the period and the person with whom Western individualism partly originated, Osborne made a remarkable dramatic breakthrough in the English theatre. Luther has the same defiant spirit of Jimmy Porter, but also has his own more complex historical voice with a historical language and sensibility which is a remarkable achievement. Rather than transposing the language and manners of the present back into the past, as Shaw did, Osborne followed Miller in attempting to produce a more formal and distanced language appropriate to the theme while remaining accessible to a modern audience. In this he was successful, creating a poetic language of materialism in a play about religious conflict. The language of course has a modern reference in the psychoanalysis of Freud and the work of the social psychologist Erik Erikson, whose study of Luther had a strong influence upon the play. The materialist emphasis is neither Büchner's cosmic atheism nor Brecht's cash nexus but rather an emphasis on the psychological basis of religious yearning, an emphasis dominated by the violent imagery of bodily and digestive functions. Private bodily obsession is linked to individual religious conscience. The sense of self is sustained in relation, simultaneously, to one's God and one's bowels.

A further advantage of *Luther* over *Look Back in Anger* is the inclusion of a public dimension and of change over time. Osborne launches his hero from the introverted world of the monastery into the public world of penances and religious corruption where his defiance and anger are put to the test. But if the historical drama goes beyond the contemporary play in this respect, it also confirms and realises its theme. Luther is seized by revulsion when his nonconformity gives rise to popular expressions of discontent, since for him only the individual conscience and not the collective will can legimately resist authority. As the conflict changes from the religious to the political arena, his hatred of mob anarchy becomes explicit. Luther finally submits to political authority when his individual conscience is affronted by a rather different kind of collective force. One feels that as an individual rebel with a hatred and fear of collective mediocrity, Jimmy Porter would have done the same. But the fate of Luther is not only illustrative in Osborne's play of the fate of religious non-conformity. It also illustrates the dilemmas inherent in the liberalism of the modern age. Osborne's heroes take seriously the liberal principles which had more or less lain redundant or unrecognised during the Imperial period.

Liberal ideals had either been attached to an ideal of unilinear human progress or been constricted to a paternalistic toleration of dissenting opinion. Osborne's eloquence is not linked either to progress or toleration but to defiant self-assertion, to the uncompromising and individualistic right to self-expression, whatever the consequences. As the tides of Empire receded and the false ideals of progress, civility and enlightened government were unmasked as rather sophisticated excuses for Imperial rule, the one irreducible benefit of British liberalism became exposed as its only excuse and its only consolation. The whole process is reflected in Osborne's two plays. But the limit of the right to self-expression is also there, the absence of any passage from self-assertion to human community. And in the failure to convert that revolt into a wider loyalty, Osborne fails to convert the alienation of his heroes into a tragic strife of wider dimensions.

In comparison with Shaffer's play, however, it is clear that Osborne had broken much more decisively with the English tradition. As a dramatic spectacle, *The Royal Hunt of the Sun* seems the more innovative play. Instead of the loosely epic, and often austere, nature of Osborne's presentation, there is exotic and sensational spectacle. The clash of different civilisations, the Spanish and the Inca, takes place on a stage dominated by a gold-petalled sun twelve feet in diameter. The dramatic moment of the first meeting Pizarro and Atahualpa, the Inca ruler, is a truly magnificent achievement. The clear divisions of culture are realised with a remarkable visual splendour—the dignified nobility of the Inca leader and the organic relationship of his Sun religion to nature are contrasted with the rapacious Spaniards and their grotesquely casuistic Catholicism. But there are also crucial defects in the two main protagonists. Atahualpa remains an exotic conception of the Irrational and the Primitive, inaccessible to the civilised world, while Pizarro has two contrasting identities which never really cohere. In the first place, he is the rapacious peasant *conquistador* determined to atone for his low social status by ruthlessly acquiring the Inca gold he covets in the name of his country. On the other hand, his disenchantment with church and state, and his crisis of faith are the dilemmas of a modern liberal conscience totally inappropriate to the historical figure who is forced by Shaffer to embody them. He is thus appalled by the human consequences of colonial brutality, as any modern liberal would be. But as the main instigator of the process he himself is responsible for what has happened. The figural dimensions of his hero are thus destroyed by an anachronistic psychology—the recognition of the Inca culture as superior, to be envied and desired, just as his sympathy for the captured Atahualpa contains his own form of suppressed sensual desire. The liberal conscience, recognising the superiority and difference of the uncivilised Other, hangs uneasily on the ruthless veteran. Pizarro, unlike Luther, has no authentic voice. The Inca ruler, magnificent yet passive in his captivity, is too much a victim to possess any heroic stature. Spectacle in the play becomes a distraction from these figural deficiencies, but once the glitter has worn off, the deficiencies remain.

Shaffer, in contrast to Osborne, is distinctly trying to evoke tragic experience in the work, an experience arising from the relationship between the Spaniard and the Inca ruler. Since Atahualpa is too dignified and external to that experience, the onus must rest on the role played by Pizarro. It would be historically absurd to suggest that Pizarro could sacrifice his life for the Sun King. Instead Shaffer opts for a compromise whereby the Spanish leader can resist the wish of his fellow Spaniards to kill the king but only to the point at which his own life is endangered. This retraction makes the scene where Pizarro allows the Sun King to confess him in the Inca manner seem basically unconvincing. The noble irrationality of the Inca leader remains an exotic mystique beyond the pale of Pizarro's own barbarous civilisation, attractive in that context but in no other, mystically superior in its fundamental inferiority.

Shaffer's bold but unsuccessful attempt to write tragedy came from a movement in theme towards the periphery of civilisation, as if he sensed intuitively that in his own stable, post-colonial society, the same dimensions for tragic drama were not apparent. While Osborne passed from the contemporary to the historical, however, Shaffer then moved in the opposite direction. In *Equus*, ten years later, he *did* try to broach similar themes within the context of the contemporary welfare state, and here the motif of authority reasserts itself more explicitly, but under conditions which make its assuredness shakier than ever. The setting is suburban middle-class southern England, the theme the violent cruelty of an adolescent boy found guilty of blinding horses. The violence itself is not gratuitous, but the dramatic framework within which Shaffer explores it, effectively disallows the tragic experience. The framework is the fixed relationship of authority which Martin Dysart the psychiatrist has over his delinquent client. It retains from the earlier play the polarity between the Rational and the Irrational, but this time the polarity is accentuated. Martin Dysart is rational, caring and perceptive. But the life he leads is mundane, prosaic and insipid. Alan Strang lives in a private world of violent poetic obsession brilliantly created on stage but he is unable to cope with the simple demands of his own everyday life. The play fails for the very reason it is supposed to be tragic. The obsession with 'equus' cannot be contained within the framework of middle-class earnestness and decency and it breaks through into sickening brutality. While this is clearly seen by Shaffer as a tragic instance of the failure of civilisation to cope with the irrational, the figural imbalance in the relationship between boy and psychiatrist is similar to that between Pizarro and Atahualpa. The figural focus is on Dysart while the portrayal of the boy, and of the events leading up to the blinding incident are unconvincing. Thus while Shaffer can give a good account of the menopausal inadequacies of his respectable hero, there is no plausible interaction in the boy's case between personality and environment. When Shaffer tries to create one in the scene where Strang accidentally encounters his puritanical father at a cinema showing a blue movie, the effect is instantly Bathetic. The subsequent blinding of the horses seems a gratuitous consequence.

Like the religion of the Sun King, the vision of equus has a cultivated mystique, Dionysian in its intent but actually infusing its middle-class audience with a purient interest in the sexually sensational. As narrator, Dysart is really a mediator between the audience and the mystified and terrifying world he unfolds through his professional probing, and to which he himself feels compellingly drawn. But the condition of that attraction is the emptiness of his own life, and that emptiness in turn obviates true heroic stature. The play therefore ends on a hollow note when Dysart, the boy unconscious at his feet, proclaims: 'There is now, in my mouth this sharp chain. And it never comes out.' The interrogator searching for psychological malady cannot change his role as interrogator, by sympathising with the obsession of his desperate client, or even by imaginatively projecting himself into it. When all is said and done, he must remain sane, normal and diminished.

An alternative to the Shafferian perspective has taken root in the sixties and seventies, which, while rejecting much of the previous English tradition, is also inimical to tragedy. The work of John Arden, Edward Bond, Howard Brenton and David Hare has all in some degree been influenced by the epic theatre of Brecht, and by a deeply ingrained sense of the objective workings of history which is the legacy of modern Marxism. But this movement towards epic theatre runs counter to the figural dimensions established by Osborne and Wesker.

To date the dialectic of the social and the political these dramatists have created is a decisive advance, but nonetheless derivative, still operating in the style and the shadow of Brecht. An alternative attempt to establish the dialectic of the social and political using naturalist techniques and adhering to figural dimensions can be found in the work of Trevor Griffiths. Griffiths is certainly closer to Osborne and Wesker, but it would be wrong to see his work as a hard politicisation of a previously unpolitical realism. It was a distinct switch of emphasis but one which revealed a failure to establish effective congruence between the social and political levels of his drama, in his two stage plays, *Occupations* and *The Party*. Griffiths' innovation in *The Party* is to present in a contemporary English setting detailed and eloquent advocacy of Marxist political argument. Yet, paradoxically, his writing is at its most *theatrically* effective in *Comedians*, where the club performance of Gethin Price is rendered through a remarkable use of alienation—effect.

The gestural theatre has, if anything, managed to remain more immune to the processes of figural decomposition that television drama, with the exception of Griffiths and David Mercer, has accelerated at the level of the single play. Its advance has to be seen in the light of decisive failures elsewhere. In an age of competing cultural forms where the theatre is often outflanked by television and film, its longevity is assured because of the pure and unique theatricality of its techniques, which do not make for easy or diluted translation. Although the epic theatre is generally opposed, as we have seen, to tragedy by its very nature there have been notable exceptions. It remains to be seen whether *The Plebeians* is a unique historical exception or whether there are any possibilities of linking tragic and epic forms in a drama which explores the dialectic of the social and the political.

One recent English work which does explore this possibility is Christopher Hampton's *Savages*. The more open structure of Hampton's work, its episodic shifting of scenes in space and time, manages effectively to combine both epic and naturalistic techniques in creating a new dimension for realist drama. The epic technique lies in the dramatic explication of a set of external political events, backwards and forwards over time, and the naturalist frame of reference is used for the kidnapping of a British diplomat and his subsequent political encounter with his guerilla captor. The play operates at two levels—the fate of the diplomat and his kidnapper, and the fate of the 'savages' of the title which is being decided independently of the two main protagonists. The superimposition works because the fate of the 'savages' becomes the focal point of the relationship between captor and captive.

As in *Equus*, the working out of the theatrical form is partially dependent on the theme. The open structure of superimposition we have mentioned can only come from the thematic importance of the Brazilian Indians in the play itself. They are at the very periphery of all human life, one of the least 'civilised' peoples in the world, their culture resistant to civilised encroachment, and therefore threatened with imminent extermination. But the vision of this barbarous process emanates from the centre, not the periphery, through the eyes of Alan West, the British diplomat, in flashback and contemporaneous encounter. Yet it is not West but the Indians who are the hero of the drama. He is the centre of the play, they its periphery. At best theirs is a ghostly and fleeting presence—mute passive suffering and peripatetic. But theirs is the tragic fate, and the personal tragedy of West's shooting which precedes it is entirely and appropriately secondary.

The play then is a tragedy but of a special and unique kind. It is a tragedy where the collective tragic hero has no voice except through its myths which a foreigner narrates, and no presence except in the final scene where their extermination is witnessed. The figural dimensions of the main personae are not tragic. Less important than what happens to them, is how they perceive contemporary Brazil and the role of the Indians within it. In terms of the tragedy written, the choric effect has been reversed. It is given to two individual personae who recount the circumstances of an anonymous collectivity, since hero and villain, diplomat and revolutionary (and the audience is left to judge for itself who is which), do not possess the noble dignity of those who are collectively doomed. The latter, in turn, are too distant to have the figural presence accorded to their lesser rivals.

The Indians are represented onstage by their ceremonies and their myths, narrated by West intermittently throughout the play. The simplicity of this method is in sharp contrast to the exotic splendour of Shaffer's Inca King and his followers, but it is more effective. The myths speak for the Indians with a kind of understanding which can be appreciated by the audience but not culturally 'understood'. Savage myth bespeaks equality of intellectual status but also signifies the immense hiatus of cultures. Theatrically it needs only the spoken word and the simple enactment of ritual to show this. The result is an alienation effect of the sort which neither Brecht nor anyone else ever conceived, but which is amazingly effective. West is not, like

Shaffer's heroes, the mediator between the audience and the mysteriously irrational. He merely narrates a myth and reveals ceremonies which are stripped of mystique and answerable only to their possessors. The play on the word 'imagineus' carved on a tree trunk in the jungle, presents the dilemma. West eventually decides it stands not for 'I'm a genius' but 'imagine us'. And that is beyond what either he, or the audience, can do.

Where understanding is possible, in the case of West or of Carlos, neither character possesses heroic status. In part it is a question of the lack of political ruthlessness. West is tolerant and ineffable, Carlos an amateur revolutionary. In the absence of the Indians the play would collapse because ultimately neither captor nor captive is strong enough to be taken seriously in themselves. It is their perception of the external political world which is important. Here Hampton reverses the Shafferian motif of 'humane authority' by having the more privileged, more civilised, person as the captive. The balance between the two men is then equal and what matters is their relative strength and weakness in their perception of events. West can understand the plight of the Indians because they are a very small and specific group of people. But in order to do so, he has to ignore the deprivation of the vast majority of the Brazilian people at the hands of dictatorship and foreign exploitation. Carlos is only too aware of the latter, but because he is obsessed by this, the plight of such a small, 'primitive' group of people as the Indians is too politically insignificant to have any real effect on him. The strength of one is the weakness of the other and vice versa. The failure of seeing here is a figural dialectic, different from the individually centred 'complex seeing' of Mother Courage or Galileo, and in its own context also more effective. It is through the confrontation that one sees through to a further truth but that truth in turn presents a dilemma which cannot be resolved.

Savages, along with *The Plebeians Rehearses the Uprising*, suggests new possible links between tragic and epic drama in the forseeable future. But the evolution of a new form, if it is to come, would differ both from the predominantly gestural theatre of Brecht and the predominantly figural theatre of Ibsen and O'Neill. It would also differ from the major forms of tragic drama in previous Western history. Whether such an artistic product evolves, as a response to the new forms of social and political consciousness in our age, is a question which is still to be answered. Significantly both the plays of Grass and Hampton are political dramas, and as we have noted, tragic drama from 1880 to 1960 has significantly absented itself from the sphere of the political. It needed the emergence of the epic form inaugurated earlier by Büchner to highlight the absence. But Büchner's quest has never really been taken up in its entirety. Grass and Hampton follow on from his example, but each has, in their departure from figural drama, significantly altered the form and altered it in a rather unique and special way. The tragic vision of Grass stems from the relationship between the committed theatre and modern politics as such, and the committed theatre is the tragic hero of the play. The collective hero of Hampton's play hardly appears on the stage at all. Its tragic nature stems from the hiatus of cultures which separates the savage mind, and its last living remnants, from a civilised world intent on destroying it. The tragedy of Grass is intrinsic to the nature of the modern theatre as a living process, that of Hampton extrinsic to all civilisation as we know it. The power of the tragic experience is still there but more widely diffused, and diminished too in comparison with what has preceded it. It represents a new kind of relationship between the fictive and the social world, between the world of imagination and the world of information. The dramatist's response to the growing social consciousness of the age is now less like the process of artistic sublimation which characterises modern tragedy as a whole, more a distanced, composed and knowing response. It is not a didactic response offering a revealed truth, but an artistic probing which presents an irreducible dilemma. That dilemma, in its totality, is written, performed and witnessed as a tragic experience. Whether the break with figural convention it entails can be sustained within the modern theatre, is crucial. Equally crucial is whether such a mode of writing can set itself apart from the by now conventional epic form stemming from Brecht. Only time will tell. But it would be true to say that the English theatre ironically absent from the third great world-historical period of tragedy, appears as socially and artistically capable of sustaining it as any. And the sociological conditions circumscribing modern tragedy up to now need not necessarily apply, in the age of advanced capitalism, to this new dramatic form.

Notes

Introduction

1. Dryden has pointed out that the unity of place is a precept of sixteenth-century French poets and is not to be found directly in Aristotle's writings at all. See 'An Essay on Dramatic Poesy', in *Selected Works of John Dryden* (London, 1964) pp. 329–40.
2. *Modern Tragedy* (London, 1966) pp. 56ff.
3. *Sociologie du Théâtre* (Paris, 1965) p. 41.
4. *The Hidden God*, trans. by Philip Thody (London, 1964) pp. 313ff.
5. See my *Tragic Realism and Modern Society* (London, 1977) pp. 41ff.
6. Duvignaud, op. cit., p. 66.
7. Williams, op. cit., pp. 121ff.
8. For the Lukácsian approach see 'Approximation to Life in the Novel and the Play', in Elizabeth and Tom Burns (eds), *Sociology of Literature and Drama* (Harmondsworth: Penguin, 1973) pp. 286ff.
9. For Auerbach's discussion of figural interpretation and figural realism see *Mimesis*, trans. by Willard B. Trask (Princeton, 1953) pp. 73–6, 156–62, 194–202 and 317f; also his essay 'Figura', in *Scenes from the Drama of European Literature* (New York, 1959) pp. 11f. and pp. 70f.; and Orr, op. cit., pp. 42f.

Part I

Chapter 1

1. For a sociological discussion of this relationship see Stein Rokkan 'Geography, Religion and Social Class; Cross-cutting Cleavages in Norwegian Politics', in S. M. Lipset and S. Rokkan (eds) *Party Systems and Voter Alignments* (New York, 1965); Harry Eckstein, *Division and Cohesion in Norway* (Princeton, 1966) chap. 2; and Francis Castles, *The Social Democratic Image of Society* (London, 1978) chap. 3.
2. 'The Quintessence of Ibsenism', in *Major Critical Essays* (London, 1948) pp. 25–32, 75–83.
3. On this period in Ibsen's life see Michael Meyer's *Henrik Ibsen: The Making of a Dramatist* (London, 1967) chaps 7 and 8.

Chapter 2

1. *The Wild Duck*, trans. Michael Meyer (London: Methuen, 1968) p. 58.
2. Ibid., pp. 73–4.
3. Ibid., p. 101.
4. *The Lady from the Sea*, trans. Michael Meyer (London: Rupert Hart-Davis, 1960) p. 101.

Chapter 3

1. *Rosmersholm*, trans. Michael Meyer (London: Rupert Hart-Davis, 1966) p. 78.
2. Ibid., p. 73.
3. Ibid., p. 97.
4. Ibid., p. 99.
5. Ibid., p. 106.
6. Cited in Meyer, *Henrik Ibsen: The Top of a Cold Mountain* (London, 1971) p. 55.
7. *Hedda Gabler*, trans. Michael Meyer (London: Rupert Hart-Davis, 1962) pp. 51–2.

Chapter 4

1. *John Gabriel Borkman*, trans. Michael Meyer (London: Rupert Hart-Davis, 1960) p. 44.
2. Ibid., p. 45.
3. Ibid., p. 53.
4. Ibid., p. 38.
5. Ibid., p. 80.
6. Ibid., p. 81.
7. Ibid., p. 83.
8. For a discussion of these productions see Frederick J. Marker and Lisa-Lone Marker, *The Scandinavian Theatre* (Oxford: Blackwell, 1975) chap. 9.
9. For an account of Bloch's naturalism see Marker and Marker 'William Bloch and Naturalism in the Scandinavian Theatre', *Theatre Survey*, xv (November, 1974) pp. 85–104. For an account of the Moscow Arts Theatre productions of Ibsen see Konstantin Stanislavsky, *My Life in Art*, trans. J. J. Robbins (New York, 1956), pp. 344–6, 378–80.

Part II

Chapter 5

1. Elizabeth Hapgood (ed. & trans.), *Stanislavski's Legacy* (New York, 1968) p. 82.
2. Ibid., p. 129.
3. Simon Karlinsky (ed.), *Letters of Anton Chekhov*, trans. Michael Heim (London, 1973) pp. 97–9.
4. Ronald Hingley (ed.), *The Oxford Chekhov*, vol. 2. (London: O.U.P., 1964–7) p. 209.
5. Ibid., p. 233.
6. Ibid., pp. 234–5.
7. Ibid., pp. 253–4.
8. Ibid., p. 257.
9. Ibid., p. 280.
10. *The Oxford Chekhov*, vol. 3, p. 74.
11. Ibid., p. 102.
12. Ibid., p. 148.
13. Ibid., p. 149.
14. Ibid., p. 153.
15. Ibid., p. 157.

16. Ibid., p. 190.
17. Stanislavsky, op. cit., pp. 553-4.
18. Ibid., pp. 398, 407.

Chapter 6

1. For a detailed study of the domestic tragedies see Edward McInnes, *German Social Drama 1840–1900* (Stuttgart, 1976) and John Osborne, *The Naturalist Drama in Germany* (Manchester, 1972).
2. See *Die verspätete Nation* (Stuttgart, 1959); Ralf Dahrendorf, *Society and Democracy in Germany* (London, 1968); Fritz Ringer, *The Decline of the German Mandarins: The German Academic Community, 1890–1933* (Cambridge, Mass.: Harvard U. P., 1969).
3. Foreword to *Pandora's Box*, in *The Lulu Plays and other Sex Tragedies*, trans. Stephen Spender (London: Calder and Boyars, 1977) p. 104.
4. 'The Sociology of Modern Drama', trans. Lee Baxendall, *Tulane Drama Review*, vol. 9 (1964–5) pp. 166–7.
5. For a detailed study of the relation between the political writings and the drama, see Maurice R. Benn, *The Drama of Revolt: a Critical Study of Georg Büchner* (Cambridge, 1976) chap. 2.
6. *The Plays of Georg Büchner*, trans. Victor Price (London: O.U.P., 1971) p. 22.
7. Ibid., pp. 56-7.
8. Ibid., p. 66.
9. Ibid., p. 28.
10. Ibid., p. 58.
11. For this aspect of Brecht's work, see Walter Benjamin's studies of the epic theatre in *Understanding Brecht*, trans. Stanley Mitchell (London, 1973) pp. 1–25.
12. 'Notes to the Threepenny Opera', in *Three German Plays* (Harmondsworth: Penguin, 1963) p. 228.
13. 'Commitment', trans. Francis McDonagh, in *Aesthetics and Politics* (London: NLB, 1977).
14. *The Days of the Commune*, trans. Clive Barker and Arno Reinfrank (London: Methuen, 1978) pp. 46–7.
15. Ibid., p. 38.
16. Ibid., pp. 73-4.
17. Ibid., p. 80.
18. For Marx's analysis of the historical significance of the Commune, see *The Civil War in France* (London, 1941).
19. The transcript of Brecht's testimony can be found in Eric Bentley (ed.), *Thirty Years of Treason* (New York: Viking Press, 1971) pp. 207–25.
20. *The Plebeians Rehearse the Uprising*, trans. Ralph Manheim (Harmondsworth: Penguin, 1972) p. 44. The 1964 address by Grass to the Academy of Arts and Sciences in Berlin is included as Foreword. Here the author presents a rationale for the drama he was subsequently to write.
21. Ibid., p. 56.
22. Ibid., p. 73.

Part III

Chapter 7

1. Joseph Holloway 'Impressions of a Dublin Playgoer', Ms. 1800, August 1902.

National Library of Ireland, Dublin.

2. *Explorations* (London: Macmillan, 1962) p. 185.

3. Ibid., pp. 197–8.

4. See 'The Tragic Theatre' (August 1910), in *Essays and Introductions* (London: Macmillan, 1961) p. 238ff.

5. Yeats, op. cit., p. 249.

6. For contrasting interpretations of the role of the Fay brothers in the early Abbey productions, see Hugh Hunt, 'Synge and the Actor—a consideration of Style', in Maurice Harmon (ed.) *J. M. Synge: Centenary Papers* (Dublin, 1972) pp. 63–75; and J. W. Flannery, *W. B. Yeats and the Idea of a Theatre* (London, 1976) pp. 176–90.

7. See the recollections of Maire Nic Shiublaigh, *The Splendid Years* (Dublin, 1955) pp. 75ff.

8. Holloway, op. cit., Ms. 1802, 25 February 1904.

9. Ibid., 26 February 1904.

10. J. M. Synge, *Plays, Poems and Prose* (London: Dent, 1958) p. 29.

11. 'J. M. Synge and the Ireland of his Time', in *Essays and Introductions*, p. 339. For contemporary reactions to the play, see James Kilroy, *The 'Playboy' Riots* (Dublin, 1971).

12. Holloway, op. cit., Ms. 1805, March 1907.

13. *Selected Plays*, (Gerrards Cross: Colin Smythe, 1975) p. 123.

14. *Selected Plays* (London: Macmillan, 1964) pp. 44–5.

15. Ibid., P. 241.

16. 'Notes to *Grania*', in Lady Gregory, op. cit., p. 216.

17. Ibid., p. 241.

18. Synge, op. cit., pp. 196–7.

19. See the important and perceptive remarks by Seán O Tuama, 'Synge and the Idea of a National Literature', in *J. M. Synge: Centenary Papers*, pp. 1–17.

20. Synge, op. cit., pp. 209–10.

21. Many Irish critics, including Holloway, saw Murray as a genuine tragedian of contemporary rural life in Ireland whose work had not received the prominence or acclaim it deserved elsewhere. Here, for example, are the comments of J. P. O'Reilly in *Irish Statesman* on *Autumn Fire*:

> 'This is one of the finest plays ever written since the founding of the Abbey Theatre. It has not the terrible intensity of *Maurice Harte*, but the tragedy is nonetheless overwhelming; its appeal is wider. Mr. Murray knows his countryside as only those can who are of the countryside. Here are no unreal peasants talking unreal dialect—the Abbey peasant or neo-stage Irishman is conspicuously absent from Mr. Murray's work. His characters are the ordinary Irishman and Irishwoman seen through the eyes of a playwright fairly and squarely . . . but Mr. Murray lacks that touch of genius which makes fine workmanship great—that gift which makes Synge's artificial peasants and their dialect immortal . . . It seems that Mr. Murray has not received the prominence of Abbey programmes, the publicity and praise that is his due. Why are we given so much that is third-rate, that is patently shoddy . . . when plays like that of Mr. Murray exist, Irish in thought and phrase, real and universal in their appeal.

Cited in Holloway, op. cit., Ms. 1899, 23 January 1926.

22. *Autumn Fire* (London: Allen & Unwin, 1925) p. 3.
23. *The Plays of Eugene O'Neill*, vol. 3 (New York: Random House, 1954) p. 144.

Chapter 8

1. See *Lady Gregory's Journals*, ed. Lennox Robinson (London, 1946) pp. 71–96.
2. *The Story of the Irish Citizen Army* (New York, 1977) p. 5. (Originally published in 1919.) On the background to O'Casey's involvement in the ICA, see C. Desmond Greaves *Sean O'Casey: Politics and Art* (London: Lawrence & Wishart, 1979) p. 56ff.
3. Ibid., p. 9.
4. Holloway, op. cit., Ms. 1897, 17 August 1925.
5. *Three Plays* (London: Macmillan, 1961) pp. 71–2.
6. Ibid., p. 90.
7. Ibid., p. 92.
8. Ibid., p. 128.
9. Ibid., p. 130.
10. Holloway, op. cit., Ms. 1899, 28 February 1926.
11. O'Casey, *Three Plays*, p. 157.
12. Ibid., p. 158.
13. Ibid., p. 204.
14. Ibid., p. 205.
15. See David Fitzpatrick, 'W. B. Yeats in Seanad Eireann', in Robert O'Driscoll and Lorna Reynolds (eds) *Yeats and the Theatre* (London, 1975) pp. 159ff.

Part IV

Chapter 9

1. See John G. Cawelti, *Adventure, Mystery and Romance: Literary Formulas as Art and Popular Culture* (Chicago, 1976) pp. 193ff.; also Leslie Fiedler, *The Return of the Vanishing American* (London, 1968) chaps 1 and 2.
2. For the open motifs of O'Neill's work see the excellent study by John Henry Raleigh, *The Plays of Eugene O'Neill* (Carbondale, 1965).
3. *The Hairy Ape* (London: Cape, 1973) pp. 13–14.
4. Ibid., pp. 17–18.
5. See the second volume of Louis Scheaffer's biography, *O'Neill: Son and Artist* (London, 1974) pp. 76–8. As Scheaffer points out, the play was influenced by Robert Wiene's expressionist film *The Cabinet of Dr. Caligari* and also by Georg Kaiser's *From Morn to Midnight* but O'Neill rejected Kaiser's abstractions and restored the figural dimensions lacking in Kaiser's treatment of an almost identical theme.
6. *The Emperor Jones* (London: Cape, 1969) pp. 153–4.
7. Scheaffer, op. cit., pp. 35–7.
8. O'Neill, op. cit., p. 26.
9. Ibid., p. 29.
10. In this respect, Holloway's remarks on the Strand Theatre production of the play in London during 1923 are extremely interesting:

> Mat Burke is a literary convention, Anna and her father living people, Mat Burke the playboy of the Eastern World after he has taken to drink and become

a Sinn Fein gunman. Now and then one catches echoes of Christy Mahon in Mat Burke's language. There's even a scene in the last act between Anna's father and Mat Burke, which instantly recalls the scene at the end of 'The Shadow of the Glen' when Dan Burke and Michael Hara sit down to drink together. Not that O'Neill repeats Synge. On the contrary he inverts him. Synge shows you the polished side of the medal, but Mr. O'Neill insists on showing the side which has not been polished. (Ms. 1897, 15 April 1923).

11. *All God's Chillun Got Wings* (London: Cape, 1973) pp. 33–4.
12. Ibid., p. 24.
13. Ibid., p. 61.

Chapter 10

1. O'Neill, *Desire under the Elms*, p. 102.
2. *The Iceman Cometh* (London: Cape, 1966) pp. 27–8.
3. Ibid., p. 164.
4. Ibid., pp. 174–5.
5. Ibid., pp. 31–2.
6. *Long Day's Journey into Night* (London: Cape, 1966) p. 58.
7. Ibid., p. 78.
8. Ibid., p. 11.
9. Ibid., pp. 90–1.
10. Ibid., pp. 128–9.
11. Ibid., p. 53.
12. Ibid., p. 113.
13. Ibid., p. 118.
14. Ibid., p. 153.
15. Ibid., p. 134.
16. Ibid., p. 135.

Chapter 11

1. For the testimonies of Odets and Kazan see Eric Bentley (ed.), *Thirty Years of Treason* (New York: Viking Press, 1971) pp. 484–533.
2. An interesting though limited study of such contradictions has been made by Daniel Bell, *The Cultural Contradictions of Capitalism* (London, 1976).
3. See Miller's Preface to his *Collected Plays* (London: Peter Owen, 1974) p. 31ff.
4. 'The Glass Menagerie' in *Penguin Plays* (Harmondsworth, 1976) p. 239.
5. 'Notebook for a *A Streetcar Named Desire*', in T. Cole and H. Chinoy (eds), *Directing the Play* (New York, 1953) p. 206.
6. *Three Plays* (Harmondsworth: Penguin, 1976) p. 169.
7. Ibid., p. 211.
8. Ibid., pp. 212–13.
9. Ibid., p. 220.
10. Tennessee Williams, *Penguin Plays* (Harmondsworth, 1979) p. 105.
11. Tennessee Williams, 'Suddenly Last Summer' in *Penguin Plays* (Harmondsworth, 1977) p. 128.
12. Ibid., p. 152.
13. Ibid., pp. 157–159.

14. For an analysis of Miller's subpoena and committee proceedings see Benjamin Nelson, *Arthur Miller: Portrait of a Playwright* (London, 1970) pp. 175–98.

15. See Robert Warshow, *The Immediate Experience* (New York, 1970) pp. 189 ff. and Morris Freedman, *American Drama in Social Context* (London, 1971) pp. 51ff.

16. *Collected Plays* (London, 1974) p. 328.

17. Ibid., pp. 409–10.

18. Ibid., p. 390.

19. Ibid., p. 438.

20. *The Zoo Story* (New York: Signet, 1971) pp. 32–3.

21. Kazan described the theatre in the following terms: 'It will be an involved theatre, a committed theatre. It will speak for the fertile against the sterile, for the free against the enslaved, for inquiry against dogma, for breadth and against constriction. It will speak against the silence of the frightened, speak of beauty and against the frightful, for life and against death.' Cited in Paul Gray, 'Stanislavski and America—a critical Anthology', *Tulane Drama Review*, vol. 9 (1964–5).

Postscript

1. On the social context of London theatregoing in this period see Raymond Williams 'The Case of English Naturalism', in Marie Axton and Raymond Williams (eds) *English Drama: Forms and Developments* (London, 1977) pp. 208ff; *Revels History of Drama in English: Volume Three 1880 to the Present Day* (London, 1978) Part 1.

2. *Look Back in Anger* (London: Faber, 1958) p. 20.

3. *The Wesker Trilogy* (Harmondsworth: 1977 Penguin, p. 173.

Bibliography

1. *Works cited in text*

T. Adorno, 'Commitment', trans. Francis McDonagh, in *Aesthetics and Politics* (London: NLB, 1977).

Edward Albee, *The Zoo Story and the American Dream: Two Plays* (New York: Signet, 1971).

——, *The Sandbox and The Death of Bessie Smith* (New York: Signet, 1963).

——, *Who's Afraid of Virginia Woolf* (Harmondsworth: Penguin, 1970).

E. Auerbach, *Mimesis: The Representation of Reality in Western Literature*, trans. Willard B. Trask (Princeton, 1953).

——, *Scenes from the Drama of European Literature* (New York, 1959).

M. Axton and R. Williams. (eds) *English Drama: Forms and Developments* (London, 1977).

James Baldwin, *Blues for Mister Charlie* (New York, 1975).

S. D. Balukhaty, *The Seagull produced by Stanislavsky*, trans. David Magarshack (London, 1952).

Samuel Beckett, *Waiting for Godot* (London: Faber, 1956).

——, *Endgame* (London: Faber, 1973).

D. Bell, *The Cultural Contradictions of Capitalism* (London, 1976).

W. Benjamin, *Understanding Brecht*, trans. Stanley Mitchell (London, 1973).

M. R. Benn, *The Drama of Revolt: A Critical Study of Georg Büchner* (Cambridge, 1976).

E. Bentley (ed.), *Thirty Years of Treason* (New York: Viking Press, 1971).

Bertolt Brecht, *Plays*, 2 vols, trans. John Willett (London: Methuen, 1961).

——, *The Days of the Commune*, trans. Clive Barker and Arno Reinfrank (London: Methuen, 1978).

——, 'The Threepenny Opera', in *Three German Plays* (Harmondsworth: Penguin, 1963).

——, *The Messingkauf Dialogues*, trans. John Willett (London, 1965).

Georg Büchner, *The Plays of Georg Büchner*, trans. Victor Price (London: O.U.P., 1971).

Mikhail Bulgakov, *The Early Plays of Mikhail Bulgakov*, trans. Carl and Elendea Proffer (Bloomington, Indiana, 1972).

——, *Black Snow: a Theatrical Novel*, trans. Michael Glenny (London, 1971).

F. Castles, *The Social Democratic Image of Society* (London, 1978).

J. G. Cawelti, *Adventure, Mystery and Romance: Literary Formulas as Art and Popular Culture* (Chicago, 1976).

Anton Chekhov, *The Oxford Chekhov*, 3 vols, ed. Ronald Hingley (London: O.U.P., 1964–7).

——, *Letters of Anton Chekhov*, trans. Michael Heim (London, 1973).

R. Dahrendorf, *Society and Democracy in Germany* (London, 1968).

J. Duvignaud, *Sociologie du Théâtre* (Paris, 1965).

H. Eckstein, *Division and Cohesion in Norway* (Princeton, 1966).

L. Fiedler, *The Return of the Vanishing American* (London, 1968).

J. W. Flannery, *W. B. Yeats and the Idea of a Theatre: the Early Abbey Theatre in Theory and Practice* (London, 1976).

M. Freedman, *American Drama in Social Context* (London, 1971).

John Galsworthy, *Ten Famous Plays* (London, 1941).

L. Goldmann, *The Hidden God*, trans. Philip Thody (London, 1964).

Maxim Gorky, *Seven Plays*, trans. Alexander Bakshy (New Haven, Conn. 1946).

——, *The Lower Depths*, trans. Kitty Hunter-Blair and Jeremy Brooks (London: Methuen, 1973).

——, *Enemies*, trans. K. Hunter-Blair and J. Brooks (London: Methuen, 1972).

Günter Grass, *The Plebeians Rehearse the Uprising*, trans. Ralph Manheim (Harmondsworth: Penguin, 1972).

Lady Augusta Gregory, *Selected Plays* (Gerrards Cross: Colin Smythe, 1975).

——, *Cuchulain of Muirthemne* (Gerrards Cross: Colin Smythe, 1976).

——, *Lady Gregory's Journals*, ed. Lennox Robinson (London, 1946).

Trevor Griffiths, *The Party* (London: Faber, 1974).

Christopher Hampton, *Savages* (London: Faber, 1974).

M. Harmon (ed.), *J. M. Synge: Centenary Papers 1971* (Dublin, 1972).

Gerhart Hauptmann, *Die Webern* (London: Harrap, 1962).

——, *The Dramatic Works of Gerhart Hauptmann*, 3 vols, ed. L. Lewisohn (London, 1912).

J. Holloway, 'Impressions of a Dublin Playgoer', Mss at the National Library of Ireland, Dublin Mss 1798–1900, Years 1900–1926.

——, *Impressions of a Dublin Playgoer: A Selection from his Unpublished Journal*, ed. Robert Hogan and Michael J. O'Neill (London, 1967).

Henrik Ibsen, *Plays*, trans. Michael Meyer (London: Rupert Hart-Davis, 1960–66).

——, *The Oxford Ibsen*, 7 vols, ed. and trans. James Walter Macfarlane and Graham Orton (London: O.U.P., 1962–77).

Denis Johnston, *The Dramatic Works of Denis Johnston*, vol. 1 (Gerrards Cross: Colin Smythe, 1977).

Leroi Jones, *Dutchman* and *The Slave* (London, 1965).

E. Kazan, 'Notebook for *A Streetcar Named Desire*', in T. Cole and H. Chinoy (eds) *Directing the Play* (New York, 1953).

J. Kilroy, *The 'Playboy' Riots* (Dublin, 1971).

S. M. Lipset and S. Rokkan, *Party Systems and Voter Alignments* (New York, 1965).

Frederico Garcia Lorca, *Three Tragedies* (Harmondsworth: Penguin, 1965).

G. Lukács, 'Approximation to Life in the Novel and the Play', in E. Burns and T. Burns (eds), *The Sociology of Literature and Drama* (Harmondsworth: Penguin, 1973).

——, 'The Sociology of Modern Drama', trans. Lee Baxandall, *Tulane Drama Review*, vol. 9 (1964–5).

Carson McCullers, *The Member of the Wedding* (New York, 1951).

E. McInnes, *German Social Drama 1840–1900* (Stuttgart, 1976).

M. Maeterlinck, *Le Tresor des Humbles* (Paris, 1908).

F. J. Marker and L.-L. Marker. 'William Bloch and Naturalism in the Scandinavian Theatre', *Theatre Survey*, xv (November 1974) 85–104.

——, *The Scandinavian Theatre* (Oxford: Blackwell, 1975).

K. Marx, *The Civil War in France* (London, 1941).

——, *Selected Writings*, ed. David McLellan (London, 1978).

M. Meyer, *Henrik Ibsen*, 3 vols (London, 1967–71).

Arthur Miller, *Collected Plays* (London, 1974).

T. C. Murray, *Autumn Fire* (Dublin, 1911).

——, *Birthright* (London: Allen and Unwin, 1934).

——, *Maurice Harte* (London: Allen and Unwin, 1925).

——, *Michaelmas Eve* (London, 1932).

B. Nelson, *Arthur Miller; Portrait of a Playwright* (London, 1970).

V. Nemirovitch-Dantchenko, *My Life in the Russian Theatre*, trans. John Cournos (London, 1968).

M. Nic Shiublaigh, *The Splendid Years* (Dublin, 1955).

Sean O'Casey, *Collected Plays*, 4 vols (London: Macmillan, 1949–51).

Sean O'Casey, *Three Plays* (London: Macmillan, 1961).
——, *The Story of the Irish Citizen Army* (New York, 1977).
Clifford Odets, *Three Plays* (London, 1971).
R. O'Driscoll and L. Reynolds (eds), *Yeats and the Theatre* (London, 1975).
Eugene O'Neill, *The Plays of Eugene O'Neill*, 3 vols (New York: Random House, 1954).
——, *All God's Chillun Got Wings and other Plays* (London: Cape, 1973).
——, *The Emperor Jones* (London: Cape, 1969).
——, *The Hairy Ape and other plays* (London: Cape, 1973).
——, *The Iceman Cometh* (London: Cape, 1976).
——, *Long Day's Journey into Night* (London: Cape, 1976).
——, *Mourning Becomes Electra* (London: Cape, 1976).
J. Orr, *Tragic Realism and Modern Society: Studies in the Sociology of the Modern Novel* (London, 1977).
John Osborne, *Look Back in Anger* (London: Faber, 1958).
——, *Luther* (London: Faber, 1961).
H. Plessner, *Die verspätete Nation* (Stuttgart, 1959).
J. H. Raleigh, *The Plays of Eugene O'Neill* (Carbondale, 1965).
Revels History of Drama in English: Volume 7: 1880 to the Present Day (London, 1978).
F. Ringer, *The Decline of the German Mandarins: The German Academic Community 1890–1933* (Cambridge, Mass.: Harvard U.P., 1969).
Peter Shaffer, *The Royal Hunt of the Sun* (London: Faber, 1964).
——, *Three Plays* (Harmondsworth: Penguin, 1976).
George Bernard Shaw, *Heartbreak House* (London, 1948).
——, *Major Critical Essays* (London, 1948).
——, *Saint Joan* (London, 1948).
L. Scheaffer, *O'Neill: Son and Playwright* (London, 1968).
——, *O'Neill: Son and Artist* (London, 1974).
K. Stanislavsky *My Life In Art*, trans. J. Robbins (New York, 1956).
——, *Stanislavski's Legacy* ed. and trans. E. Hapgood (New York, 1968).
John Millington Synge, *Collected Works*, 4 vols (London: 1966 O.U.P., 1966).
——, *Plays, Poems and Prose* (London: Dent, 1958).
Leo Tolstoy, *The Power of Darkness*, trans. G. R. Noyes and G. Z. Patrick in N. Houghton (ed.), *Great Russian Plays* (New York, 1960).
R. Warshow, *The Immediate Experience* (New York, 1970).
Frank Wedekind, *The Lulu Plays and other Sex Tragedies*, trans. Stephen Spender (London: Calder and Boyars, 1977).
Arnold Wesker, *The Wesker Trilogy: Chicken Soup with Barley, Roots, I'm Talking about Jerusalem* (Harmondsworth: Penguin 1977).

R. Williams, *Modern Tragedy* (London, 1966).
Tennessee Williams, *The Theatre of Tennessee Williams*, 5 vols (New York, 1971).
——, *Three Plays* (Harmondsworth: Penguin, 1976).
W. B. Yeats, *The Collected Plays of W. B. Yeats* (London: Macmillan, 1954).
——, *Essays and Introductions* (London: Macmillan, 1961).
——, *Explorations* (London: Macmillan, 1962).
——, *Selected Plays*, ed. and intro. A. N. Jeffares (London: Macmillan, (1964).

2.   Other Works

W. H. Bruford, *Chekhov and his Russia: a sociological study* (London, 1947).
R. Brustein, *The Theatre of Revolt* (London, 1965).
E. Burns, *Theatricality* (London: Longman, 1972).
E. Burns and T. Burns (eds), *The Sociology of Literature and Drama* (Harmondsworth: Penguin, 1973).
E. Coxhead, *Lady Gregory* (London, 1969).
M. Egan (ed.) *Ibsen: the Critical Heritage* (London, 1972).
U. Ellis-Fermor, *The Irish Dramatic Movement* (London, 1939).
——, *The Jacobean Drama* (London, 1958).
G. Lloyd Evans, *The Language of Modern Drama* (London, 1977).
R. Gaskell, *Drama and Reality; The European Theatre since Ibsen* (London, 1972).
Lady Gregory, *Our Irish Theatre* (Gerrards Cross, 1972).
R. Hare, *Maxim Gorky: Romantic Realist and Conservative Revolutionary* (London, 1962).
R. Hayman (ed.), *The German Theatre: a Symposium* (London, 1975).
C. D. Innes, *Erwin Piscator's Political Theatre* (Cambridge, 1972).
T. Komisarchevsky, *The Theatre and a Changing Civilisation* (London, 1934).
C. Leech, *Tragedy* (London, 1969).
E. K. Mikhail (ed.), *A Bibliography of Modern Irish Drama: 1899–1970* (London, 1972).
——, *Lady Gregory: Interviews and Recollections* (London, 1977).
Massachusetts Review, 'Irish Renaissance', ed. R. Skelton and D. Clark (Dublin, 1965).
J. Northam, *Ibsen's Dramatic Method* (London, 1953).
M. OhAodha, *Theatre in Ireland* (London, 1974).

J. Osborne, *The Naturalist Drama in Germany* (Manchester, 1972).

L. Robinson (ed.) *Our Irish Theatre* (London, 1939).

M. Slonim, *Russian Theatre* (London, 1963).

J. L. Styan, *Chekhov in Performance* (Cambridge, 1971).

J. Russell Taylor, *The Rise and Fall of the Well-Made Play* (London, 1967).

M. Valgemae, *Accelerated Grimace: Expressionism in the American Drama of the 1920s* (London, 1972).

M. Valency, *The Breaking String; the Plays of Anton Chekhov* (New York, 1966).

R. Williams, *Drama from Ibsen to Brecht* (London, 1968).

Tulane Drama Review, vol. 9, nos 1 and 2 (1964–5), 'Stanislavski and America'.

W. B. Yeats, *Autobiographies* (London, 1955).

Index

Using literary and sociological perspectives John Orr explores, through detailed analysis of key plays, the nature of tragedy in modern drama from Ibsen's *Ghosts* to Grass's *The Plebeians Rehearse the Uprising*. From 1870 onwards, tragic drama is seen as a peripheral cultural creation in the work of Ibsen, Strindberg, Chekhov, Lorca, Yeats, Synge and O'Casey, emerging at the geographical margins of modern Europe rather than its metropolitan centres. The social and literary causes of this unique occurrence are examined, as is the subsequent development in the United States where its themes are more centrally related to the urban and industrial life of the most advanced capitalist society of the twentieth century. From this perspective, the common themes in the work of O'Neill, Williams, Miller and Albee are analysed and contrasted with their European predecessors.

There is also detailed exploration of the role of women in modern tragedy, which links the European to the American drama, and also helps to explain the persistence of the naturalistic domestic setting on the contemporary stage. In addition, reasons are suggested as to why the political theatre, unlike the political novel, has been non-tragic in its general development. Modern tragedy, it is claimed, is essentially a drama of social alienation creating a literary affront to bourgeois society in its portrayal of social estrangement and the forms of human loss which ensue.

In conclusion, some suggestions are made about the possible fusion of tragic and epic modes of theatre in future playwriting, an achievement created by Georg Büchner prior to the central period of modern tragedy but subsequently neglected for over a hundred years.

For a note on the author, please see the back flap